99

3000 800046 54231
St. Louis Community College

D1635950

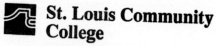 **St. Louis Community College**

Forest Park
Florissant Valley
Meramec

Instructional Resources
St. Louis, Missouri

politics, gender, and

the Islamic past

St. Louis Community College
at Meramec
Library

politics, gender, and

the Islamic past

the legacy of

'A'isha bint Abi Bakr

D. A. Spellberg

new york   columbia university press

columbia university press
new york   chichester, west sussex

Copyright ©1994 Columbia University Press
All rights reserved

Library of Congress Cataloging-in-Publication Data

Spellberg, D. A. (Denise A.)
   Politics, gender, and the Islamic past: The Legacy of ʿAʾisha bint Abi Bakr / D.A. Spellberg.
   p.   cm.
   Includes bibliographical references and index.
   ISBN 0-231-07998-2 (alk. paper)
   1. ʿAʾisha, ca. 614-678. 2. Women, Muslim. 3. Muhammad, Prophet, d. 632—Family—Bib-
liography, 4. Women, Muslim—Saudi Arabia-Biography.   I. Title.
   BO80.A52S64   1994
   297'.64—dc20
   [B]   94-25025
                                                                                                  CIP

Casebound editions of Columbia University Press books are
printed on permanent and durable acid-free paper.

Printed in the United States of America

c 10 9 8 7 6 5 4 3 2 1
p 10 9 8 7 6 5 4 3 2 1

For my parents, two people who inspire courage

Angelina Pavone Spellberg
and
Israel Abraham Spellberg

contents

preface and acknowledgments

I started this book when I was young. Now in my venerable middle years I look fondly back on a decade of on-and-off devotion to thinking about the legacy of a difficult woman. The struggle has convinced me both that youth is exhaustible and the richness of my subject limitless. I do not profess any truths but these. The rest is interpretation.

My thanks go to Richard W. Bulliet for sharing his extraordinary historical insight, support, and sense of humor. Kate Wittenberg, my editor, deserves both praise and thanks for her wise and enthusiastic supervision of the project. Although I recall with clarity all the scholarly advice I never took, I also remember the intellectual generosity of many, who in agreeing, disagreeing, or simply suggesting, helped to sort out the tangle. I am profoundly grateful to them.

Peter J. Awn
Caroline W. Bynum
M. E. Combs-Schilling
Fred Donner
R. Stephen Humphreys
Rhoads Murphey
George Saliba

Granting agencies who provided support for the project include: Whiting Fellowship; Pennar Fellowship; Josephine de Karman Fellowship; Woodrow Wilson Women's Studies Research Grant; Fulbright-Hays Dissertation Research Abroad Fellowship; Social Science Research Council Dissertation Research Fellowship and the Women's Studies and Religion Program of Harvard Divinity School.

Throughout, when I use dates, I give both the A.H. (anno Hegirae) year and the A.D. (anno Domini) year, first the Islamic one, separated by a slash from the Christian one.

politics, gender, and

the Islamic past

one *approaches to the study*
of a legacy: an introduction

> *Men have had every advantage of us in telling*
>
> *their story. . . . the pen has been in their hands.*
>
> —*Jane Austen*

$\mathcal{A}$ life and a legacy are not always the same. Time and perspective collude to shape the latter, promoting a definitive semblance of
the former. Yet of any life, the legacy is only a semblance—a vision of reality generated by those who thought and wrote about their subject, for
their own reasons, after the life to be retold had ended. Ostensibly, the
focus of this investigation is `A'isha bint Abi Bakr (d. A.H. 58/A.D. 678), a
woman known most succinctly in works of Islamic history as the third and
favorite wife of the Prophet Muhammad (d. A.H. 11/A.D. 632). Realisti-
cally, however, it is about the construction and presentation of `A'isha bint
Abi Bakr's historical persona by a select group of medieval Muslim men
who shaped the memory and meaning of her life for their fellow believers. It is their story not hers, for she is the object not the subject of their
written remembrance and evocation. `A'isha's legacy demonstrates the
power of interpretation in the formation of historical meaning. Her life,
as retold in an increasingly elaborate series of reflections and contexts,

refracts the emergence of a complex Islamic communal identity in the medieval period. In writing about `A'isha, Muslims honed their own vision of themselves. They used her example to define their past in new ways for a community that sought always to follow the precedent of the Prophet Muhammad and his first followers, male and female.

`A'isha and Communal Identity

Ultimately, every study of history contends with an implicit conflict between the lure of the past and the implications of the present. In many ways the past remains forever removed by chronology and context, but continues to be "shaped by today's predilections" with "its strategies domesticated by our own preservation of its vestiges."[1] Modern approximations of the seventh century, the first Islamic century in which `A'isha lived, must contend with the absence of contemporary written sources from that critical period. What is true of modern evaluations of the medieval past also applies to the work of the Muslim authors who, generations after `A'isha's death, began the task of reconstructing her life. These male scriptors began to preserve their Islamic past and its significance within a later context, a different present. Although they were much closer chronologically to `A'isha's real life than we, they were also removed from her existence in significant ways. For example, Ibn Sa`d, the author of `A'isha's most detailed early written biography, died in Baghdad in 230/845. `A'isha's life, according to him, ended in 58/678.[2] More than one hundred and fifty years had passed before his written preservation of `A'isha's life began.[3] A comparable span of time, framed in the much shorter national record of the United States, would mean that a historical work written in 1994 sought to record a woman's life which ended in 1827, relying not on written materials but, as in `A'isha's original Islamic milieu, on oral reports transmitted over three to four generations. Thus, even the earliest Arabic written sources on `A'isha's life already capture that life as a legacy, an interpretation, not simply because of the issue of chronology or mode of transmission, but because of the distinctly different historical contexts in which the later written preservation of her recorded life took place. Aspects of `A'isha's life were known, discussed, and debated before their placement in the earliest written records to which we retain access. Medieval Muslim scriptors never knew `A'isha, but they were forced to contend with her presence in their past and to reckon repeatedly with the controversial wife of the Prophet Muhammad in their continuing elaboration of their communal record. No other Muslim woman had had such a life; no other woman would generate such a legacy. Yet what appear as `A'isha's most immutable core biographical components remain objects of dispute within the Muslim record. Even this brief outline of her life might promote debate between Sunni and Shi`i Muslims in the modern as in the medieval period:

A.H. 1/A.D. 623. Married to the Prophet Muhammad at the age of nine in Medina; `A'isha becomes his favorite wife and an exemplary female figure for all Muslims.

A.H. 5/A.D. 627. Accused of adultery at the age of fourteen; `A'isha is vindicated by a divine revelation received by the Prophet Muhammad and recorded in the Qur'an.

A.H. 11/A.D. 632. `A'isha becomes a childless widow at eighteen. Her father, Abu Bakr, a trusted companion of the Prophet Muhammad, becomes the first political leader of the Islamic community and rules for two years. `A'isha's father is chosen to lead the Muslim community because Muhammad had no male heirs and designated no other political leader before his death.

A.H. 36/A.D. 656. `A'isha and two male allies oppose `Ali ibn AbiTalib, the fourth political successor to the Prophet Muhammad. The conflict over political control of the Islamic community escalates into the first Islamic civil war.

Defeated in a single military encounter near Basra, known as the Battle of the Camel, `A'isha returns to Medina as a virtual prisoner and retires from further direct political involvement.

A.H. 58/A.D. 678. `A'isha dies at the age of sixty-six after spending her final two decades in Medina transmitting her detailed observations of the Prophet Muhammad's words and deeds to male and female Muslims. These oral reports of `A'isha's, along with those of the Prophet Muhammad's other companions, became central to the later written historical record and establish her reputation as a key source for the Muslim preservation of the past for generations to come.

Conflict and controversy are at the core of what we know about the life of `A'isha. She was born, raised, married, and buried in an Islamic environment, but even the chronology of her life is disputed in the early sources.[4] Although Muslims might disagree about ʾAʾisha's symbolic meaning in the medieval period, they agreed fundamentally about key aspects of her centrality and import in a shared past. If these elements had not been present, the formulation of this inquiry into the evolution of her legacy would not have been possible.

Genealogy and Politics

ʾAʾisha's high historical profile in the Islamic record proceeds from two key factors: marriage and genealogy. She is first present in early Islamic historical works by association with her husband and father. ʾAʾisha's relationship to her husband Muhammad, the spiritual and political leader of the first Islamic community, amplifies her husband's biography and, by extension, the earliest accounts of the first Muslim society. Her status as wife was further enhanced by her father Abu Bakr's religious and political prestige as one of the first converts to the new faith of Islam. After Muhammad's death, ʾAʾisha's father Abu Bakr (d. 13/634) became the first man to hold the position of caliph, or political successor to the Prophet Muhammad. Aʾisha's name, derived from the Arabic root for "alive," also directly links her to the patriline and defines her as *bint Abi Bakr*, "the daughter of Abu Bakr."[5] ʾAʾisha's natural proximity to her husband and father ties her permanently, if normatively, to the male heart of the first *umma*, or Islamic community. She is thus inextricably bound to all later evocations of that initial, precedent-laden Muslim society, the ideal community to which believers look for inspiration in the medieval and modern periods.

During Muhammad's lifetime no Muslim used the designation Sunni or Shiʿi. Both of these adjectives represent Muslim definitions which emerged only after the Prophet's death. Muhammad had been for Muslims the last prophet, the bearer of the final and perfect divine revelation contained in the Qurʾan. There could, by definition, be no spiritual successor to his prophetic mission, but the question of political succession became critical to communal survival and identity. ʾAʾisha's father became the Prophet Muhammad's first political successor. Abu Bakr, defined as a trusted companion to the Prophet, was also bound to him as a son-in-law through ʾAʾisha's marriage. ʾAʾisha's status as Muhammad's widow and Abu Bakr's daughter cast her forever as a figure of honor among those

Muslims who considered the first caliph's appointment as a true and representative reflection of communal ideas of leadership. Abu Bakr became the first caliph and thus the first to define the responsibilities of a new position of authority for the fledgling Muslim community in the absence of their Prophet.

At the time of Abu Bakr's appointment by committee, there was no Sunni ideological position on leadership within the Islamic community. Indeed, Sunni political theory was solidified centuries after the events that would later be defined as pivotal in the majority's communal reading of the past. Retrospectively, the Muslims who would eventually be termed "Sunni" and continue today to represent the vast majority of the faithful accepted a range of political leadership options as long as they served to promote the preservation of the Islamic community.[6] The adjective *Sunni* is derived from the more descriptive phrase *ahl al-sunna wa al-jama`a,* "the people of the example [of the Prophet] and the community." The consensus-minded majority of Sunni Muslims revered Abu Bakr as the close companion of the Prophet and the first caliph. Support for the father as an exemplary figure for the Sunni majority also prompted parallel positive treatment for his daughter `A'isha. Politically, the development of her legacy as a positive reflection of the past placed her securely in the Sunni Muslim sphere and developed a key component in the construction of a father-daughter duo.

Just as `A'isha's link to her father as the first caliph had signal implications for her legacy, so too did her political opposition to the fourth caliph, `Ali ibn AbiTalib (d. 41/661), the man whom Shi`i Muslims would identify as their first true political leader. `Ali, the first cousin of the Prophet, his son-in-law, and the fourth caliph of Islam, faced a serious threat from within the Muslim community on his accession to power. `A'isha's active opposition to `Ali determined the initial phase of the first Islamic *fitna* or "civil war," prompted a major battle, and caused the formation of the Shi`a, or "party" of `Ali. `Ali's supporters were, by definition, initially opponents of `A'isha. After `Ali's death, his supporters, as Shi`i Muslims, would eventually press their claim that only `Ali's patrilineal descendants had the right to rule the Islamic polity. Shi`i Muslims evolved increasingly complicated arguments about spiritual and political authority as a familial concept that provided the closest blood link to the Prophet Muhammad. Genealogical and political considerations among this Muslim minority created subsets of Shiʿis who accepted five, seven, or twelve direct descendants of ʿAli, known as *imams*. The majority of Shiʿi Muslims who currently reside in Iraq and Iran are known as Twelvers because they believe that the last rightful descendant of ʿAli was the twelfth imam in this genealogical continuum.

For Shiʿi Muslims, ʿAʾisha would retain the negative distinction of having opposed their first political leader, while her father would be designated as the usurper of ʿAli's right to the caliphate.[7] Even the Sunni Muslim majority would be forced to contend with the aftermath of ʿAʾisha's political involvement and her prominent part in the destruction of the unity of the first Islamic community. If Shiʿi Muslims cast ʿAʾisha as the persecutor of ʿAli, their first legitimate leader, Sunni Muslims delicately assessed her role as the opponent of their attested fourth caliph, the father of the Prophet Muhammad's only grandchildren. Indeed, the more equivocal Sunni stance at once sought to defend ʿAʾisha as the Prophet's favorite wife from Shiʿi condemnation, while effectively defining ʿAʾisha's political persona as a negative dimension of her legacy laden with lessons for all later Muslim women. Both Shiʿi and Sunni Muslims shared a common past, but would be forced to contend with ʿAʾisha's part in the same events quite differently. In this process, medieval debate about political authority harked back to the divisive events of the first civil war and channeled ideological programs through key historical figures. The development of ʿAʾisha's historical persona definitively demonstrates the nexus between the personal and the political in Islamic historiography. The first civil war pitted ʿAʾisha against ʿAli in a retrospective divide which increasingly manifested the strain of emerging Muslim communal identities.[8]

Gender

Although the definition of ʿAʾisha's historical persona would be inextricably bound with key males in the development of Muslim historiography, her exceptional visibility as a pointedly female presence in the communal record documents male discussion about her as both a real woman, a female, and a symbol of the feminine. The remembrance of ʿAʾisha charged Islamic historiography with crucial lessons for all Muslims about politics, gender, and the representation of the past as presented exclusively by men. Although Sunni and Shiʿi Muslims disagreed vehemently about the question of `A'isha as an exemplary female figure, they concurred at critical junctures about the force of her function in that debate.

`A'isha's marriage to the Prophet Muhammad defined her as an exceptional and, in the Sunni record, exemplary female figure. The depiction of her life with the Prophet in early Muslim sources focuses on the components of her definition as the most excellent of his wives. Praise for `A'isha emphasizes aspects of her genealogy and uniqueness. Divine intervention in both her marital selection and defense against the charge of adultery also figures prominently in defining her exceptional legacy. `A'isha's sexuality and the sacred intersect in the Islamic record to enhance both the Prophet's preference for her as his wife and the initial communal conflict threatened by the suggestion of her infidelity. The link between concepts of honor and shame, truth and falsehood, belief and unbelief are interwoven in early accounts and expand with later polemical consequences for both Sunni and Shi`i believers. Sunni Muslims believe in `A'isha's exoneration from the charge of adultery as recorded in the Qur'an, the divinely revealed source of their faith and practice. Yet `A'isha's name is not explicitly attached to this incident as part of Qur'anic revelation. Only in later sources is `A'isha clearly linked to the revealed verses concerning the charge of adultery. It is not insignificant that early accounts of the incident record `Ali's doubts about `A'isha's innocence. Later Shi`i interpretations of the same Qur'anic verses reveal distinctly different results and consequences for `A'isha's historical persona. Interpretation, as focused through the accusation of adultery made against `A'isha, becomes a prism for male definitions of Sunni communal identity. `A'isha's part in the first Islamic civil war and her opposition to the fourth caliph `Ali ibn Abi Talib also tie her historical persona to crucial questions of religiopolitical legitimacy as imaged through the parameters of female conduct and control. Indeed, these two controversial biographical components represent both a sectarian divide in Islamic historiography and a series of charged lessons directed to all women, through `A'isha's example, about female sexuality and political influence.

`A'isha's singularity is, however, qualified in relation to other Muslim women, most notably the Prophet's first wife Khadija bint Khuwaylid (d. 619) and their daughter, Fatima (d. 11/633). `A'isha, Khadija, and Fatima are represented frequently in early sources in terms of their contested closeness to the Prophet Muhammad in varied interactions and utterances which signal nuanced dimensions of his preference for each of them. Descriptions of these female figures evolve into an implicit and then explicit Sunni doctrinal and Shi`i sectarian debate about which of the three exemplifies the most excellent woman of the first Islamic community. The debate about the best of Muslim women, in the definition of their symbolic significance, hinges on Qur'anic precedent. Thus, `A'isha's historical persona also demonstrates Islamic religiohistorical continuity in relation to a spectrum of Qur'anic feminine exemplars including Maryam, the mother of the prophet Jesus; Asiya, the wife of pharaoh; Zulaykha', the temptress of the prophet Joseph; and the wives of the prophets Lot and Noah. In the debate over definitional control of `A'isha's image, the figure of Maryam, the mother of Jesus, is by far the most pivotal. Both `A'isha and Fatima, by association with one another and the Qur'anic mother of Jesus, will be defined more clearly in terms of their oppositional feminine attributes.

Fueling the discussion of female excellence within the first Muslim community are issues of genealogy and political legitimacy. Thus, `A'isha becomes an extension and reflection of her father Abu Bakr's historical persona, just as Fatima's definition depends, increasingly, on that of her husband, `Ali. In this sense, female historical figures define not just male projections of the feminine; they also ramify argument about male authoritarian personae and definitional control within Islamic society. In `A'isha's capacity as a mediating figure for communal identities, she also becomes an Islamic cultural symbol of great versatility, one that embodies "multiple (and often contradictory) representations."[9] The construction of `A'isha's meaning, with its explicit emphasis on the legacy of a historical female figure as the basis for discussions about the nature of the feminine, also confirmed gender categories as inherently dual as represented in the emergence of intricate Islamic definitions of both male and female, masculine and feminine.

`A'isha's legacy also included practical definitional precedents for the lives of Sunni Muslim women as represented in Islamic law and ritual practice. Although `A'isha's name and example are frequently cited in these medieval sources for Islamic social legislation, we have no accounts authored by medieval Muslim women that attest to their response to `A'isha as her legacy was represented to them for emulation or rejection.[10] We cannot deduce from the male debate about ʾAʾisha the experience of real medieval Muslim women's lives, or surmise positions they might have articulated without documentation.[11] Nor is it judicious, as some might suggest, to cease analysis of the premodern historical record because there were no female contributions to this written corpus. However, we can attempt to understand the particular historical contexts in which male imagination worked on multiple definitional levels within medieval Muslim society to shape ʾAʾisha's viability as a point of reference for shared Muslim communal concerns and qualified self-definition.

The Representation of the Past

If marriage and genealogy cast ʾAʾisha in a central historical role in the first Islamic community, then her part in the preservation of the past also promoted her high visibility as a source for the Muslim written record. ʾAʾisha's posthumous stature as a frequently named authority for the Prophet Muhammad's words and deeds contributes to a critical dimension of her religious prominence in the Sunni Muslim sphere. As the oral point of origin for later *hadith*, the written reports or traditions that preserve the Prophet Muhammad's precedent, ʾAʾisha's keen memory is repeatedly praised in the earliest written sources. Each hadith has two parts: the *isnad*, or chain of named transmitters who formed the original oral conduit for the *matn*, or core content of the report.

The first problem in dealing with this abundant written material is that these sources, as written, are not contemporary with the events they describe, including the life of ʾAʾisha. The hadith format, with its written emphasis on a meticulously preserved prior oral phase of communal memory, is critical to the later elaboration of Muslim faith and history as inspired by the Prophet Muhammad's example and the words of his close associates, including his wives and family. Other early Islamic written genres, such as chronicle and biography, were also composed of thousands of discreet hadith-like sources, organized by chronology or human subject, respectively. In this regard, it is important to distinguish between hadith, as *hadith al-nabi*, "sayings of the Prophet Muhammad;" *hadith al-sahaba*, "sayings of the Prophet's companions," including ʾAʾisha; and *khabar*, "a short narrative or bits of related information from whatever source available."[12] Although they purport to be primary sources written down after scrupulous oral transmission, hadith and khabar may more accurately represent secondary accounts selected for preservation and written down at a later date.

Only Sunni Muslims define ʿAʾisha as an esteemed authority for the preservation of their past. Shiʿi Muslims, relying on their own version of authoritative oral transmission, with the best chain of authorities originating with the Prophet Muhammad via ʿAli, his descendants, and supporters, dismissed ʿAʾisha along with her father and many of Muhammad's other companions as partisan and, hence, suspect sources of information.[13] Those Muslims who had usurped ʿAli's rightful claim to be the first successor to the Prophet Muhammad or opposed him as the fourth caliph were, by Shiʿi definition, accorded neither religiopolitical legitimacy nor unqualified contributions to the Shiʿi Muslim historical record. Yet ʿAʾisha is present in avowedly Shiʿi sources. Indeed, her historical persona is critical to the presentation of their sectarian past. ʿAʾisha, as subject or foil in certain traditions, enhances those in the Shiʿi Muslim sphere whom she antagonizes, most especially ʿAli ibn AbiTalib, and his wife, the Prophet's daughter Fatima. In her capacity as an exemplary antithesis to Shiʿi religiopolitical authority, ʿAʾisha's persona defines by contrast both male and female Shiʿi ideals. Thus, Shiʿi accounts do not expunge ʿAʾisha from their past, but instead selectively utilize her presence to emphasize the emergence of their own distinct vision of the communal record.

Sunni Muslim hadith collections emerge in their written, definitive form by the third/ninth century, with six key collections finally accepted as canonical slightly later in the fourth/tenth century. These collections are composed of those hadith that record the Prophet Muhammad's precedent in word and deed. By this later period, Shiʿi hadith collections had also been formulated as distinctly partisan alternatives to the Sunni majority record. While ʿAli and the Prophet's daughter Fatima are included as figures of honor and reverence in Sunni hadith and are cited as oral authorities in written accounts, Abu Bakr and ʿAʾisha are rejected in the Shiʿi canon as sources of religiohistorical truth. The fluidity of early hadith and the importance of ʿAli as the Prophet's first cousin and son-in-law created a shared reverence for him, his wife Fatima, and their descendants among both Sunni and Shiʿi Muslims. Shiʿi sources thus often cite early non-Shiʿi materials especially when they concur about the excellence of ʿAli or Fatima or are inherently critical of `A'isha. If Sunni Muslims were inclusive in their ability to maintain `A'isha's legacy, they did so, in part, in support of her much-lauded contribution to their communal record. `A'isha's legacy as a contributor to Sunni precedent featured the wife of the Prophet not just as a source of hadith, but as a major figure, summoned through these sources, in the later, more elaborate articulation of Sunni law and theology.[14] In this context, Shi`i rejection of `A'isha clearly signaled rejection of the entire Sunni edifice of scholarly consensus. Sunni defense of `A'isha's reputation and legacy became fully synonymous with the Muslim majority's defense of the foundations of their past. All Muslims, in the evolution of their communal identities, defined themselves in relation to the posthumous legacies of the men and women of the first Muslim community. In their attempt to create a definitive historical record ex post facto, Muslim authors both preserved memory and created meaning. Their collective attempt to control the past was contingent on elaborate, interactive definitions of prominent Muslim figures whose legacies outlived their real historical lives, taking on new religiopolitical resonances over time.

The process of hadith transmission may include in the chain of authorities the names of both men and women, but the final stage of written preservation features only male authorities as compilers. There is, to date, no evidence of female Muslim scriptors in the medieval period. The rise of the `ulama' as a group of Muslim scholars who controlled the articulation of the Islamic faith in the medieval period would categorically exclude both Sunni and Shi`i women from the study of theology and law, the most advanced courses of Islamic education in which debate about `A'isha's legacy reached its apex. Sunni Muslim women might be enjoined to relate hadith, following the example of `A'isha and other early Muslim women in the continued medieval emphasis on orally transmitted communal memory, but they were not permitted access to the exclusively male environments in which the implications of `A'isha's legacy most directly contributed to their own lives as the prescriptive basis for social and legal definition.[15]

The import of `A'isha's life, as an active force in the first Muslim community, would be rendered entirely by men in a social milieu vastly different from their subject's original Arabian setting. Whereas `A'isha and her co-wives had been present in battlefield and bedroom more than one hundred and fifty years before, the elite women of the `Abbasid period

(132–656/750–1258), the dynastic frame from which our earliest preserved written sources date, lived lives in imperial Baghdad defined by
their strict separation from the male sphere of action and education.[16]
When considering ʿAʾisha's life at a later date, Muslim male scholars
could not fail to have been influenced by the emergence of a very different Islamic status quo for their female coreligionists.

A word should be stated at the outset about the role of ʿAʾisha as a con-
tributor to her own legacy. A number of hadith and khabar that feature
ʿAʾisha in their matn, or report, also cite her as the originating authority
in the chain of transmission. Such dual placement suggests apparent control over her own presentation in the Islamic historical record, but this
work does not assume that ʿAʾisha was the point of origin for the thousands and thousands of words attributed to her in either Sunni or Shiʿi
sources. Instead, the written format, with its potential to support or
defame ʿAʾisha, provides the perfect vehicle for the medieval embellishment of her historical persona. Her interpretation in the written record
depends not merely on her presence in what was once an oral process, but
on the selectivity employed by later Muslim scriptors. Once ʿAʾisha's life
and words enter the early Islamic corpus, her interpretation then continues in a wide variety of genres in which the chain of transmitting authorities often disappears. Hadith and khabar represent the triumph of both
selectivity and the pen as the arbiters of communal Islamic truths.
ʿAʾisha's life, as cast in these early accounts and later sources in a wide
range of genres, exemplifies the power of the written word over the spoken, of the scriptor over his subject, and of the living over the memory of
the dead. In none of these sources does ʿAʾisha have the last word. She
speaks words as attributed to her or created for her, but she herself does
not ultimately select or record them. The pen, in the creation of her legacy, is wielded by other hands.

Hadith and khabar have been criticized by Western scholars as the
repositories of unauthentic fictions which offer the historian unverifiable
content based on spurious chains of transmission.[17] There has been opposition to such an extreme, cynical position about these early materials by
both Muslim and Western scholars.[18] However, most Western historians
who use this material remain cautious despite acknowledgment that Muslims established safeguards for weeding out forgeries and false chains of

transmission.[19] The problematic of these early sources speaks to the difficulty with which any historian may accurately analyze the lives of the members of the first Islamic community. In trying to deal with this body of
texts, certain scholars have attempted to circumvent these early Muslim
materials by utilizing alternative accounts from other Middle Eastern religious communities.[20] Others have attempted to work on specific Muslim
texts as the repositories of both sectarian and literary invention in conjunction with hermeneutic and literary critical theory.[21] The content of
these early sources often grew in the telling over time in detail and import
for those who expanded early narrative accounts and there is increased
Western scholarly interest in the study of early religiohistorical literature
as a partially creative rather than exclusively factual form of recorded historical evolution.[22] However, the ability to isolate certain topics or narrative conventions in Islamic history is still in the formative stages.[23] Indeed,
in some instances the process of transmission of the Islamic past depends
less on issues of authenticity and more on the later contingencies of detailing a particular event or expanding specific patterns of argument. No matter who the chain of transmitting authorities featured, as investigated in
detail by Muslim scholars in the medieval period, it is the core of content
that becomes critical in later communal debate. Parts of the process of
transmitting hadith and khabar, as an originally oral phenomenon, may be
more closely related to the mode of storytellers whose public recitations
about crucial Muslim lives and events may best account for the presence of
content variation over time.[24] Khabar, in particular, while transmitted with
a chain of authorities, is critical to the creation of both our earliest forms
of Islamic chronicle and biography during the third/ninth and fourth/
tenth centuries. As confirmed time and again, part of the problem with
these sources is not just the issue of authenticity, but the question of the
compilers' basis for inclusion of circulating materials.[25] The compiler's
intent is not recorded explicitly in these sources, but lies submerged,
charged with meaning in a supposedly inchoate method of inclusion.

Thus far, the twin dilemmas of core authenticity and authorial selectivity have remained a vexing problematic in the study of early Islamic historiography. There are varied Western-inspired critical approaches to the
use of this pivotal early material. Two major analytical paths stand out in
Western analysis of early Islamic historiography: assume these sources are

critically flawed and exploit them primarily to undermine any notion of authenticity in the early Islamic record; or analyze their chains of transmission and the individual biographies of relaters for clues as to the geographical origins and doctrinal ambitions of the material preserved as well as its authenticity. The first option has already been suggested by some Western scholars and leaves the historian of medieval Islamic society with much early material and, seemingly, no worthy options for historical research except the confirmation of Muslim duplicity and the omnipresence of negative historical evidence.[26] Many more works of early Islamic history have been conducted according to the second alternative and have directed their attention to the individual chain of authorities in early accounts with a variety of revealing results.[27] These studies, by definition, focus exclusively on issues of authenticity and politicization with their gaze focused backward in time. Even when verifiable content is supported by modern scrutiny of chains of transmission, the drive to define authenticity and potential fabrication limits the amount of positive information which may be drawn from these earliest written materials. Often, despite scrupulous care, the result of such studies only confirms a confused, highly qualified sense of an unreachable true core for the earliest Islamic period, the time during which ʾAʾisha lived.[28] Moreover, even when this approach acknowledges politically inspired reshaping of the past, it seeks to work around such present-centered Muslim problems of historiography rather than pursue them directly as an intrinsic object of study.[29] Rather than exploit Muslim selectivity and interpretation in written materials, these studies hope always to transcend them in the never-ending hunt for objective data from the earliest, undocumented period of Islamic history.

In a study such as this one, a focus on the relaters in the chain of transmission as an exclusive methodology would certainly yield a highly qualified understanding about a reduced body of early written material, but it would tell us little about ʾAʾisha's legacy as an evolving, later medieval interpretation. Moreover, such scrutiny would seek only to authenticate materials whose importance Muslims themselves confirmed by repeated use or rejection over time from the third/ninth century far into the late medieval and even modern periods. The struggle to understand the reasons for the selection and inclusion of these materials, traced in the case of a highly controversial historical figure, allows interpretation to function as a key to Muslim sources and not a closed door. The approach chosen represents a third option and seeks to analyze select trajectories of Islamic thought as evolving narratives which contributed with authorial care and intent to important arguments within the Islamic medieval community. In the process of building `A'isha's legacy, Muslims preserved her life in reports that sometimes were at odds with one another, but eventually transcended written contexts that featured the chain of transmission. Thus, rather than concentrate on the vicissitudes of individual relaters, their geographical and doctrinal positions, this work argues that scholars judiciously utilized these materials to build written arguments about `A'isha in which authenticity, after a time, was of less import than the overall interpretive strategies which make reference to the earliest written sources. Concentration on the matn, or content, of these early materials allows the historian to trace patterns selected by the authors who preserved and expanded aspects of `A'isha's legacy. Such an approach attempts to glean insight about difficult material that has until now been viewed as suspect.

Although some selective attention will be paid to the issue of individual relaters in chains of authority, this work does not seek to consistently document these purported oral remnants, in part, because the object of this inquiry is not to confirm a verifiable seventh/first century core of data about `A'isha bint Abi Bakr's real life or the events in which she took part. Instead, it takes as a given the problematic of early hadith and khabar and exploits that corpus as an introduction to the later selection and preservation of a medieval Muslim record. The question of authenticity, an issue of heated debate in Western scholarship on early Islamic sources, becomes less critical in the focus on the placement, repetition, and divergence of these materials as they contribute to ongoing, evolving written arguments in the medieval period. Muslim scholars elaborated with care and great acumen the reliability of those men and women who related hadith in their search for authenticity, a true core for their past. In this process they parallel the painstaking modern quest for insight into what really happened in the earliest undocumented period of Islamic history.[30] However, once placed in an accepted Muslim corpus these written materials implicitly redefine authenticity in a later cultural context as not simply a retrospective inquiry, but an ever-present intellectual endeavor. If historians of the modern period cannot definitively know ʿAʾisha, they may at least begin to understand her significance for those determined medieval Muslim scholars who shaped her meaning by virtue of their later interpretations of her example. Thus, recorded time, previously presumed in Muslim sources as always past, functions in this work to enhance and not deny meaning. Authenticity, to be culturally effective, must in Islamic historiography continue to be reconfirmed after its initial written preservation.[31]

This study seeks to find a new definition for cultural authenticity and, in so doing, enhance our understanding of authorial intent as it expanded contextually to fit a variety of debates in the medieval Islamic community. The book traces ʿAʾisha's legacy as it evolved in internally generated directions as reflected in a complex intertextuality, a web of texts in which medieval male authors responded with argumentative zeal to communal issues and one another.[32] Obsession with authenticity in the chain of transmitted ideas in such an approach is less important than the routes these surviving kernels of content took over time. They existed in the medieval period and were used repeatedly with great flair and imagination by Muslim scholars and men of faith who understood their potent importance within the community. Once beyond certain types of elaborate scholarly scrutiny, the brilliance of Muslim imagination continued to argue within the framework of set patterns, motifs, and polemical programs. These narrative conventions were accepted and utilized with great skill and logical intent at the time of their written preservation and beyond.

ʿAʾisha's presence in the historical record would be utilized by male scholars to emphasize important lessons about a shared past for the Muslim community. The remembrance of what ʿAʾisha did or said became, in effect, the platform for more divisive issues. Her relevance for communal discussion was renewed each time Muslims recalled the details of the accusation of adultery, the first civil war, and the multitude of observations attributed to ʿAʾisha herself in the written Islamic record. Issues of female sexuality, political influence, and the preservation of the past lurked beneath the surface of ʿAʾisha's controversial legacy. In each of these critical areas, Sunni and Shiʿi Muslims read ʿAʾisha's significance differently. Increasingly, these key features of ʿAʾisha's remembered life would overlap within the medieval historical record, emerging as an interactive tissue of charged associations. The life of one woman inspired a spectrum of interpretation among those who shaped her posthumous legacy. Indeed, her historical persona became a lightening rod for their emerging religiopolitical distinctions. `A'isha's legacy, ultimately, forced Muslims to consider which of the women closest to the Prophet Muhammad would be considered the most excellent and why. Her symbolic valence posed crucial questions about the nature of female flaws and feminine idealization in Islamic society.

Beyond Biography: `A'isha and Modern Sources

In modern works from the Muslim Middle East `A'isha's life has been the focus of much discussion as a model for women and a source of Islamic tradition. In the Sunni Islamic world, most notably Morocco, Egypt, Syria, Turkey, and Pakistan, `A'isha continues to be the subject of both learned and popular reflection. Her absence as a figure of reverence among Shi`i populations, especially in Iran, is a result of the medieval legacy that is the subject of this book. Nevertheless, except as an object of derision, the silence on the subject of `A'isha in current Shi`i works is deafening: "Thus `A'isha, the vivacious young wife of the Prophet and the daughter of Abu Bakr, carries on a feud with `Ali for a variety of fairly obvious reasons; but in Shi`ite homiletics this conflict is reduced to admonitions about the proper place of women."[33]

The preponderance of supportive Sunni treatments of `A'isha issue from the Arabic-speaking world.[34] There are great variations in the focus and quality of these works, but all are united in their assertion of a special reverence for `A'isha. Some may be classed as instructional literature designed with didactic rather than scholarly intent to reach younger Muslim audiences.[35]

All modern Islamic writing on `A'isha has the potential to carry explicit and implicit messages about the proper role of women, their behavior, and status. Using `A'isha as a prism, the most unsubtle of these works may utilize her persona to argue either for change or enforcement of a variously defined Islamic status quo. Thus, the Egyptian feminist author Nawal al-Sa`dawi argues that `A'isha represents a "tradition" of "those who stood

up for themselves and their rights" while others utilize the same historical figure to deny those same rights to women.[36] Evocations of `A'isha
continue to be included in the more recent works of the Moroccan
authors Magali Morsy and Fatima Mernissi who also analyze `A'isha's sig-
nificance within the broader sphere of the Prophet Muhammad's wives.[37]
The work of Mernissi, like that of al-Sa`dawi, appears driven by increas-
ing Muslim feminist concerns with the status of women in the contemporary world. Pressing issues of self-definition in Sunni Muslim countries
allow `A'isha to serve simultaneously as both role model for a more tra-
ditional Islam or symbol for a greater need for female access and participation in public life.[38]

In the scholarly vein, the best, most detailed modern biographies by
Muslim scholars are those of `Umar Kahhala and `A'isha bint `Abd al-Rah-
man.[39] Kahhala's work is part of a larger biographical dictionary of
notable Arab and Muslim women. `Abd al-Rahman's biographical dictio-
nary is dedicated exclusively to the women of the Prophet's family. Both
Kahhala and `Abd al-Rahman draw their materials from early Arabic
sources. Neither editorializes about the bases of `A'isha's importance for
the Muslim community. They take her significance to be self-evident and
often cite early Islamic sources verbatim in sketching her life. A more spe-
cialized study is contained in Sa`id al-Afghani's work on `A'isha and politics, which details the implications of the participation of the Prophet's
wife in the first civil war.[40] Although al-Afghani's work mines much
medieval material, the conclusions he draws for his modern audience are
pointed in their condemnation of any role for Muslim women in politics.[41] His pronouncements promote `A'isha as the perfect Islamic exam-
ple for the exclusion of all Muslim women from any public role. Muslim
feminists such as Mernissi find themselves in the unenviable position of
refuting not just al-Afghani, but his presentation of `A'isha's prominent
example in the Islamic past.[42]

`A'isha bint Abi Bakr has been the focus of renewed interest in recent
Western scholarship on Islamic history, most of which has been generated
by the study of gender initiated by the relatively new discipline of
women's studies. In Middle Eastern history the study of medieval women
has been implicitly defined as a subversive sideshow of a sideshow.[43]
Recent scholarly literature, with few exceptions, cites `A'isha's example

as evidence for more general questions relating to the roles of women before and after the advent of Islam.[44] These brief treatments are suggestive, but are no more conclusive in their reading of `A'isha's legacy than are the discussions of their modern Muslim counterparts. Many of these Western analyses are tied explicitly to highly politicized contemporary questions concerning the status of women and Islam.[45] One Western assessment of `A'isha bint Abi Bakr contains a survey of translated anecdotes relating to her life and concludes succinctly that she "played an important role" in Muhammad's life which in turn "made her an influential figure" in the Islamic community.[46] The details of that influence receive no expansion. Selective attention to `A'isha in recent anthropological, literary, and historical works which utilize gender as a primary category of analysis has also expanded her visibility in Western scholarship.[47]

The most thorough Western study of `A'isha's life to date remains the biography by Nabia Abbott, written in 1942. In her introduction Abbott notes that her work was prompted by "the urge to make known more of the life of this First Lady of Islam."[48] Abbott was keenly aware of the political implications of her work on `A'isha as of "special interest" to "the progressives of both East and West in a world so rapidly contracting."[49] In this regard, she cites the Muslim women's movement and its renewed interest in the historic women of Islam. Abbott's observations about `A'isha's viability as a modern mediating figure for Muslim women have been confirmed more recently in the distinctly different context of the Sunni Islamic resurgence in the Arab world, where an observer of the phenomenon in the 1980s wrote: "a new generation of Muslim women, many of whom are not only educated in the liberal arts and sciences, but have also acquired an Islamic literacy—through study of the Qur'an and the Hadith . . . are taking as their models the founding mothers of Islam—the Prophet's wives [including] `A'isha."[50]

Abbott's biography is thorough in its analysis of medieval materials, but is confined to a concept of linear chronology in which the subject is traced from birth to death. `A'isha's legacy is summarized in one final brief paragraph in a chapter in which she is referred to as "sage and saint."[51] Despite the Sunni acceptance of her importance as a sage, this work and others dispute `A'isha's designation as a saint as both inaccurate and misleading.[52] In Abbott's presentation of `A'isha's life, little allowance is made for the

divergent accounts which reflect `A'isha's more controversial compo-
nents in the medieval record. No biography can adequately treat the
process of communal debate about `A'isha's posthumous meaning which
is the focus of this work.

When Muslim authors began to capture `A'isha's past on paper, they
did so from a variety of perspectives, in a number of genres, faced always
with the implicit understanding that she was difficult to categorize. Yet
these written sources represent only the beginning of the oft-repeated
medieval process of selectively retelling and emphasizing parts of her life
and its meaning. They do not yield a complete personality so much as a
suggestion of the varied aspects of a past life presented as a dubious coher-
ence.[53] `A'isha's life as written was, from the first, a composite of remem-
brances which represent different angles of a difficult subject, one whose
presentation was of critical interest to all members of the Muslim community for whom she would serve repeatedly as a central figure in their
discussions of the past.

We do not have `A'isha's autobiography, but even when we encounter
the oral remnants which purport to be `A'isha's own words frozen in
writing, the effect is not unlike that described by Morton Smith in his
attempt to ascertain the essence of religiohistorical personality: "Personality is so complex and changeable that even a good autobiography is a
high-speed photograph of a waterfall: it imposes a fixed form on a process
falsified by fixation."[54]

`A'isha's depiction represents a portrait revealed in a range of sources
which may be likened to that of a historical waterfall: a process fixed,
repeatedly and distinctly over the centuries by later efforts to capture the
significance of her image for Muslim society. The image of the waterfall,
like that of the historical `A'isha, appears the same, but it is, in fact, ever-
changing. However, unlike Smith's description of the waterfall "falsified by
fixation," it may be argued that male Muslim scholars, in refining and
expanding aspects of `A'isha's historical personality, implicitly verified the
difficulty of presenting her controversial existence as a coherent whole.
In so doing, they compensated for their distance from the existence they
sought to describe, the historical presence about whom they had heard so
much, but never witnessed. However, the depiction of `A'isha's life also
prompted by its very repetition great refinement and variation. Her

essence was not "falsified by fixation," rather it was confirmed anew in its relevance to emerging Muslim communal identities.

A waterfall summons a vision of fluidity of movement, unerring gravity of direction. In the realm of intellectual and cultural processes, ideas may also be similarly propelled, for they too move and establish patterns of direction through repeated expression. In the multiple trajectories of `A'isha's depiction, the historian must simultaneously account for the place of both women and invention in the past. The construction of historical reality in all cultures must allow room for some fiction, a logical manifestation of historicity. In describing a reluctant student of history, the novelist Jane Austen dispatched both issues succinctly:

I read [history] a little as a duty, but it tells me nothing that does not either vex or weary me . . . with wars or pestilences on every page; the men all so good for nothing, and hardly any women at all—it is very tiresome; and yet I often think it odd that it should be so dull, for a great deal of it must be invention. The speeches that are put into the heroes' mouths, their thoughts and designs—the chief of all this must be invention, and invention is what delights me in other books.[55]

As a response to these conjectures, another female character replies that she is "very well contented to take the false with the true, . . . and as for the little embellishments you speak of, they are embellishments, and I like them as such." Even such a fictive exchange suggests that the utilization of historical sources need not focus on explicit historical data, a usual object of the modern scholarly quest, but may also reveal attitudes. Austen's formulations about invention or presumed invention may be applied to the scrutiny of Arabic sources concerning `A'isha bint Abi Bakr. In the context of this study the challenge to the modern historian is to reconcile "the false with the true." Indeed, the historian must also find value and meaning in the expression of detail and dialogue which grows rather suspiciously over time and fits the category suggested by Austen as embellishment. In this study, invention will not be shunned, but will instead be examined and utilized. The life of `A'isha, replete as it was with controversial events prompted contradictory depictions, interpretations, and attitudinal biases. Not to exploit these observations, especially in cases where a tale grows in the telling or is selectively used in polemic, is to miss the development of a dialogue fixed in time. Indeed, this is the stuff of which legacies are made and through which we gain access to their evolution.

W. Montgomery Watt, a noted Western biographer of the Prophet Muhammad, warned about the problem of invention in Arabic sources by taking the phrase "tendential shaping" from a predecessor and then expanding upon it. What Watt did in explicating his understanding of tendential shaping was to unintentionally paraphrase Austen. Watt states that with some effort, one can identify fact in terms of event-related explicit data by warily defining invention most particularly "in the attributing of motives for historical acts" to their actors. Watt explains: "The distinction between external acts and alleged motives should therefore be kept firmly in mind. The actor himself and his friends will suggest the praiseworthy motives; his enemies will assert that the motives were dishonorable. But there can be little dispute about the external acts except within narrow limits."[56]

What Watt and most historians who assert that there is explicit historical data to be found in early Muslim sources want to discard is exactly what Austen identified as embellishment and Nabia Abbott, ʿAʾisha's single Western biographer, described as "tares among wheat . . . readily weeded out."[57] It is at this juncture in Watt's argument that he inserts a historical example. Not surprisingly, he chooses ʿAʾisha to clarify the disjunction between tendential shaping and explicit event-related data. "Thus," suggests Watt concerning the events leading up to the first Islamic civil war, "nobody denies that ʿAʾishah left Medina shortly before the murder of the caliph ʿUthman, but whether her motives were honourable, dishonourable, or neutral is vigorously debated."[58] Watt's method, such as it is, works if one assumes that the event in question, ʿAʾisha's timely departure from Medina, is accurately related and the embellishment represented by ex post facto reaction or attitudinal overlay, merely reveals the patina of fiction on fact. However, through the application of this method, Watt tosses out ideas which he himself admits were "vigorously debated" at the time they were set down. In this process of exclusion, a later medieval discourse resonant in Arabic sources about the meaning of these events and ʿAʾisha's part in them is ignored.

Watt assumes that questions of motivation and personal qualities add little to the writing of history because these attitudes are replete with opinions which may warp the representation of people and events. As a fellow biographer, Abbott seems to have applied a similar approach to the selection and utilization of materials about ʾAʾisha. Both Watt and Abbott shape the depiction of their subjects accordingly: "The modern historian will therefore largely discount allegations of motives in his sources and will suggest his own motives in the light of what he knows about the total pattern of the external actions of a man."[59] In this case, we may extend Watt's remarks to include the external actions of a woman. In contradistinction to previous studies and biographies, the focus and methodology of this book promotes access to a hitherto ignored historical debate.

Chronology, Sources, and Organization

The primary focus of this inquiry is the majority Sunni Muslim community who perceive ʾAʾisha as an exemplary figure, but who alone faced the dilemma of reconciling her more controversial aspects within the communal record. Shiʾi Muslim texts, which maintain greater uniformity in their rejection of ʾAʾisha as an exemplary female figure, will be utilized only for points of obvious contrast to the more nuanced Sunni position in this study. ʾAʾisha's centrality to the Islamic past meant her presence could not be ignored, but must be shaped in Sunni sources to merit praise, meet attack, or counter derision. The Sunni Muslim struggle to maintain a female historical persona who could not be easily idealized, but who would remain a multifaceted and important figure within the realm of their past, is the essential conundrum at the heart of this work. Since this is not a biography, but a critical inquiry into the implications of a woman's life, this work may be categorized as a study of Muslim historiography refracted through the example of ʾAʾisha bint Abi Bakr.

Although I seek to document the medieval interpretation of ʾAʾisha, in so doing, I simultaneously present an interpretation of my own. In this process, I acknowledge that just as Muslims shaped their past to fit their own internal definitional categories in a vast span of times and texts, so too did I construct an analytical framework, following Muslim clues, that is clearly distinct from them.[60] Selectivity and authorial intent remain as central to this attempted reading of the past as to any current study of the earliest Muslim sources. Thus, I make no claim that this book is either

exhaustive or encyclopedic in its treatment of ʿAʾisha's legacy. Her presence in the medieval Islamic written corpus is so frequently represented,
so persistently present, that many lifetimes and volumes would be requisite to fully explore the totality of her historical implications.[61] Those who
would seek out the definitive ʿAʾisha bint Abi Bakr may find more of their
answers in biography, but they should be warned that ʿAʾisha's legacy, as
constructed in the medieval Islamic past or the present day, is, in its
essence, always redefined by those driven by the need to know, to remember, and to interpret.

ʿAʾisha's symbolic valence did not emerge full-blown in the historical
record as a static representation. Rather, in its complexity, her legacy
exemplifies a contextually construed evolution, one that responded to
reflect both continuity and change in an Islamic medieval milieu where
both promoted the representation of truth. All of the works featured in
this study date, as written, from the period between the third/ninth century and the eighth/fourteenth century. All but three of the sources are
written in Arabic, with two other selections in Persian and one from a
Turkish text. Those materials that fall beyond the eighth/fourteenth century, include a series of miniatures which illustrate an Ottoman Turkish
life of the Prophet Muhammad from the sixteenth/eleventh century
based upon an earlier Turkish work composed in the eighth/fourteenth
century. Late biographical dictionaries dedicated to the women of the
Prophet Muhammad's family also mark an endpoint in the discussion of
ʿAʾisha's legacy during this latest medieval phase of her evolution.

The sources for each chapter begin with the earliest written Arabic
accounts, including *tabaqat*, "biographical dictionaries," *siyar/maghazi*
works on the life of the Prophet and the early expeditions of the first
Islamic community, hadith collections, *ta'rikh*, "chronicle," and *tafsir*,
"Qur'anic exegesis." They are supplemented in thematic relevance with
selections from *adab*, "belles-lettres," poetry and reference to theological
and doctrinal works from the third/ninth–sixth/twelfth centuries. This
four-hundred-year period produced examples of the most fluid definitional debates about ʿAʾisha's legacy, but the essence of their resolution
appears most distinctly defined in the fourth/tenth century as both Sunni
and Twelver Shiʿi identities are solidified separately and in relation to one
another. During this period, praise of her historical persona is present,

but definitively qualified in the Sunni record, in part, as a response to a volatile medieval environment. `A'isha's meaning in Muslim memory is a composite product of the earliest compilations undertaken in Arabia at Medina as well as later elaborations and definitional debate centered in the Islamic urban centers of Iraq and Iran.

The devastating Mongol invasions of the mid-seventh/thirteenth century put an end to the `Abbasid imperial heartland as a medieval center of Islamic scholarship. A hundred years later, in the eighth/fourteenth century, a geographical shift occurs in the locus of additional works concerning `A'isha's legacy. Most of the sources generated about `A'isha after that time are the product of the Egyptian and Syrian-based urban scholarly elite who had survived the Mongol onslaught. These later works represent a brief period of primary emphasis on `A'isha as a source of hadith, a symbol of the survival of Sunni Muslim civilization and communal memory. Sunni scholars based the boldest of their redefinitions of `A'isha on the precedent of those Muslims who had preceded them by as much as four hundred years. Even a change in the terms of her relevance in the later medieval period would not be undertaken without reference to the earliest, most positive sources of her definition. The continuity of the embellishment of `A'isha's legacy during this later period suggests that overt political disjunctions did not disturb Sunni Muslim scholarly impetus so much as redirect it, a clear sign of civilizational vitality. Thus, in the last phase of `A'isha's medieval evolution, Sunni scholars celebrated her anew as part of a reaffirmation of their own self-definition in the aftermath of external threat and continuing internal division.

two *privileges and problems: the shaping of `A'isha's historical persona*

> *If it is permissible to take two-thirds of the religion from `A'isha, the truthful, then it is also permissible to receive religious benefit from one of her handmaidens . . . When a woman [walks] on the path of Allah like a man, then it is not possible to call her a woman.*      —Farid al-Din`Attar

C ontested issues of religiopolitical precedence and praise shaped the historical persona of `A'isha bint Abi Bakr in the earliest written sources. Unique positive qualities attributed to the Prophet's wife first appear as attempts to promote her distinctive place in the Islamic past, a position with critical ramifications for an emerging Sunni Muslim majority. `A'isha was only one wife among the thirteen women married by the Prophet Muhammad.[1] Her placement within the category *azwaj al-nabi,* "the wives of the Prophet," is consistent throughout several early genres. `A'isha's inclusion within this model group of women in the first Islamic community represents a significant female frame for her remembered life. In the Qur'an, the wives of the Prophet are defined as special, different from other women. They are described as like "the mothers," of the Muslims, a phrase which promotes their collective honorific *ummahat al-mu'minin,* "the mothers of the believers," the category of address and record within which these women are found in most early sources. They were singled out within the Islamic community because of the Prophet's marital selection, but also as a result of the Qur'anic injunctions addressed specifically to them concerning their behavior, dress, and inability to remarry after the Prophet's death.[2]

As represented in the earliest written sources, `A'isha's life is documented in works that describe the life and exploits of the Prophet Muhammad.[3] What first sets `A'isha apart as a female figure of religiohistorical significance is her role in the life of the Prophet Muhammad. Her marriage to the Prophet is thus the primary distinguishing factor in the creation of her legacy. In this process, biographical details about `A'isha's life with her husband may be read as data distilled from perceptions about Muhammad, the Islamic community's most important figure. References to `A'isha abound in early biographies of the Prophet Muhammad, but they do not include detailed reference to either her uniqueness or her marriage, the cornerstones of her historical centrality.[4]

`A'isha's posthumous recollection in the written record fixes her within the first Muslim female religious elite, but the attempt to separate her from her co-wives could not emphasize mere distinction without acknowledging a confluence of factors that made her simply different in Muslim memory. As she was one of the Prophet's wives, early sources would both promote and contest her superiority, a historiographical debate in which emerging Sunni and Shi`i concerns about political succession and communal identity were embedded. Her legacy as one of the Prophet's many wives thus had a key practical component in `A'isha's case, for her status as wife also promoted her father Abu Bakr's remembrance as the first legitimate political successor to the Prophet. `A'isha, as the key link between the two men, may have been ostensibly present in the historical record as the Prophet's wife, but the terms of her meaning would be charged for both Sunni and Shi`i Muslims by the implications of her role as the daughter of the first caliph. Additional factors of difference, enhanced by the politics of genealogy and succession, simultaneously set her apart from the other wives of the Prophet and infused later historiographical debate in the Muslim community about the accusation of adultery and her participation in the first civil war. If genealogy and controversy provided a higher historical profile for `A'isha than for the rest of Muhammad's wives, these biographical factors also insured that

control of her memory in the written record would remain for her supporters both different and difficult.

The question of what made `A'isha special was pursued most directly
in biographical dictionaries, chronicles, and hadith collections of the
third/ninth and fourth/tenth centuries. It is in the indigenous genre of
tabaqat, a term synonymous with biographical dictionaries, that `A'isha's
earliest and fullest representation may be found in the third/ninth century. Biographical dictionaries began as an attempt to preserve the lives of
those Muslims who related traditions from the Prophet Muhammad. The
most expansive, early written source of information on `A'isha's life is the
entry dedicated to her in the biographical dictionary of Ibn Sa`d (d.
230/845). Born at Basra, Ibn Sa`d later settled in `Abbasid Baghdad and
became secretary to al-Waqidi (d. 207/823), an early biographer of the
Prophet. Ibn Sa`d's biographical dictionary includes notices of more than
four thousand Muslims who narrated hadith. Nearly six hundred women
are included in the work, one of whom is `A'isha bint Abi Bakr. `A'isha's
placement among the biographies of women contained in Ibn Sa`d's work
is further qualified by her designation within the more specific category
of the wives of the Prophet. Ibn Sa`d's information on the wives of the
Prophet, in particular, was most probably culled from an earlier, no
longer independently extant work of al-Waqidi. Each entry is composed
of a selection of hadith, arranged roughly from the subject's birth to
death.[5] A contemporary with a brief section on women, but with a focus
on Arab tribal genealogy rather than biographical detail is found in Khalifa Ibn Khayyat al-`Usfuri (d. 240/855) and the later, more detailed bio-
graphical dictionary of al-Baladhuri (d. 279/892).[6] These sources are also
supported with reference to major Sunni hadith collections of the
third/ninth century, six of which Sunni Muslims would accept as canonical within the next century.[7]

Ibn Sa`d's biographical dictionary contains two separate lists of attrib-
utes that explicitly distinguish `A'isha. These claims are related on the
authority of `A'isha herself, a device which appears to cede the wife of the
Prophet control over the terms of her own praise. Taken together, these
nineteen items, although sometimes repetitive, emphasize privileges that
pertain to `A'isha alone. They record the singularity of distinctions that
made her preferred over and above the other twelve wives of Muhammad

and form a composite picture of her life with him. The lists serve, ostensibly, to define and defend the bases of his preference for her. They reinforce Muhammad's choice of `A'isha in a later, distinctly different historical context. Written more than one hundred and fifty years after the death of both husband and wife, the Prophet's choice of `A'isha as his *habiba*, his "beloved" favorite, is justified once again. These items are, collectively, an attempt to promote and praise her as unique and superior to all the other wives of the Prophet. Even as a partisan attempt, these qualities emphasize key attributes in `A'isha's remembered life. They provide a succinct form of access to the most positive features of her presence in the communal record which remain as remarkable for what they select as omit. The fact that these attributes represent a form of praise does not mean that there were not alternative representations of `A'isha's unique significance presented in similar forms. Within a hundred years of Ibn Sa`d's death, his two lists of unique qualities dedicated to `A'isha would be significantly qualified in the hands of another compiler, a chronicler named al-Tabari (d. 310/923). During this critical century in Baghdad, `A'isha's legacy would be recorded, rewritten, and variously preserved. Both the attributes first found in Ibn Sa`d in the third/ninth century and implicitly qualified in the fourth/tenth-century version of al-Tabari, not only survived, but proved remarkably resilient in later Sunni sources. The difference between the lists of Ibn Sa`d and al-Tabari suggests that `A'isha's legacy formed part of the attempt by Sunni Muslims to define themselves through the representation of the past and its most prominent personages. It is in the fourth/tenth century that scholars first applied the term "Sunni" to themselves as the majority of believers.[8] The emergence of a forged collective identity during this period represented not only a conceptual evolution, but a more definitive response to definitional pressure articulated by Twelver Shi`i coreligionists whose different vision of the same past also effectively challenged the majority's interpretation of `A'isha.[9]

Ibn Sa`d records the following privileges accorded `A'isha in order. They are narrated in the first person and are introduced by the phrase "I was preferred above the [other] wives of the Prophet by ten [attributes]":

1. He [Muhammad] married no other wife as a virgin except me.

2. He didn't marry anyone else whose mother and father were both emigrants.

3. Allah sent down my innocence from heaven.

4. Gabriel brought him [Muhammad] my likeness in silk from heaven saying, "Marry her for she is your wife."

5. He and I used to wash from a single vessel and he didn't do that with any of his wives except me.

6. He used to pray while I was in his presence. He did that with none of his wives except me.

7. He received revelation while he was with me. This didn't happen when he was with any of his other wives.

8. He [Muhammad] died in my arms.[10]

9. He died on a night which had been turned over to me.

10. He was buried under my house.[11]

Shortly thereafter in Ibn Sa`d's entry, the wife of the Prophet narrates a second list of nine characteristics. Cast once more in her own voice, `A'isha announces: "I received attributes which were not granted [any other] wife."

1. The Prophet of Allah took me as his wife when I was a girl of seven.

2. The angel brought Muhammad my likeness in the palm of his hand.

3. He [Muhammad] consummated the marriage when I was nine.

4. I saw Gabriel and no other wife saw him except me.

5. I was the most beloved of his wives.

6. My father was the most beloved of his companions.

7. The Prophet of Allah fell ill in my house.

8. I nursed him.

9. Muhammad died and no one witnessed it except myself and the angels.[12]

Five major themes emerge from these nineteen items. They refer to `A'isha's genealogy, her proximity to the Prophet during his performance of ritually significant acts, and her presence during the final days of his life.[13] The two remaining major categories describe aspects of `A'isha's marriage to the Prophet and the demonstration of divine intervention in her married life.

Genealogy: The Father-Daughter Linkage

`A'isha's genealogy is referred to in both lists. In the first, her mother and father are described as *muhajirun*, "emigrants." They followed the Prophet from Mecca when he departed for the oasis town of Medina in the year 622. The importance of this event, called the *hijra*, marks a turning point in the Islamic community and begins the Muslim era proper as the year 1. Those Meccans who followed Muhammad to Medina confirmed both their loyalty and preeminence among other Muslims as the first group of converts to Islam. Not only does her parents' designation as emigrants enhance `A'isha's prestige in the religious community, it confirms the solidity of her own parental lineage as fully Islamic. Moreover, it emphasizes the implicitly political dimension of her father's importance as the first temporal successor to Muhammad. Sunni Muslim reverence for Abu Bakr thus reinforces `A'isha's exalted status. She is defined primarily as the wife of one man, secondarily as the daughter of another, two key ascriptive aspects of her legacy.

In the second list of privileges, `A'isha declares that her father Abu Bakr "is the most beloved" of the Prophet's companions. Such praise and pride in her paternal ancestry parallels the terminology which in these early sources links father and daughter in the superiority of the Prophet's esteem. Abu Bakr's early conversion to Islam and staunch support of the Prophet created a close bond between the two men. Thus, it is no wonder that Abu Bakr initially viewed the Prophet's intention to marry `A'isha with some trepidation. Abu Bakr reportedly queried Muhammad about the situation, asking "How can I marry my daughter to the man who is my brother?" The Prophet replied, "You are my brother in religion."[14]

Clearly, certain of the first Muslim lineages based on faith projected more prestige than others. The exchange between Abu Bakr and the Prophet suggests a new basis for communal relationships forged in faith rather than blood. As a community of believers, drawn from an increasing variety of tribal genealogies, the Prophet's message ideally created a religious community in which tribal conflict would be superseded by a new unity shared by all Arabs who had adopted Islam. In matters of political succession, Sunni Muslims would retrospectively argue that after the Prophet's death, Abu Bakr's precedence in faith mattered more than genealogy. Moreover, Muhammad and Abu Bakr had cemented their religious commitment through the marriage of `A'isha, a marital tie with immediate and longterm consequences for the Islamic community. In contrast, Shi`i Muslims would opt for leadership drawn from an Islamic genealogy based on both faith and collateral descent from the Prophet. For Shi`i Muslims, the designation of Abu Bakr as the Prophet's "brother in religion" could not challenge the superior spiritual and political claims of `Ali ibn Abi Talib, the Prophet's closest male relative and son-in-law. The male descendants of `Ali and the Prophet's daughter Fatima would represent the majority of Shi`i Muslim challengers to later Islamic dynasties, a fact already repeatedly, if unsuccessfully, demonstrated by the third/ninth century.

Many of `A'isha's honorary titles are closely tied to and, in some instances, replicate those of her father. Abu Bakr is described in his most famous title as *al-siddiq*, "the truthful," as conferred, in one account, by the angel Gabriel.[15] Abu Bakr's designation as "the truthful man" is the reward for his staunch support of the Prophet's account of his miraculous journey from Arabia to Jerusalem and back in one night.[16] In this sense, Abu Bakr's honorary title refers to his speaking the truth in support of Muhammad.[17] The term is also used as an epithet in the Qur'an in conjunction with the prophets Abraham and Joseph.[18] `A'isha becomes, seemingly by extension, *al-siddiqa bint al-siddiq*, "the truthful woman, daughter of the truthful man."[19] The designation doubly emphasizes the paternal precedent of exemplary faith and character. However, in `A'isha's case, the honorary title *al-siddiqa* may also contain specific connotations about the matter in which she testifies to the truth. Abu Bakr professes his faith in the Prophet's account of his night journey; `A'isha will tell the truth in her own defense against a charge of adultery.

Another instance of father-daughter replication in honorary designations occurs in the second list. There, Abu Bakr is defined as "the most beloved" of the Prophet's male companions and his daughter is designated as "the most beloved" of his wives. A separate tradition found in Ibn Sa`d confirms the linkage of these claims and distinguishes categories of priority by gender. Thus, the Prophet was asked, "Whom do you most love among the people?" "`A'isha," he replied." The interlocutor continued, "And among men?" The Prophet said, "Her father."[20] The political implications of this, apparently, harmless question reverberated in medieval Islamic society as an extension of communal identity and a later provocation for violence throughout the `Abbasid period, the very time when these traditions were finally preserved and codified. Although her father's reputation enhanced `A'isha's standing in the Sunni Islamic community, those who supported the primacy of `Ali's claim to the caliphate perceived Abu Bakr as a usurper. In her list of unique qualities, `A'isha proudly made reference to her father as the most beloved, hence the best, of the Prophet's companions, but that claim would be challenged by accounts about the Prophet's love for `Ali. Competing statements concerning the Prophet's affection for his most prominent followers were often cast in terms of the most beloved male and female pair. In some hadith, `A'isha and Abu Bakr would emerge triumphant, in others Fatima and `Ali.[21] For Shi`i Muslims, however, there would be no question that `Ali was the most beloved male.[22] In sixth/eleventh-century Baghdad the Sunni judge and preacher Ibn al-Jawzi (d. 597/1200) was approached during one Sunni-Shi`i riot. He was asked to mediate between the two groups who could not agree about the merits of Abu Bakr and `Ali. When pressed to state which of the two was the best man, Ibn al-Jawzi astutely replied, "He whose daughter married the other." Each faction interpreted the mediator's response in their own favor. The Sunni Muslims believed that the male in question was Abu Bakr since `A'isha had married the Prophet. With equal ease, Shi`i Muslims concluded that the statement referred to `Ali, since the Prophet's daughter Fatima had married him.[23] Moreover, as a scholar who knew that in the earliest traditions both men were separately designated as the best, Ibn al-Jawzi demonstrated not merely cleverness, but the variability of the truth. He provided a persuasive demonstration of the power of partisan interpretation.

Although the primary association of both `A'isha and Fatima was to the Prophet, their distinctive secondary relationships to prominent male Muslim leaders would cause them to be irrevocably opposed in communal debates after their deaths. At the verbal level, the confrontation between Shi`i Muslim supporters of `Ali and Sunni Muslim partisans of Abu Bakr resulted in competing claims for superiority. The opposition between `A'isha and Fatima as conflicting female images was merely an extension of the more overtly political Abu Bakr-`Ali terminological tension. These claims, made by both camps, were ostensibly linked to individuals not causes. Thus, when Abu Bakr's reputation was maligned by supporters of `Ali, so too was `A'isha's. However, in the case of `A'isha and Fatima, the conflict of words was also a debate about these women's meaning and example for later members of the Islamic community, written about by men for the edification of women.

The battlefield in this contest for merit and demonstrable closeness to the Prophet Muhammad took place both in this world and the next. Both Abu Bakr and `Ali are described as the first converts to Islam, with disagreement about their precedence sometimes taking place within the same tradition.[24] The attribution of this honor held great significance throughout the Muslim community, but its determination drew upon conflicting accounts to suit political necessity. Thus, there was no doubt for Shi`i Muslims that `Ali was the first convert. Both men are also recorded in early sources as having been "promised paradise" by the Prophet.[25] Nor were Abu Bakr and `Ali alone in their final heavenly destination. Each of the key women close to the Prophet also held a future place in the next world. His first wife, Khadija, would have a house in paradise, while Fatima would reign as mistress of the female community of believers in heaven, along with her sons who would be the chiefs of the Muslim young men there.[26] `A'isha would also appear as Muhammad's wife in "this world and the next" and "in heaven."[27] The burgeoning population of heavenly inhabitants reflected an earthly Islamic hierarchy of belief about human precedence in the first Muslim community.

Just as the Christian inhabitants of fifth- and sixth-century Constantinople were provoked to violence over theological differences about the nature of Jesus, Muslims in third/ninth- and fourth/tenth-century Baghdad and Nishapur came to blows over the reputations of Muhammad's companions and wives.[28] Issues of political authority and religious identity continued to be transmitted through association with specific human examples from the first Islamic community. A fourth/tenth-century chronicle describes an incident in which the third/ninth-century `Abbasid Caliph al-Mutawakkil (d. 247/861) ordered the torture and death of a man accused of cursing the first two caliphs, Abu Bakr and `Umar, and their daughters, the Prophet's wives `A'isha and Hafsa.[29] The behavior of the accused clearly suggests a Shi`i Muslim identity. By the late third/ninth century, the majority of Muslims, including the `Abbasid ruling authority, would have identified such behavior with *al-Rawafid*, "the rejectors," those Shi`i Muslims whose faith prompted them to declare the first three caliphs illegitimate successors to the Prophet.[30] As part of this Twelver Shi`i doctrinal practice, ritual curses were heaped upon these men. `A'isha's name, as the daughter of Abu Bakr and the opponent of `Ali in the first civil war, was not surprisingly part of this Shi`i practice. In the year 241/855, the accused man was killed by "a thousand blows of the whip." On his death, the body was thrown into the Tigris river without benefit of any prayers. He was, in fact, treated as an apostate. Special mention is made in a later chronicle of this same incident and the importance of the man who "slandered" `A'isha, the verb used most probably represents a delicate reference to the accusation of adultery, a charge Sunni Muslims refute with reference to her Qur'anic vindication.[31]

In the Iranian city of Nishapur, local history records the partisan implications of mentioning the name of the third caliph `Uthman (d. 35/656) in the fourth/tenth century. `Uthman, like `A'isha's father Abu Bakr, was also regarded by Shi`i Muslims as a usurper. The nexus of illegitimate successors to Muhammad who had thwarted the Shi`i Muslim vision of `Ali's rightful primacy of place, included `A'isha by extension and demonstration. Her genealogy and active opposition to `Ali in the first civil war made her a double object of Shi`i scorn. In Nishapur, one man, assumed to be a Shi`i Muslim, referred to the third caliph `Uthman with unusual reverence saying, "the martyred caliph may God be pleased with him" and describing `A'isha as "the truthful" and "the beloved of the beloved of God." Praise for both `Uthman and `A'isha suggests that this man was not a Shi`i Muslim. Indeed his words of praise could "easily have sparked serious rioting" in Shi`i neighborhoods of Nishapur.[32]

The Prophet's preference for `A'isha resulted in recorded resentment on the part of some of his other wives. In one instance, certain disgruntled spouses sent the Prophet's daughter Fatima to him demanding equity of treatment. The Prophet queried his daughter about her mission, asking, "Do you not love what I love?" When Fatima responded in the affirmative, her father replied that he "loved `A'isha." Fatima left vowing never again to press the matter. The Prophet's wife Zaynab bint Jahsh made a similar complaint, but `A'isha silenced her co-wife with Muhammad's tacit support. `A'isha defended herself with such verbal zeal and ire that the Prophet noted a family resemblance, remarking with pride, "She is the daughter of Abu Bakr."[33] `A'isha's historical persona, as defined by these accounts, underscores a pointed triumph of her prestige and that of her father. The Prophet in this anecdote praises them both. Their implicit linkage in the Prophet's esteem is, retrospectively, a political asset. Aided and applauded by her husband, `A'isha is allowed to publicly thwart her powerful female challengers Fatima and Zaynab, not just in past encounters, but for the purposes of third/ninth-century promotion. Thus, both Fatima and Zaynab serve in the written record to inadvertently demonstrate `A'isha's special status as a confirmation of her father's prestige.[34]

Ritual: `A'isha as a Source of Religious Knowledge

The Prophet's attested preference for `A'isha during his lifetime enabled her to observe acts of ritual Islamic practice. Her claims in the first list of her privileges to have washed with the Prophet from the same vessel and to have watched Muhammad pray in her presence are both followed by the assertion that she alone had been a favored witness to these situations.[35] `A'isha's proximity to the Prophet in washing, a critical part of Islamic prayer and, later, ritual purity laws, emphasizes both her physical and spiritual worthiness. An extension of this marital intimacy may be found in references to `A'isha's involvement with the Prophet's habit of cleaning his teeth. He used a twig in this process which `A'isha first chewed in order to soften it for her husband. Reference to this practice is amplified in the biographical dictionary of al-Baladhuri, who records, on the authority of the Prophet's wife, that she used to "brush and take the Prophet the toothstick. He cleaned [his teeth] with the help of my saliva."[36] `A'isha, apparently, also followed her husband's lead in dental matters.[37] The most famous instance of `A'isha softening the Prophet's toothstick occurred during his final illness.[38] Her special knowledge of significant acts of prayer, ablution, and cleanliness performed by the Prophet Muhammad made her an especially valued source of ritually significant information for the Sunni Muslim community, who in all matters looked to the Prophet's human example in the performance of their daily lives.[39]

`A'isha's proud claim to have been the only wife present during Muhammad's reception of divine revelation also figures as a critical point in her prominence as literal witness to the faith. The juncture between jealousy and `A'isha's special privilege is demonstrated by Umm Salama, another of the Prophet's wives. Umm Salama also once lodged complaints about `A'isha's favored treatment in a pattern reminiscent of the objections raised by Fatima and Zaynab. Three times Umm Salama is said to have demanded equity of her husband in the matter of Abu Bakr's daughter. She was dismissed, finally, by the Prophet's testimony that only in `A'isha's presence, sharing a single blanket, had he received revelation from Allah.[40] Once again, the scenario functions as a vehicle of seemingly inadvertent praise for `A'isha whose strengths are demonstrated in stark contrast to the weakness of her female challengers, other wives of the Prophet without equally demonstrable privileges.

Deathbed: The Prophet's Final Preference for `A'isha

Six of the nineteen privileges accorded `A'isha concern her role in the last illness and death of the Prophet. Three references to Muhammad's death are found in each list of `A'isha's unique attributes. The first list includes the triad of statements that Muhammad died in `A'isha's arms,[41] on a night turned over to her, and was buried under her house.[42] It was the Prophet's usual habit to stay one night with each of his wives, but when he became ill, he chose to be taken to `A'isha's house by asking, "Where am I tomorrow? Where am I tomorrow?"[43] Muhammad thus broke his previously established order of rotation and marital equity in order to be nursed by his favorite wife.

The three claims made by `A'isha in Ibn Sa`d's second list of privileges focus more on the illness of the Prophet. The Prophet became ill in her house,[44] she nursed him, and when he died she and the angels were the only witnesses.[45] Each of these ideas indicates `A'isha's uniqueness by emphasizing the Prophet's marked preference for her presence during his last crisis on earth. `A'isha, according to these traditions, is the wife whose company and comfort the Prophet chose in his final moments. In these claims, `A'isha is proven, even at the end of her husband's life, to have maintained her superior status over her co-wives. The political implications of her proximity to the Prophet on his deathbed and, by extension, that of her father is suggestive in the matter of succession. For Sunni Muslims the fact that the Prophet died in 'A'isha's house indirectly supports the nomination of Abu Bakr as the first caliph. Her presence during his last illness and death would be used to confirm that the Prophet designated no one to rule the Islamic community after his death, a position which supported Abu Bakr's subsequent choice by a committee of Muslims. Shi'i Muslims would not interpret 'A'isha's deathbed proximity to the Prophet in such a positive political light. Their own accounts of this critical period would assert that 'Ali had been previously designated by the Prophet at a place called Ghadir Khumm, but that this instruction was ignored and later thwarted by Abu Bakr and his supporters.[46] 'A'isha's role in attempting to prevent the dying Prophet from summoning 'Ali, presumably in order to designate him once more as his choice to lead the Islamic community, is also emphasized in Shi'i sources.[47]

Marriage and Physical Attributes: Age, Virginity, and Childlessness

'A'isha's married life with the Prophet spanned only twelve years. As recorded, she narrates key aspects of this brief marital chronology: "I was six years old when the Prophet married me and I was nine when he consummated the marriage. When he died, I was eighteen years old."[48] 'A'isha would live almost fifty additional years within the Islamic community as a widow, forbidden by the Qur'an to remarry along with Muhammad's other wives.[49] Having benefited from the ascribed status conferred by the prestige of her husband and father, she would maintain her prominence in the community despite actions for which she alone would be responsible.

Four factors found in the two lists of Ibn Sa'd make specific mention of 'A'isha's marriage. In the first list, 'A'isha states that she was the only woman the Prophet married "as a virgin."[50] This obviously prized though fleeting physical asset allowed 'A'isha to remind her husband that all his other wives, as widows, had been physically intimate with other men. Reference to her unique virginity, narrated on 'A'isha's authority, caused the Prophet to smile.[51] 'A'isha's virginity, defined as special attribute, emphasizes her sexuality as the Prophet's marital prize, a mark of distinction which supports male definition and control of female honor and chastity. Unlike the Prophet's daughter Fatima, whose designation in later medieval sources as *al-batul*, "the virgin," will allow her to transcend aspects of more mundane female biology, not in the conception of her children but in matters of menstruation and parturition, `A'isha's virginity merits no honorary epithet, but remains part of her sensual legacy as the Prophet's spouse.

The second list confirms the particulars of the marriage by explaining that `A'isha was seven when she married the Prophet and nine when the union was consummated. `A'isha's age is a major preoccupation in Ibn Sa`d where her marriage age varies between six and seven; nine seems constant as her age at the marriage's consummation.[52] Only Ibn Hisham's biography of the Prophet mentions that `A'isha may have been ten years old when the Prophet consummated the marriage.[53] All of these specific references to the bride's age reinforce `A'isha's pre-menarcheal status and, implicitly, her virginity. They also suggest the variability of `A'isha's age in the historical record.[54]

As if in summation of her marital status, it is recorded among `A'isha's privileges that she was "the most beloved of his wives."[55] Although not mentioned in either list, it is perceived in other third/ninth-century sources attributed to `A'isha as a mark of additional esteem that the marriage occured in the tenth Islamic month of Shawwal.[56] After stating the month of her marriage, `A'isha raises the clearly rhetorical question: "Which of his wives had more favor with him than me?"[57] `A'isha believed the month so propitious that she preferred the women of her family to marry in that month.[58] The idea was not immediately popular with the populace.[59] The month of Shawwal had, before the advent of Islam, apparently been considered unlucky because of its association with outbreaks of the plague. It has been suggested that `A'isha wanted to demonstrate that the month was an exemplary time in which to wed.[60] Thus, `A'isha sought not only to reverse prevailing practice, but to create another mark of distinction for herself.

`A'isha's marriage with the Prophet produced no children. Yet the Prophet distinguished `A'isha with a *kunya*, an honorary parental designation. Apparently, `A'isha complained that all of his other wives had these titles. She became Umm `Abd Allah, "the mother of `Abd Allah," a reference to her sister Asma's son ʾAbd Allah ibn al-Zubayr (d. 73/692).[61] Al-Zubayr, the father of ʾAbd Allah, (d. 36/656) would join with ʾAʾisha when as a widow she fought the fourth caliph, ʾAli, in the first civil war. His son, ʾAʾisha's nephew ʾAbd Allah ibn al-Zubayr, would also assert his political will in the Islamic community. He sided with his aunt ʾAʾisha in the Battle of the Camel, the military confrontation in the first civil war in which his father would lose his life. After ʾAʾisha's death, ʾAbd Allah ibn al-Zubayr would unsuccessfully challenge the Umayyad dynasty (41/661–132/750) in the second civil war.[62] ʾAʾisha's kunya is both a mark of the Prophet's favor, an admission of her childlessness, and a tacit reflection of her political involvement in the Battle of the Camel. In comparison with the fecundity of Muhammad's first wife Khadija, ʾAʾisha's childlessness remained an insuperable disadvantage. Only one of Muhammad's concubines after Khadija would bear children and that single son did not survive infancy. Thus, without direct male heirs, the children of Muhammad's daughter Fatima also become particularly important figures in the Islamic community. ʾAʾisha's maternity remained strictly honorary.

The Angel Gabriel: Heavenly Intervention

According to third/ninth-century evocations, the marriage of ʾAʾisha and the Prophet Muhammad was truly made in heaven. The protagonist in this heavenly intervention was the angel Gabriel. Gabriel's primary significance in Islamic tradition rests on his critical role in the Prophet's mission. The angel was the conduit of revelation to Muhammad from Allah. Only Muhammad ever saw the angel Gabriel in the shape in which he was created. The rest of the angel's manifestations were in human form. Most often he resembled Dihya al-Kalbi, the man acclaimed as the most handsome of the Prophet's time. When in human form, only Muhammad understood Gabriel's true identity, a knowledge of the celestial presence within the power of prophets, but denied other mortals.

The angel Gabriel appears in ʾAʾisha's list of special attributes as a divine envoy in the arrangement of her marriage. Not only does the angel bring Muhammad ʾAʾisha's likeness from heaven, he also commands the Prophet: "Marry her for she is your wife."[63] This intent is reiterated with some variation in the second list found in Ibn Saʾd's biographical dictionary, where the angel who is not named brings `A'isha's likeness "in the palm of his hand," but does not order the Prophet to marry her.[64] These two statements represent the only true, if incomplete, repetition in the two lists. As a part of `A'isha's legacy, the intervention of the angel Gabriel enhances her marriage and places it in the realm of spiritual determinism. Muhammad, in a related tradition, explains that he saw `A'isha twice in his dreams: "I saw a man carrying [your likeness] in a piece of silk cloth. He said, 'This is your wife.' " Gabriel is not specified as the man who holds her image in silk, but Muhammad himself later identifies the vision as the work of Allah.[65] In one account, the context of Gabriel's intervention is made clear in the aftermath of the death of the Prophet's first wife, Khadija. `A'isha is described by the angel as "a successor to Khadija" who will "obliterate some of your grief."

There are in Ibn Sa`d six variations on this theme of angelic intervention in `A'isha's marriage. All of the hadith are attributed to `A'isha as the originator, with one exception. Five out of six of these traditions are transmitted on the authority of men related directly to `A'isha in what is often called a family isnad. Most popularly represented are her maternal nephew `Urwa ibn al-Zubayr (d. 94/712) and his son Hisham.[66] `Urwa was one of the most famous authorities of hadith and history based at Medina. If `A'isha's legacy was to have heavenly inspiration, it would be helped along on earth by its attribution to, and possible propagation by, those male relatives who, in relating these traditions, aided in her praise.

Four other sources for these narratives concerning `A'isha's marriage and the angel Gabriel may be examined in third/ninth-century sources outside of Ibn Sa`d. All of them originate with `A'isha and three out of four perpetuate the family chain of authorities through `Urwa ibn al-Zubayr and his son.[67] There is, however, some minor variation between the hadith found in the third/ninth-century collections of al-Bukhari and Muslim. The former states that the Prophet saw `A'isha's likeness twice in his dreams in accord with the sources in Ibn Sa`d.[68] Muslim reports that the Prophet saw `A'isha thrice.[69] Although this minor discrepancy matters little, the tradition found in al-Tirmidhi suggests the accretive potential of the content. `A'isha's likeness is brought not just in silk cloth, but in green silk.[70] Green is a color associated with the Prophet. In this tradition, `A'isha is not just defined as the Prophet's wife, but his wife "in this world and the next," a phrase that effectively links her divinely ordained marital arrangement with her posthumous place in heaven.[71] The association of 'A'isha as a wife so special on earth that she would retain her status in paradise is found elsewhere in the early record in conjunction with both praise and defense of the Prophet's favorite wife. However, it is not usually articulated by the angel Gabriel.[72]

The role of Gabriel in the arrangement of 'A'isha's marriage is no less significant than the intervention of the divine in the defense of her marital reputation. 'A'isha's vindication from the charge of adultery, as revealed to Muhammad by a revelation recorded in the Qur'an, is also found in Ibn Sa'd's list of special privileges. In it, 'A'isha voices the positive outcome of the scandal, "Allah sent down my innocence from heaven."[73] The only other reference to this matter in Ibn Sa'd is an account which apparently refers to the end of her life. On her deathbed, 'A'isha reminds two visitors that she was the most beloved of the Prophet's wives. One visitor responds in confirmation of her words intended as praise: "Then Allah sent down your innocence from the seven heavens." These two indirect references form the only mention of the accusation of adultery in the biographical entry in Ibn Sa'd dedicated to 'A'isha. Al-Baladhuri also makes only two references to this critical event in her life in his biographical dictionary. He presents the evidence of 'A'isha's vindication as a divine triumph for the wife of the Prophet which resulted in Qur'anic inspiration for the entire community and poetic celebration of the character of the Prophet's wife.[74] The absence of greater detail about this incident in early biographical entries about 'A'isha may suggest that despite a decided emphasis on the positive outcome of the accusation, the matter was generally regarded as too controversial and potentially harmful to her legacy to be treated in other than a detailed description. Both Ibn Sa'd and al-Baladhuri were well aware that extended descriptions of this incident in 'A'isha's life could be found in early biographies of the Prophet Muhammad and hadith collections.[75]

In addition to the arrangement of her marriage by Gabriel and her exoneration from the charge of adultery conveyed by the angel to Muhammad from Allah, 'A'isha claimed a third and final divine privilege: "I saw Gabriel and no other woman saw him except me."[76] This claim occurs in the second list of privileges in Ibn Sa'd. 'A'isha's actual sighting of the angel appears to be amplified in two traditions, one found in Ibn Sa`d and the other in al-Baladhuri's history of the early Islamic conquests. These two references represent two different glimpses of the angel Gabriel. In each, the Prophet is present and it is he, not his wife, who communicates directly with the angel. The version found in Ibn Sa`d originates with `A'isha and is cast in her voice as remembrance.

I saw Gabriel standing in my chamber. He was mounted on a horse and the Prophet of Allah was whispering to him. When the Prophet approached [me], I said, "O Messenger of Allah, who is that with whom I saw you whispering?" The Prophet replied, "You saw him?" I said that I had. He said, "Who does he look like?" I said, "Dihya al-Kalbi." The Prophet said, "What you saw is a great blessing. This is Gabriel." She said, I hesitated until the Prophet said, "O `A'isha, this is Gabriel who says, `Peace be with you.'" I said, "And upon him be peace and may Allah bless him."[77]

The account emphasizes that `A'isha's special privilege is only made possible through the Prophet's mediation. Gabriel, in his earthly resemblance to the Prophet's handsome contemporary Dihya al-Kalbi, appears, initially, as an ordinary mortal to `A'isha. She derives a blessing first by being in the presence of the angel, but also in becoming the recipient of Gabriel's traditionally Muslim salutation "peace be with you," as conveyed through her husband Muhammad. Although `A'isha claims in her list of privileges that she alone among the Prophet's wives saw Gabriel, it is recorded in the hadith collection of Muslim that her co-wife Umm Salama also saw Gabriel. Umm Salama's account, like `A'isha's, emphasizes that the angelic presence took the human form of Dihya al-Kalbi. Umm Salama asserts that she had no knowledge of the angel's presence until after he had departed and she heard the Prophet explain his true nature.[78] Umm Salama "saw" Gabriel in much the same fashion as `A'isha, but with two critical differences: only `A'isha knew of the angel's presence and, even if indirectly, was saluted by him.

The second record of `A'isha sighting Gabriel is recorded in al-Baladhuri in conjunction with a specific time and place. The account is placed within the reports from the fifth Islamic year when the Muslims fought the Banu Qurayza, a clan of Medinan Jews. The Banu Qurayza refused to convert to Islam and eventually negotiated with the Meccan tribe of Quraysh, Muhammad's own tribe, but during this period, his chief military antagonists. The tradition, which originates with `A'isha, reveals that Muhammad's massacre and enslavement of the Jewish clan was inspired by the angel Gabriel's directive.[79] The Prophet had just returned from battle, when the angel appeared.

Then Gabriel came to him and said, "O Muhammad, you have put down your weapons, but we have not yet put down ours. Assault the Banu Qurayza!" Then `A'isha said, "O Prophet of Allah, I saw him [Gabriel] through a crack in the door and dust encircled his head."[80]

`A'isha serves as an observer in this tradition who, apparently, overhears Gabriel's directive without being acknowledged by either Muhammad or the angel. `A'isha's primary role as narrator and relater of the account parallels the intent of al-Baladhuri's work, which is to detail the incident involving the Banu Qurayza. As witness, `A'isha is meant to testify to the angel's presence in order to confirm the Prophet's military action and validate its divine inspiration. Her presence authenticates the Prophet's motive and, indirectly, justifies it.

The majority of traditions in which `A'isha notes Gabriel's presence feature only an exchange of greetings, some of which state explicitly that `A'isha did not see the angel even though Muhammad did. "One day, the Prophet said, 'O `A'isha, this is Gabriel who says, "Peace be with you."' She replied, 'And upon him be peace and the mercy of Allah and His blessing.' I didn't see him. He [Muhammad] saw him, but I did not."[81]

Other references repeat the exchange of greetings, which are always initiated by Gabriel and conveyed through the Prophet without `A'isha explicitly stating whether she saw the angel.[82] In all these cases, `A'isha's numerous contacts with Gabriel are presented as a demonstration of her unique relationship to Muhammad. Through the Prophet's preference for her, now defined as the logical extension of Gabriel's initial and singular intervention in arranging her marriage, `A'isha embodies a marital proximity to the divine.

Khadija, the Prophet' first wife, was also recorded as having indirect contact with the angel Gabriel. The account is located in Ibn Hisham's biography of the Prophet and originates on the authority of Khadija. When the Prophet first began receiving revelation, his wife Khadija tested Gabriel in order to establish his divine nature. She asked Muhammad to inform her when his visitor appeared.[83]

When Gabriel came to him, the Prophet said to Khadija, "This is Gabriel who has just come to me." "Get up, O Muhammad," she said, "and sit by my left thigh." He did. Then she asked, "Can you see him?" "Yes," he replied." Then she said, "Turn around and sit by my right thigh." He did so and she asked, "Can you see him?" When he said that he could, she said, "Sit in my lap." When he had done this, she asked if he could see him [the angel]. He said, "Yes." Then she became distressed and cast aside her veil while the Prophet continued sitting in her lap. She said, "Can you see him? "No," he replied. She said, "O Muhammad, bear witness and rejoice, for by Allah, he is an angel and not a devil."[84]

When Gabriel visits the Prophet, his wife cannot see the angel, nor does he acknowledge her in any verbal way. Khadija's test relies on Muhammad as the intermediary. Through his eyes, Gabriel confirms his true angelic nature by demonstrating respect for the wife of the Prophet. The angel does not transgress what appear to be implicit rules of female modesty as would a devil and departs when Khadija throws off her veil. The word *khimar*, "veil," did not in the early Islamic period necessarily refer to a face covering. In the Qur'an, 24: 31, the term is used to remind Muslim women that they should "draw their khimars over their bosoms" as a part of a prescription for modest female behavior. The verse was revealed at Medina after Khadija's death, as was the "verse of the veil," which commanded only the Prophet's wives, as a mark of distinction, to speak "from behind a *hijab*," or curtain.[85] Thus, in this source, one cannot assert that Khadija threw off her veil in the sense that she uncovered her face. Indeed, such an assumption may represent, should it be so interpreted, an anachronism based on later Islamic practice. Khadija, in this account, does not directly encounter the angel and unlike `A'isha she does not claim in these early sources to have seen him. Her brief, but important, role in this part of Muhammad's life story is to confirm that even in the earliest phase of her husband's prophetic career his instructions originated in heaven.

Gabriel's repeated involvement with `A'isha emphasizes the unique-
ness of her position in relation to all other women, but most particularly
the other wives of the Prophet. The vast majority of these incidents are
related on the authority of `A'isha herself and many are transmitted from
her by members of her extended family. Whether the chains of transmission are authentic or created at a later date and attributed ex post facto,
the content of these reports consistently enhances the legacy of `A'isha's
religious prestige. As a support to the prophetic mission of her husband
and witness to Gabriel as Allah's divine messenger, `A'isha also confirms
for the Muslim community the truth of their faith. Her title *habiba habib
Allah*, "the beloved of the beloved of God," attests in these early biographical sources to her mediated, yet powerful proximity to the divine.[86]

The nineteen attributes listed as key to `A'isha's life with the Prophet
provide an entry point to the examination of her legacy. As part of her earliest biography, the three most critical categories of the five examined are
marriage, divine intervention, and genealogy. In the third/ninth century-
depiction of `A'isha's preeminence, her marriage embodies both a sexual
and sacred reality. As wife, `A'isha's distinct humanity, virginity, youth,
and childlessness is delineated in marked contrast to her role as a divinely designated spouse. The implicit tension between these distinct aspects
of `A'isha's presentation in early written sources suggests that her desig-
nation as the Prophet's favorite wife was built upon a complex combination of factors. These reflect a posthumous attempt to present the
Prophet's wife as more than just another wife. Muhammad's marked preference for `A'isha is detailed as a combination of female distinction and
divine direction. As a historical persona, `A'isha had an edge over her co-
wives manifest in her youth and virginity and enhanced by the manner of
her heavenly presentation, selection, and defense. The memory and the
meaning of `A'isha's marital legacy served to consolidate a vision of
`A'isha as an earthly wife chosen not by the Prophet, but for the Prophet
by heaven.[87] `A'isha's unique marital prestige is also elaborated as an
extension of Muhammad's preference for her father. In both lists, her
prominence appears to be enhanced by that of her father. However, as a
retrospective act of recorded memory, Sunni Muslim scholars understood
that praise of `A'isha was politically interactive in the third/ninth centu-
ry. Thus, the demonstration of `A'isha's preeminence among the Prophet's

wives also served to solidify the bases of her father's importance at a time when Shi`i Muslims refuted the majority's reading of the past and the order of legitimate political leaders of the first Islamic community.

`A'isha's Importance as a Point of Communal Contention

If Ibn Sa`d's two lists represent a partisan attempt at praise of `A'isha and, through her, her father Abu Bakr, then the single list found in al-Tabari less than one hundred years later affirms a contested vision of `A'isha's meaning within Muslim memory. Al-Tabari's chronicle makes reference to `A'isha's marriage briefly as an event of the first Islamic year and allows `A'isha, when prompted by two visitors, to detail her nine unique qualities. These attributes at once consolidate features found earlier in Ibn Sa`d while presenting striking new qualifications and omissions. It is worth noting that the chain of transmission in al-Tabari is utterly different from that found in Ibn Sa`d and is, indeed, suspiciously weak in that one link is recorded as an anonymous man of the tribe of Quraysh. The anonymity of this relater might have been grounds for invalidating the content of the report. Yet the compiler included the flawed chain of authorities along with its core and, in so doing, made a conscious effort to bypass or ignore Ibn Sa`d's earlier references to `A'isha's special qualities. We cannot know what prompted the compiler to include this version of attributes, but the content variation acts implicitly as a curb on Ibn Sa`d's earlier, more fullsome account.

Al-Tabari's introduction to these unique qualities includes two key additions. First, `A'isha asserts that the nine qualities she is about to enumerate belong to no other woman but herself and Maryam, the mother of Jesus. The mention of Maryam, the only woman named in the Qur'an and the explicit object of praise as a model for believers chosen by Allah, appears to have no obvious linkage to `A'isha's special attributes. However, as will be demonstrated later in this work, the association of Maryam with `A'isha indirectly reflects a more substantial discussion of Islamic female ideals based on hadith and Qur'anic exegesis during this period, a process in which al-Tabari as exegete was intimately involved. Even if the links between Maryam and `A'isha appear misplaced and unsubstantiated in this particular context, there was ample reason for the association of

the Qur'anic archetype with `A'isha during the third/ninth and fourth/
tenth centuries. In addition to the curious reference to Maryam in al-
Tabari, `A'isha also declares that by elaborating the nine qualities that per-
tain to her alone she had no intention of placing herself above the other
wives of the Prophet. In fact, `A'isha's protestations, as documented in al-
Tabari, confirm quite the opposite. As a rhetorical device, `A'isha's words
are designed to emphasize these unique details as praise. Indeed, the reference to Maryam here makes `A'isha's claims applicable to only two
women, placing the Prophet's wife by definition above all the other wives
of Muhammad as well as all the other women of the Muslim community.

The nine attributes in al-Tabari's chronicle are a curious fusion of the
characteristics present in both of Ibn Sa`d's lists. Even though there are
the same number of attributes found in Ibn Sa`d's second list and the
placement of the first three and last two items therein is quite similar,
al-Tabari's content, cast once more in `A'isha's voice, contains critical
differences:

1. The angel brought my likeness.
2. I was married at seven.
3. The marriage was consummated at nine.
4. He married me as a virgin without having shared me with any
   other man.
5. He received revelation when we were beneath a single blanket.
6. I was among the most beloved of people to him.
7. A verse of the Qur'an was revealed [about me] when the community was almost destroyed.
8. I saw Gabriel and none of his other wives did.
9. He died in my house and there was no one with him except the
   angel and myself.[88]

The details of `A'isha's marriage are substantially consonant with Ibn
Sa`d's second list, with its emphasis on divine intervention and marriage
age. However, `A'isha's virginity as emphasized in Ibn Sa`d is now qualified with the phrase that "no other man" except Muhammad had "shared"
her, a deft reference to her sexuality and, possibly, her chastity in the
aftermath of the accusation of adultery. Reference to the fact that Muham-

mad received divine revelation while in her presence is detailed with a phrase not found in either list in Ibn Sa`d, but reported in another hadith during which Umm Salama challenged the Prophet's preference for `A'isha. Thus, in al-Tabari, not only did the Prophet receive revelation while he was in `A'isha's presence, but while they were "under a single blanket."[89]

`A'isha is no longer described in the superlative form as the most beloved of the Prophet's wives as she was in Ibn Sa`d. Instead, al-Tabari's version states that she was only "one" of the most beloved people in the Prophet's estimation. Her status as the favorite wife here appears to be undermined and, despite the introductory claims of the passage, severely qualified. Nor is there any reference to her father in al-Tabari's list, an omission that is critical to the dual prestige of `A'isha and Abu Bakr and had been present in both of Ibn Sa`d's versions. Finally, whereas Ibn Sa`d's first list mentioned that her innocence was sent down by heaven during the accusation of adultery, al-Tabari states only that a verse of the Qur'an "was revealed when the community was almost destroyed." The application of Qur'anic revelation to `A'isha's dilemma is implicit, but nowhere is her innocence or exoneration emphasized. The addition of the phrase in al-Tabari pertaining to the original turmoil in Medina underscores the accusation made against `A'isha as a communal dilemma rather than a personal triumph of divine intervention in the life of the Prophet's wife. Further emphasis on the accusation of adultery made against `A'isha as both the occasion of revelation and crisis, qualifies her exoneration as a celebration and instead retrospectively casts the event as a pivotal point of communal conflict for the first Muslim community. By the fourth/tenth century the incident once more had become a point of dispute between Sunni and Shi`i Muslims who vehemently disagreed about the nature and interpretation of this incident as a part of `A'isha's biography. The reference in al-Tabari to the Qur'anic verses as applicable to `A'isha's dilemma would in themselves be disputed by Shi`i Muslim sources.[90]

If Muslims were elaborating their evolving religiopolitical identities through the prism of the past, then `A'isha's presence was central to their shared communal debates about meaning and memory. If `A'isha's prestige depended on praise which could be qualified with regard to the accusation of adultery, then how much more contentious would Muslims become about her presence in an even more significant crisis—the first civil war, an event not part of her life with the Prophet nor recorded in any of these lists, but remembered as a second communal trauma which, like the accusation of adultery, almost destroyed the first Islamic community. Both of these critical dilemmas and `A'isha's centrality to them provoked Sunni–Shi`i self-definition and polemic in the medieval period. As a demonstration of a difficult historical legacy, al-Tabari's version of `A'isha's importance articulates the vulnerability of her claims for preeminence among the wives of the Prophet. More importantly, this source emphasizes the problems inherent in the medieval Sunni Muslim attempt to present her praise as an extension of their communal identity. The denial of her superiority as Muhammad's most beloved wife is paralleled by the omission of her father's status as the most beloved of his male companions. This absence may represent an attempt to extricate Abu Bakr's reputation from a contentious context of praise for his daughter.

It is conflict over `A'isha's meaning in Muslim memory with which al-Tabari's list of nine attributes ultimately contends and it is the difficulty of presenting her historical persona as other than a point of contention in a more complex, elaborate medieval Muslim society that makes this list so revealing. Selectivity and emphasis are key in this version of the representation of `A'isha's past. Yet later medieval Sunni authors also appear to have exercised their options in choosing between the lists of Ibn Sa`d and al-Tabari to detail their vision of `A'isha's historical legacy. In biographical works dedicated most specifically to the Prophet's wives and `A'isha's role in hadith transmission, later medieval works from the seventh/thirteenth century through the tenth/sixteenth century drew almost equally upon both Ibn Sa`d and al-Tabari as definitive forms of Sunni Muslim praise for `A'isha and her uniqueness.[91]

Memory and Example: `A'isha As A Source of Hadith

It is significant that `A'isha's ability to contribute to the knowledge of the Islamic community about its past is not listed by her among the privileges that exalted her above her co-wives. `A'isha would not define herself as exceptional in this regard, but the male Sunni scholars who relied upon

her authority in their representation of the past would champion her contributions to the faith. Unchallenged among Sunni Muslims as a source
of hadith, `A'isha's reputation for the transmission of tradition forms a
critical dimension of her achieved religious prestige within the medieval
record. Unlike the special privileges surrounding her marital union,
`A'isha's ability to recall and transmit aspects of the Prophet's example
would be undertaken by her as a widow. However, her contribution to the
Islamic record as a widow remained contingent on her former status as a
wife. The transmission of hadith is a process which depends upon proximity and memory. `A'isha's status as the Prophet's favorite wife suggests
her unique ability to both hear and observe her husband's practice in both
public and private matters. In the earliest third/ninth-century sources
`A'isha's contribution to the preservation of the faith is lauded. Over
time, her praise in Sunni sources evolves into the superlative mode. In
contrast, Shi`i Muslims perceived `A'isha as an object of censure, a negative example for the faith who would never be defined as a reputable
source for the transmission of their past. Instead, they relied upon alternative chains of authority from which `A'isha was excluded according to
their own religiopolitical definitions.[92] `A'isha's persona and words were
not expunged from Shi`i communal memory, but her contributions
would be applied selectively to enhance their most important personages
and to confirm a vision of events that served to separate them from the
Sunni Muslim majority.

The biographies of `A'isha found in the third/ninth-century works of
Ibn Sa`d and al-Baladhuri make explicit references to her memory and
knowledge. The majority are related on the authority of persons other
than `A'isha. Both cite sources who confirm her knowledge of poetry.[93]
Such knowledge might appear peripheral to her contributions to the
preservation of the Prophet's example, but her skill served as a demonstration of both her prodigious memory and her mastery of the Arabic language. Her memory is the cause for both praise and a position of primacy
in the earliest written sources. "I didn't see anyone who was more knowledgeable than `A'isha about sunna [the Prophet's example in word and
deed], nor more learned in opinion when it was needed, nor anyone who
knew more verses of the Qur'an or about inheritance matters."[94]

Her knowledge of pre-Islamic lore and medicine is repeatedly cited in early sources.[95] Al-Baladhuri offers a tradition which explains how 'A'isha learned so much about medicine. In this account 'A'isha explained that since the Prophet was often ill, she watched those he consulted and learned from them.[96] The range of topics preserved by 'A'isha is vast and includes such categories as prayer, fasting, marriage, pilgrimage and ritual ablutions. Many matters of particular interest to Muslim women were transmitted by 'A'isha regarding marriage, dowries, clothing and menstruation.[97]

'A'isha's unique proximity to the Prophet and reliable memory made her an unavoidable point of reference for the male companions of the Prophet. Both Ibn Sa'd and al-Baladhuri state that Muhammad's male companions used to ask her opinion about matters of inheritance.[98] After the Prophet's death, 'A'isha's opinion was also sought as a consultant in political matters by the second caliph 'Umar and the third caliph 'Uthman. 'A'isha's superiority as a source of hadith is acknowledged in the third/ninth century and forms a substantial part of her portrayal. In these sources, the superlative mode is applied to 'A'isha alone: "'A'isha was the most knowledgeable of people. The greatest of the Prophet's companions used to ask her questions."[99] Apparently, the male companions of the Prophet did not just consult 'A'isha, they often deferred to her final opinion in the determination of which version of a hadith was correct. 'A'isha's ability to act as the arbiter in cases of conflicting traditions allowed her to figure prominently in the Sunni genre dedicated to hadith criticism. In the role of critic, 'A'isha is cited as a final authority in a work of this type by Ibn Qutayba (d. 276/889). In one instance, 'A'isha's correction was preferred to the versions of Muhammad's male companions including the caliphs 'Umar and 'Uthman.[100] In his defense of Sunni beliefs, Ibn Qutayba was quick to point to the heterodox interpretations of Shi'i Muslims by citing the aspersions they cast upon 'A'isha in their suspect exegesis of the Qur'an.

'A'isha's authority as a source of tradition figured prominently in the acceptance of hadith as the basis for the foundations of Sunni Islamic jurisprudence according to the jurist al-Shafi'i (d. 205/820). Al-Shafi'i defined 'A'isha as the preferred source in the face of contradictory traditions for a variety of reasons: "If there is a tradition contradictory to 'A'isha's it would be obligatory on both of us to accept her tradition rather than another, for her tradition should be the standard according to which you and I make our choice."[101]

In the continuation of this exchange, framed as a dialogue, al-Shafi'i is asked to explain the bases for the reliability of traditions. He stated that if two traditions contradict one another, the one more consistent with the Qur'an should be chosen. However, in the event that there is no relevant link to the Qur'an, the most critical criterion for acceptance is the reliability of the originator. The best hadith will be the one "related by an authority better known as an expert in transmission and who has a greater reputation for knowledge, or better memory." Al-Shafi'i also emphasized the conditions which maintain the integrity of the chain of relating authorities who transmitted from `A'isha. Although `A'isha's authority as a source of hadith was highly valued, the preservation of the content of the tradition is dependent on the reliability of those who followed her. A tradition might originate with `A'isha or be attributed to her, but it was those who came after her whose reputations and reliability collectively determined the preservation of the content. In such a system, `A'isha could not control her final contribution to the communal record of the Islamic community. `A'isha might be the first link in many oral chains of authority, but no tradition ever rested on her word alone. Her memory and observations were at the mercy of those who came after her. Information that began with the wife of the Prophet was passed along by others and ultimately recorded in writing by male authorities in the third/ninth century. In recounting the words and deeds of the Prophet as well as the particulars of her own life in the first/seventh century, `A'isha never exerted final control over the Islamic record or her contribution to it as preserved more than one hundred and fifty years after her death. In such a system, the editing of a large oral corpus was an implicit part of the process. This explains why of the thousands of hadith attributed to `A'isha, the canonical third/ninth-century Sunni collections of al-Bukhari and Muslim retained only fifty-four and sixty-eight respectively.[102] In contrast, the contemporary collection of Ibn Hanbal cites `A'isha as the source for more than two thousand traditions.[103]

After the third/ninth century, Sunni biographers of `A'isha bint Abi Bakr often repeated traditions about her contribution to their communal memory. During this later medieval phase, scholars in Syria and Egypt emphasized `A'isha's knowledge as an attribute that made her superior to all other Muslim women. "If I collected the knowledge of `A'isha from her and combined it with that of all the wives of the Prophet and [then] combined that with [the knowledge of other] women, then `A'isha's knowledge would be the greatest."[104]

In the eighth/fourteenth-century work of al-Dhahabi (d. 749/1348), `A'isha's biographer includes a superlative phrase to emphasize her critical role in the transmission of hadith. He refers to her as "the most knowledgeable of the women of the Islamic community." Al-Dhahabi then lists the names of one hundred and seventy-five people, including twenty women, who related tradition from `A'isha.[105]

During this same period Sunni authors began to focus exclusively upon `A'isha's criticisms of the hadith of the male companions of the Prophet. These works built upon the third/ninth-century example of more general treatises of hadith criticism, such as the work of Ibn Qutayba. However, these later sources did not merely depict `A'isha as an astute critic of variant traditions, they also became a vehicle for enhancing her religious prestige as an important dimension of her medieval legacy. In this process, one author would define `A'isha as the most exalted female in the Sunni community. Only in the eighth/fourteenth-century work of al-Zarkashi (d. 795/1392) is there an attempt to fully integrate `A'isha's special attributes as the wife of the Prophet with her unique contribution to Islamic memory as his widow. Al-Zarkashi's work is a treatise dedicated to `A'isha's criticisms of the hadith of the Prophet's male companions including the first four caliphs of Islam.[106] The author states in his introduction that the Prophet once said, "Take half of your religion from *al-humayra*," "the little ruddy one," his pet name for `A'isha. Al-Zarkashi claims that `A'isha "added to [the community] in knowledge what no one else provided." Such an admonition serves as the rationale for al-Zarkashi's treatise and the elaboration of what he he defines as her forty special attributes. In fact, the number of these qualities as listed is forty-two, but it would seem the author designated the number forty consciously because of its medieval resonance as a type of hadith collection which featured the same number of traditions.

Thirty-one of these forty-two special attributes amplify those privileges listed in the third/ninth-century sources that earlier defined `A'isha as superior to her co-wives. They emphasize her importance in relation to her marriage to the Prophet and reiterate her status as a virgin bride and favorite wife. `A'isha's pivotal role during the Prophet's last illness and death is also outlined. In the midst of the list, al-Zarkashi also makes reference to the nine attributes conferred upon no one but `A'isha and Maryam bint `Imran before her. This aspect of `A'isha's uniqueness was initially presented in the fourth/tenth-century chronicle of al-Tabari. Al-Zarkashi's intent in linking Maryam and `A'isha is to enhance the latter's prestige. Elements of divine intervention in `A'isha's life form a major division of her special attributes in this work. Emphasis is placed on the role of the angel Gabriel in `A'isha's life. The angel arranges `A'isha's marriage to the Prophet, vindicates her from the charge of adultery and is seen by her, albeit in disguise. The importance of `A'isha's linkage with her father is also underscored by al-Zarkashi as a positive feature of her Sunni persona. References to Abu Bakr include some embellishment of his stature within the medieval Sunni community. Not only is Abu Bakr the most beloved man in the Muslim community after the Prophet Muhammad, but, al-Zarkashi declares, "those who disavow her [A'isha's] father are infidels."[107] Once again, both `A'isha and Abu Bakr personify critical components of Sunni communal identity.

Al-Zarkashi's unique contribution to the depiction of `A'isha bint Abi Bakr in the medieval record rests upon the fact that within the special attributes accorded the Prophet's wife he includes ten which detail her religious prestige. Her piety is praised in terms of her "religious devotions," "generosity," and "asceticism." He also cites traditions which utilize the superlative to demonstrate `A'isha's unique contributions to the transmission of hadith. Thus, he asserts that she "was the greatest of his [the Prophet's] wives regarding the science of hadith." `A'isha is also described as "the most eloquent" of people and her words are praised as both better and "more intelligent" than the Friday sermons of the first four caliphs of Islam. Al-Zarkashi's portrayal of `A'isha's historical persona implicitly joined ascribed and achieved aspects of her prestige within the Sunni Muslim community. His emphasis on `A'isha's key role in the transmission of hadith expresses the devotion of the male Sunni scholarly community to the precedent passed on to them by the Prophet's wife. In the tenth/sixteenth century al-Suyuti would author another short treatise on `A'isha's hadith criticism in which he would draw directly upon al-Zarkashi's earlier work.[108]

The generations of Muslim women that followed `A'isha in their involvement with the transmission of tradition were no doubt inspired by her example. Indeed, the transmission of hadith by women was perceived as a legitimate avenue of religious participation throughout the medieval period.

Women achieved greater recognition in hadith than in any other branch of Islamic knowledge. One of the reasons for this was that women had always been accepted as transmitters of tradition, because the wives of the Prophet had naturally played a very important role in transmitting reports of the Prophet's words and deeds.[109]

It has been suggested that the reason women were consistently involved in the transmission of hadith throughout the medieval period had to do with the centrality of memory as the essential component in the process. Yet for Muslim women who came after `A'isha, hadith transmission became increasingly like an intellectual revolving door. While the men associated with the collection and criticism of hadith became renowned for their commentaries on the Qur'an, their histories and collections of law, all based on the transmission of tradition, women remained unable to participate in these most challenging intellectual undertakings.[110] Women, even those who were literate, were not the scriptors of any known works in the medieval Islamic world. As a form of secluded education, the transmission of hadith was the only acceptable option open to women. It required memory, but not literacy and it could be undertaken at home or with a group of other women in a mosque. In many cases, women transmitters were the recipients of traditions from within their own families.[111] The ability of Sunni Muslim women to transmit hadith, to follow in the footsteps of exemplary women such as `A'isha bint Abi Bakr, was controlled by a combination of male social attitude and access to education. Limitations that affected a Muslim's potential to excel in forms of Islamic knowledge other than tradition were applied only to the female gender. Indeed, while religious memory could be cultivated by both Muslim men and women, restricted access to higher branches of Islamic learning was placed upon women alone. Just as `A'isha could not control the preservation or selection of her words by those who transmitted from her, neither could those women who continued to preserve traditions in the medieval period hope to define or apply the meanings of such memory within Islamic society.

`A'isha and Rabi`a: Exemplary and Exceptional Female Religious Figures

The conflict between gender and religious prestige was emphasized, inadvertently, by the biographer `Attar (d. 627/1229). In his biography of Islamic saints, `Attar describes a female mystic named Rabi`a al-`Adawiyya (d. 185/801), a woman whom he places among the ranks of men: "If anyone were to ask me, "Why did you mention her among the ranks of men?" I would reply, "[Muhammad], chief of all prophets, used to say, Allah does not look on outward appearance."[112] In his response to this categorization of a woman as a man, he articulates the Islamic mystical doctrine that Allah does not look on outward forms.[113] Such a perception expresses an ideal nullification of any gender restrictions faced by Muslim female mystics. Thus, he suggests, bodily forms, obvious sex differences, do not matter as a factor in spiritual identity. However, in addition, `Attar's description of the outward forms argument implicitly documents the manner in which two women, one a mystic and one a transmitter of hadith, may be defined as both exemplary and exceptional.

If it is permissible to take two-thirds of the religion from `A'isha, the truthful, then it is also permissible to receive religious instruction from one of her handmaidens [that is, Rabi`a]. When a woman [walks] on the path of Allah like a man, then it is not possible to call her a woman.[114]

`A'isha as sage and Rabi`a as saint exemplify the two main paths of faith in medieval Islam. Indeed, `Attar also describes Rabi`a as "a second pure Maryam," invoking the Qur'anic example of the mother of Jesus earlier associated with `A'isha. `Attar's statement that men learned about the faith from `A'isha, as mystics learned from Rabi`a, embodies a lesson directed by a man to other men about the meaning of medieval female spiritual identity. Although he categorically states that Allah considers irrelevant the differences between male and female believers, `Attar demonstrates that while God may not note such differences, male authors certainly did. In `Attar's estimation, it is not possible to call Rabi`a a woman because she transcends his definition of the female gender as an unqualified form of spiritual identity. Indeed, the power of his categorization relies not simply on Rabi`a's honorary designation as a man, but on her contrived disassociation from the rest of her gender. It is not possible to call her a woman, he proves, because she is superior to other women. Rabi`a's definition is thus strategically linked to two other exceptional female models of religious prestige—Maryam and `A'isha. `Attar's construction of their interactive symbolic import is an attempt to idealize these three females within his constricted understanding of the feminine as a manifestation of Islamic spiritual identity. A near contemporary confirmation of this male tendency may be drawn from a history of Yemen authored by al-Hakimi (d. 569/1173). In his description of a Shi`i female ruler of Yemen allied with the Sevener theology of the Fatimids, the author inserts an anecdote about `A'isha. Although, he claimed, the female ruler Arwa dealt with many men at court they, like the men who once heard hadith from `A'isha bint Abi Bakr, never forgot that she was a woman.[115]

In the development of `A'isha bint Abi Bakr's medieval legacy as a source of hadith, `A'isha represented both an example for women and an exception to them. In the medieval community Muslim women continued to transmit hadith, but `A'isha's example alone did not enlarge their collective access to other branches of Islamic learning. `A'isha transmitted much information about Islam, but no Muslim woman after her would be allowed to interpret it. Rabi`a also had many spiritual insights attributed to her, but neither could she control her posthumous contributions nor depiction in Islamic mysticism. Modern Western scholars of Islamic mysticism and gender continue to describe Rabi`a as exemplary, but not exceptional.[116] They promote her as a woman whose medieval praise implied a positive and practical precedent for all Muslim women.[117] Yet, the depictions of Rabi`a and `A'isha as both exemplary and exceptional suggest a theoretical, ex post facto closure of options for real women: "Exceptional women are the chief imprisoners of nonexceptional women, simultaneously proving that any woman could do it and assuring, in their uniqueness among men, that no other woman will."[118]

When compared to a Sunni female saint, `A'isha's example would be cited in opposition to the limitations of her gender: "If it is permissible to take two-thirds of the religion from `A'isha, the truthful, then it is also permissible to receive religious benefit from one of her handmaidens [that is, Rabi`a]."[119] Alone this statement suggests the possibilities inherent in `A'isha's example for all women. However, combined with its qualification, it demonstrates the limitations implicit in exceptional female religious figures: "When a woman [walks] on the path of Allah like a man, then it is not possible to call her a woman."

three the accusation of adultery and communal debate

> *For better or for worse, the wagging of tongues is inescapable.*   Women of Deh Koh

𝒯he accusation of adultery made against ʾAʾisha in 5 A.H./A.D. 627, as remembered by Muslims, remained a critical, controversial part of her medieval legacy.[1] The majority of Muslims termed the incident *hadith al-ifk,* "the account of the lie," the tale of the slander and vindication of ʾAʾisha by a divine revelation recorded in the Qurʾan. However, the event also contained the seeds of conceptual conflict regarding issues of honor and shame, belief and unbelief, and truth and falsehood. Each of these three apparently dichotomous pairs would become the object of Sunni–Shiʿi polemic. The medieval interpretation of the accusation of adultery became synonymous with definitions of communal honor and identity. Both Sunni and Shiʿi Muslims integrated the accusation into the broader framework of their disputes about faith and politics. Sunni Muslim praise of ʾAʾisha's reputation included a celebration of her divine vindication. Shiʿi Muslims did not accept either ʾAʾisha's vindication or innocence and found in the incident a potent weapon in their polemic against the entire Sunni community.

At the most fundamental level, the accusation challenged the preservation of male honor directed through an assertion of female shame. The incident also represented a challenge to the Prophet's mission and the faith of Islam. As the Prophet's wife, ʿAʾisha embodied his honor and the accusation against her chastity threatened to undermine both the Prophet's male honor and the prestige of his religious mission. ʿAʾisha became central to a divine drama in which her exoneration also demonstrated the larger truth of Muhammad's revelation. In the earliest third/ninth-century records that detail the incident, ʿAʾisha's assertion of her own innocence serves to frame Qurʾanic verses 24:11-20. In these injunctions, ʿAʾisha's name and situation are never explicitly mentioned. The interpretation of the revelation thus becomes critical to sectarian definitional differences as projected through ʿAʾisha's historical persona.

Honor and Shame: Male and Female

The accusation of adultery made against ʿAʾisha presents an ostensibly personal dilemma as a communal crisis. The hadith al-ifk is not about private conduct or matters of conscience, but about public definitions of social control, behavior, and gender. Anthropologists continue to study the function of these concepts in modern societies, particularly in the Mediterranean, where cultural definitions of honor and shame suggest a striking unity regardless of Christian or Islamic religious frameworks.[2] Even in the time of the Prophet Muhammad, these concepts do not appear to have been unique to Arabia, where male honor was demonstrated through emphasis placed upon female chastity codes.[3] In this conceptual context, ʿAʾisha's situation reflects male honor as threatened by the allegation of female shame. The confusion provoked in the Islamic community by the hadith al-ifk reflects a complex reaction to a charge of adultery among people whose primary affiliations at the time of the scandal were tribal rather than religious. The female role in the pre-Islamic definition of honor was tied to male maintenance of the purity of tribal lineages.[4] Female offspring were perceived as potential sources of familial dishonor, described in modern Mediterranean contexts as the "weak link" in the chain of masculine virtue.[5] Modern studies of bedouin values suggest that female sexuality in particular "threatens the whole male-oriented social order."[6] Mediterranean and Middle Eastern societies which value honor and shame divide "social beings into two fundamental categories, those endowed with honour and those deprived of it."[7]

The account of the lie is implicitly a story about female chastity before it becomes a tale of divine vindication. It is a dilemma in which male honor is threatened by the sexual aspersions cast upon a woman. The attack upon ʿAʾisha's chastity was in fact aimed through her at her husband, the founder of the Islamic community. In this sense, Muhammad's male honor was merely maintained by ʿAʾisha as a woman. Women are not active in promoting or attaining honor, but demonstrate only passive proof of its maintenance in the public vigilance of male control and protection. Thus, "men are responsible for the shame of their women" and when they fail in that charge they are "diminished in relation to other men."[8] A woman's sexual misconduct did not reflect on her primarily as an individual, but represented an affront to her entire family. The defense of ʿAʾisha's reputation was not about her alone, but about the effect of this charge on the larger kin group and religious community of which she was a member. It is in this sense that the defense of her reputation became at once a matter in which the gendered social values inherent in the concepts of honor and shame merged with the new faith of Islam.

The Accusation in the Earliest Written Sources

The remembrance of the hadith al-ifk in the written record from the first places the event solidly in the communal realm. This emphasis is reflected in the placement of the most detailed accounts of the incident in the earliest written genres. In Sunni Muslim sources the event is developed most fully in the literature dedicated to the biography of the Prophet Muhammad and the exploits of his community. The account of the lie as ʿAʾisha's divine vindication is thus initially more about the first Muslim community as a group than the individual woman who is the object of the accusation of adultery. In third/ninth-century biographical accounts mention of the hadith al-ifk in entries devoted to ʿAʾisha is both brief and indirect. In Ibn Saʿd, the revelation vindicating ʿAʾisha is noted as part of her ten special privileges.[9] The only other reference to this matter is taken from an account at the end of her life. On her deathbed, ʿAʾisha reminds two visitors that a revelation had been sent on her account. Her visitors respond with reference to the incident as praise: "Then Allah sent down your vindication from the seven heavens." Al-Baladhuri also makes only two references to the accusation in his biographical entry about ʿAʾisha. He emphasizes ʿAʾisha's vindication as a divine triumph by citing the Qur'an 24: 23: "As for those who slander virtuous, believing women [who are] careless, cursed are they in this world and the next. Theirs will be an awful doom." These are particularly interesting verses to select, for while they are drawn from the chapter of the Qur'an which defends ʿAʾisha's reputation, they are not the exact verses said to be revealed on her behalf. The second and final reference to the accusation in al-Baladhuri once again supports ʿAʾisha's innocence and exoneration as a form of divine rather than human support: "When Allah sent ʿAʾisha's vindication, Abu Bakr went to her and kissed her on the head. She said, 'Praise be to Allah, not to you or your friend [Muhammad].'"[10]

In both Ibn Saʿd and al-Baladhuri, the incident is not central to her biographical depiction. Their scant, incomplete references to the event suggest that the whole story was well known outside the biographical genre. Moreover, it is clear that in recounting this tale, deliberate choices were made by early Muslim authors to detail the accusation of adultery more fully as part of the communal past rather than ʿAʾisha's individual record. The placement of the event in the written corpus suggests possible strategies for controlling the meaning of the account. As part of Islamic communal memory, the incident becomes the provocation for Qur'anic revelation as communicated through the Prophet Muhammad. Emphasis is thus on both the mission of the founder of Islam and the Qur'an. The frame and incentive for these divinely communicated injunctions is ʿAʾisha's dilemma, the aspersions cast upon her chastity. The implications for the new Islamic community combined the sacred and the sexual. The delicacy of the accusation against the favorite wife of the Prophet also resounds to the pre-Islamic social chords of honor and shame. Although the community would record the incident in detail as an ex post facto divine triumph, mention of ʿAʾisha's exoneration would forever recall the initial slanderous accusation as a threat to her chastity, a potential source of shame. In Sunni sources ʿAʾisha would retain the honorary epithet *al-mubarraʾa*, "the vindicated," but the sensitivity of the issue required a defense of her reputation in the communal record, a representation of the past that would vindicate ʿAʾisha and the Muslim community.

The earliest, most detailed references to the hadith al-ifk appear in third/ninth-century sources in hadith collections, accounts of the military exploits of the first Islamic community, and the earliest biography of the Prophet.[11] In Sunni collections of hadith, full accounts of the accusation are presented in the compilations of al-Bukhari, Muslim, and Ibn Hanbal.[12] The subject divisions for the placement of this information vary widely and include tafsir, the section dedicated to the explication of specific Qurʾanic verses, and maghazi, the details of the Muslim community's raids against other Arab tribes. Just as the Qurʾanic commentary emphasizes the verses revealed in response to the accusation, the military context is established through its linkage to the specific raid against the tribe of the Banu Mustaliq.[13] Despite their disparate subject headings, these hadith references are alike in two crucial ways.[14] None of them places the incident among the biographical qualities of excellence attributed to ʿAʾisha among the women closest to the Prophet and all of them are related on ʿAʾisha's authority through a chain of individuals which include members of her extended family. The most consistent relater in the chain of transmission besides ʿAʾisha is her maternal nephew ʿUrwa ibn al-Zubayr (d. 94/712), a figure also consistently present in biographical sources which promote ʿAʾisha's connections to the angel Gabriel in the arrangement of her marriage. (See chapter 2.) ʿUrwa died more than forty years after his aunt ʿAʾisha, but he was of great significance in the transmission of aspects of her life, apparently, as she related them to him. The Medinan school of hadith and history which would come to be associated with Muhammad al-Zuhri (d. 124/741) appears to be the primary source represented in the preservation of the accusation.[15] Although scholars have suggested al-Zuhri was not partisan in his preservation of the past, the Medinan collective of scholars, including the presence of ʿAʾisha's own family members, conclusively promoted a positive, detailed defense of her reputation. It is their vision of the past, channelled through her own words, which is most consistently presented in the earliest written sources and it is their positive, implicitly partisan representation of this incident which provoked contradiction and attack by Shiʿi Muslims one hundred years later in the fourth/tenth century.

The version of the hadith al-ifk recorded in the biography of the Prophet Muhammad by Ibn Hisham (d. 219/834) and based on the earlier edition of Ibn Ishaq who died in the late second/eighth century originates with the Medinan school through the authority of ʿAʾisha's relatives and al-Zuhri.[16] As captured in Ibn Hisham, the incident has been termed "the longest hadith of all."[17] In Ibn Hisham, as in other third/ninth-century accounts, the accusation becomes ʿAʾisha's story, ostensibly related in her own voice. Even if the tale related by ʿAʾisha has negative implications, it also reveals a deeply felt personal crisis in the life of the then fourteen-year-old wife of the Prophet. There is an implied element of control given to ʿAʾisha by ceding to her the entire narrative and allowing her to detail it in the first person. ʿAʾisha thus appears to testify to her innocence on her own behalf in the historical record. Yet the nature of her narrative is clearly a carefully structured retrospective version of past events. As the purported narrator, ʿAʾisha's presence suggests control over her own story. Ironically, the written content underscores her vulnerability to the charge of adultery and her inability to convince her family or her husband of her innocence. Although she appears to have the final word regarding these events, her record of them definitively captures the fact that despite her protestations, her own words alone could not exonerate her from the charge of adultery. The account of the lie may have been cast through ʿAʾisha's collected observations, but the selective scripting and final detailed shaping of her role and reactions would be done after her death.

The Accusation

According to Ibn Hisham, the slanderous rumors about ʿAʾisha began on the raid made by the Prophet against an Arab tribe called the Banu Mustaliq. ʿAʾisha was the only one of Muhammad's wives to accompany him on this journey. She was inadvertently left behind on the return to Medina. The caravan moved off and she was assumed to be seated in her covered camel litter, or howdaj, but she was not. Stranded alone in the desert, ʿAʾisha was rescued by a young Muslim man named Safwan ibn al-Muʿattal al-Sulami. On her return, enemies of the Prophet and his wife claimed that ʿAʾisha had betrayed her husband with her young rescuer.

This is the synopsis of events that precipitated the rumor of adultery and the aspersions made against `A' isha's chastity.

`A' isha narrates her tale in Ibn Hisham with a provocative attention to detail. She outlines the confluence of reasons that explain why she was accidentally left behind in the desert and the appropriately modest manner in which she comported herself when she was rescued. Her account reads as if the final scriptor, if not the purported narrator, had in hindsight anticipated the need to defend the wife of the Prophet and her sensitive situation in the hadith al-ifk. Each of `A' isha's actions is explicated in detail. At every stage in the events her motivations are rationalized. `A' isha's narrative appears designed as a response to the range of questions which must have been previously, repeatedly raised in discussions about the incident within the Muslim community. The narrative reflects the anticipated refutation of tough questions about `A' isha's dilemma and the resounding importance of the maintenance of the Prophet's honor as threatened by the suggestion of his wife's potential shame.

When the Prophet had completed his journey, he started back. When he was close to Medina, he halted and stayed for part of a night. He then ordered [the troops] to start and the men began to move forward. I went out [to the bathroom] wearing a necklace of Za`far beads around my neck. When I returned, unknowingly, [the necklace] had slipped from my neck. I returned to the camel, but could not find [my necklace]. The troops began to move out.[18]

At this point `A' isha establishes the reason she was not missed when the rest of the company moved off without her.

I returned to the place [where I had lost my Za`far beads] and looked for my necklace until I found it. The men finished saddling my camel and lifted the covered litter [onto the camel] assuming that I was already in it, since that was the usual procedure. Then they picked up the litter and tied it onto the camel not doubting I was within.[19]

Since the account `A' isha gives is built on a wealth of detail, it is no wonder that at the very beginning of the hadith she explains that the Prophet's wives weighed very little since they did not eat meat.[20] Her slenderness and its explanation thus confirms why the suspicions of her bearers were not aroused when they placed the empty litter on the camel. `A'isha's weight, due to diet, was negligible and thus her absence was not noted. In addition, `A'isha outlines the procedure by which members of Muhammad's entourage covered the litter atop the camel. In deference to her position as the wife of the Prophet and the new Qur'anic regulation that Muhammad's wives veil themselves, `A'isha would have seated herself in the covered litter prior to its placement on the camel. The men securing the contraption to the camel assumed that `A'isha was in her habitual place.

When she returned to the place where her camel had been, she found no one there.

The men had gone. I covered myself in my wrap and lay down. I knew that if I was missed, they would come back for me. No sooner had I lain down when Safwan ibn al-Mu`attal al-Sulami came by. He had remained behind the main part [of the troops] and had not spent the night with them. He saw me and came over. He had seen me before the veil had been imposed upon us, so when he realized who I was he was surprised and said: "The wife of the Prophet!" He asked me why I had been left behind, but I did not speak to him. He led his camel up and told me to ride [it] while he stayed behind [it]. I rode the camel and he led the animal, moving quickly in order to find the army. By Allah, we did not catch up to them and I was not missed until [the next] morning. The army was resting when we came upon them with Safwan leading me. At that point the liars [began] spreading their tales. The army was very upset, but by Allah, I knew nothing about this.[21]

Male Responses: The Prophet, Abu Bakr, and `Ali ibn Abi Talib

On arriving in Medina, `A'isha became very ill and so claims that she knew nothing of the lies her accusers were spreading about her. However, the story reached both her husband and her father although they did not tell her of it. The Prophet was disturbed by the rumors about his wife and his treatment of `A'isha changed markedly. As she noted, "When I was ill he used to be kind and understanding toward me, but he did not act this way during this illness. I missed his attentions." Eventually, `A'isha asked to be taken to her mother's house to be nursed. The Prophet's estrangement and confusion concerning the rumors he had heard about `A'isha continued until she recovered about twenty days later. When `A'isha was well again, she heard from a female relative of her father's that she had been accused of adultery. Her mother told her not to worry because all beautiful wives were the object of such gossip from their rivals.[22] Until this time she claimed she knew nothing of the lies that had been spread about her.

In the meantime, the Prophet addressed the men of the community and referring to the trouble concerning `A'isha he said: "Why are some men worrying me about my family? They are saying false things about them. By Allah, I know nothing but good about them. They say these things of a man about whom I only know good and who never enters my house except in my presence."[23] The reference in this speech is not to `A'isha, but, it would seem, to Safwan, her male rescuer. It is possible that Muhammad also sought to protect `A'isha's father, Abu Bakr, who would also have born some responsibility for the actions of his daughter. The Prophet tried to keep `A'isha's name out of the scandal, a reason for his oblique reference to his family. However, the rumors threatened both `A'isha's husband and father. Their honor and that of the fledgling Islamic community was clearly challenged by the account of the lie. The rumors about `A'isha nearly undermined the fragile cohesion of the first Islamic society at Medina as the rival tribes of Aws and Khazraj, both of whom had accepted Muhammad's leadership, accused each other of starting the rumors about the Prophet's wife.

The Prophet was confused enough by the situation and fearful enough of its personal and communal implications to ask the advice of `Usama ibn Zayd and `Ali ibn Abi Talib. `Usama declared the circulating stories to be "a lie and a falsehood." The threat of communal strife may have prompted `Ali to suggest to the Prophet that the scandal made his favorite wife a liability. Thus he said, "There are many women. You can easily replace one with another."[24] `Ali's statement implies that the prime asset of any married female is her chastity. Once lost, the woman in question is expendable and should be cast out of the family since she brings dishonor on its male members. In `Ali's assessment, `A'isha is typical of the gender to which she belongs. She is sexually vulnerable, inclined to err and, therefore, interchangeable. Thus, `Ali urged the Prophet to repudiate his favorite wife, `A'isha. This utterance of `Ali's would be cited in later Shi`i Muslim sources on the Battle of the Camel as one of the prime reasons for `A'isha's hatred of `Ali and her subsequent military action against him.[25] Despite his own negative testimony, `Ali also suggested that `A'isha's servant girl Barira should be consulted. After he beat the girl soundly, urging her to tell the Prophet the truth, she spoke no ill of `A'isha.[26]

The Active Defense of Male Honor: Safwan ibn al-Mu`attal al-Sulami

The Prophet solicited the opinions of his most trusted male companions, but the male accused of adultery took the defense of his honor into his own hands. He attacked one of his accusers, the poet Hasan ibn Thabit, with his sword. In Ibn Hisham's account, `A'isha's very last words concern Safwan. She states that Safwan was known to be impotent and that he "never touched women."[27] In this heavily detailed story, it is perhaps one detail too many that Safwan was found, after the accusation and its divine resolution, to be impotent. One wonders about the necessity for the clarification of Safwan's physiological condition. `A'isha's testimony about Safwan's impotence certainly serves to obliterate any possibility of sexual intercourse between the wife of the Prophet and her young rescuer. The inclusion of such a biographical note about Safwan may also suggest that `A'isha's reputation had not been completely cleared by Muhammad's revelation. Between Qur'anic revelation and male impotence, however, the divine and the human would combine to fully safeguard the Prophet's honor. It is further narrated by `A'isha that Safwan later died a martyr in battle, the ultimate demonstration of his faith in Islam and his honor as a Muslim male.[28]

`A'isha's Dilemma: Female Passivity and Divine Intervention

When the Prophet himself finally visited `A'isha, he did not assume her innocence, but rather asked her to repent. Muhammad's approach to his wife's situation demonstrates little faith in her: "`A'isha, you know what people are saying about you. Fear Allah, and if as men say, you have done wrong, repent to Allah. He accepts repentance."[29] On hearing these words, `A'isha, who had been weeping, stopped. At the critical moment in this crisis she realized that no one would defend her against the general presumption of her guilt: "I waited for my parents to answer the Prophet, but they said nothing."[30] The lines which follow immediately in the story have a predictive continuity which underscores the vantage point of the narrator's hindsight. With a decidedly high degree of retrospective humility, `A'isha recreates the scene of silence and tension in which her innocence will be revealed by Allah.

By Allah, I believed I was too unimportant for God to send down a [Qur'anic] recitation which could be read in the mosque and in prayer. I hoped that the Prophet would see something in his sleep through which Allah would exonerate me from the lie, because Allah knew my innocence. Regarding a revelation or other news coming down on my account, by Allah, I thought myself too insignificant for that.

After this soliloquy, `A'isha asked her parents why they wouldn't speak to the Prophet in her defense. They replied that "They did not know what to answer." In the end, `A'isha herself found the words to answer the Prophet, words not of defense, but despair because no declaration of innocence spoken by her would be acceptable.

"By Allah, I will never repent about what has been said. If I were to admit to what the people are saying about me, Allah knowing that I am innocent, I would be confessing to what did not occur. If I deny what they said, you still would not believe me." Then I tried to recall the name of Jacob, but I could not remember it. I said, "I will say what the father of Joseph said: "[My course is to show] comely patience. The help of Allah needs be sought [to defend] me against what you describe."[31]

The dilemma of the lie serves as a test of `A'isha's faith in Allah and her commitment to the truth. Without the support of her husband or her parents, `A'isha refuses to lie as a defense against the falsehoods being spread about her. She refuses to accept the communal rumors that suggest her guilt, just as Jacob, the father of Joseph, in the Qur'anic verse 12:18 she cites, refuses to believe the false evidence of his son's bloodied shirt. `A'isha's speech illuminates her own perilous position. She will not lie to suit liars, but she also realizes that her own truthful words do not provide either a believable or adequate defense of her innocence. Caught in the most serious crisis of her married life, `A'isha understood that her testimony in the face of communal slander and doubt was worthless. At this critical juncture in her life, only divine intervention could exonerate her because the true danger of the accusation, now common knowledge in the community, would never be completely undone. At best, a higher source could contradict the charge of adultery since no earthly authority had come forward to defend the Prophet's wife. At this penultimate moment of her trial she is reduced to passivity, the static object of the divine intervention which she herself had earlier protested she would be too insignificant to receive.

By Allah, the Prophet had not stirred from where he sat when he was overcome by Allah as he used to be. He was wrapped in his cloak and under his head was placed a leather pillow. When I saw this I was not afraid because I knew that I was innocent and [I believed] Allah would not be unjust to me. When the Prophet recovered I thought that my parents would expire from fear that what the people had said about me would be confirmed. Then the Prophet recovered and he sat up and . . . began to wipe the sweat from his brow exclaiming, "Rejoice, `A'isha! Allah has sent down your vindication." I replied, "Praise be to Allah." Then the Prophet went out to the people and addressed them, reciting to them what Allah had sent about the matter.[32]

The Prophet then proceeded to order punishment for the three people who had been most public in promoting the slander against `A'isha: Hamna bint Jahsh, the sister of the Prophet's wife Zaynab, Mistah ibn Uthatha, and the poet Hasan ibn Thabit. Each received the eighty lashes required by the Qur'an 24:4 for the crime of false accusation against a woman without four witnesses. Zaynab, claimed `A'isha, was the only wife who could rival her in the Prophet's favor. According to `A'isha, Hamna's part in the scandal, perpetuated without her sister Zaynab's participation, was part of an intrigue to increase her sister's prestige as a rival wife.

The hadith al-ifk as recorded in Ibn Hisham closes with an example of Hasan ibn Thabit's poetry. It is a poem composed after `A'isha's exoneration that seeks to excuse the poet's behavior in the form of a panegyric to the Prophet's wife. Her praise is couched in terms which defend her reputation. The poet emphasizes her chastity and thus reaffirms the honor of the Prophet's family. He describes `A'isha as "chaste," "above suspicion," and "purified" by Allah of all "falsehood."[33] The theme of praise attached implicitly to the idea of blame in the accusation of adultery is the first example of this bivalent employment of poetry that seeks to praise and defend at the same time. Indeed, `A'isha's reputation, as much as the poet's, is the object of retrospective vindication.

Yet another poem about the punishment meted out to those who slandered `A'isha more explicitly details the event as an attack against the entire Islamic community.[34] Hasan, Hamna, and Mistah are described as getting what they deserved for lying about the Prophet's wife. Not only did they spread false rumors, but through `A'isha, "they harmed the Prophet of Allah." The anonymous poem suggests that the Prophet's honor was injured by the hadith al-ifk and the prestige of the entire Islamic community threatened.

This aspect of the event underscores the male control of female chastity as an extension of personal and tribal honor. The attempt to undermine the Prophet's standing as the leader of the Islamic community at Medina was also directed by `Abd Allah Ibn Ubayy, the leader of the *munafiqun*, those Medinans who had converted only nominally to Islam and thus were termed "hypocrites" because of their unbelief and covert opposition to the Prophet. Ibn Ubayy took a leading role in propagating the lies about `A'isha in Medina in an attempt to compromise Muhammad's authority. Thus the hadith al-ifk was both an affair of male honor and a contest over religiopolitical control of Medina, a confluent demonstration of the values of honor and shame, belief and unbelief, and truth and falsehood in the nascent Islamic community.

In the earliest third/ninth-century sources, the hadith al-ifk provides the narrative framework for the Qur'anic revelation exonerating `A'isha.[35] Although neither her name nor the context of the raid against the Banu Mustaliq is ever mentioned, early written sources confirm the connection between `A'isha's exoneration and revelation. Thus, in Ibn Hisham, verse 24:11 of the Qur'an, the first of nine revealed in `A'isha's defense, becomes part of the earliest biography of the Prophet and the communal record.

Those who spread the lie are a gang among you. Do not regard it as a bad thing for you; no, it is good for you. Every one of them will receive what he has earned of sin; and he who has the greater share therein, for him there will be an awful doom.[36]

In the Qur'an, references to false accusations of adultery are directed primarily against women. The number of male witnesses required to convict a woman of adultery makes the conviction of any woman for such a crime, at least theoretically, difficult. In 'A'isha's case, one of the verses revealed on her account specifically asks why those who spread the rumors about her did not produce four witnesses. Thus, verse 24:13 of the Qur'an concludes, "Since they produce no witnesses, they are liars in the sight of Allah."

The divine, although indirect, proof of 'A'isha's innocence would seem to be a blessing for all those Muslim women accused of adultery who came after her. In practice, however, divine intervention in 'A'isha's case did not protect other Muslim women from the unsupported charge of adultery. With four male witnesses, according to verse 24:2 of the Qur'an, both men and women are punished for adultery by one hundred lashes. In verse 4:15, adulterous women charged by the requisite four male witnesses should be confined to their houses "until death." Although a woman accused of adultery may ask Allah to punish her if she testifies to a falsehood and is technically innocent without the requisite proof of four witnesses, such aspersions were, in themselves, often life-threatening. Unlike 'A'isha, whose innocence was revealed by revelation, other Muslim women could appeal for divine support, but never again would heavenly intervention exonerate the accused. 'A'isha's own words had mattered little in the defense of her reputation; the words of other Muslim women in similar situations would count for even less. Death remained the customary rather than the Islamic penalty for a woman whose male family members believed her guilty of bringing them dishonor through adultery. Even into the modern period, local family justice often prevailed and with it the assertion that "One washes the honor of the family in blood."[37]

Susanna and 'A'isha: Two Accusations of Adultery

The story of Susanna, found in the Apocrypha, reveals striking parallels with the tale of 'A'isha as told in the hadith al-ifk. The Apocrypha is a series of fifteen books considered by Christians as part of their Greek version of the OldTestament, but not accepted by Jews as canonical.Written somewhere between the second and first centuries B.C., the story of Susanna "is based on the familiar motif of the triumph of virtue over villany, the narrow escape from death of the innocent victim."[38] The tale also contains themes not unfamiliar in the much later Islamic context: honor and shame, belief and unbelief, and truth and falsehood. In Hebrew, the name Susanna means "lily." Her story is part of a cycle of traditions concerning Daniel. Although the story takes its name from Susanna, its true protagonist is Daniel, the male who, with the help of God, will save Susanna from the false charge of adultery.

Both `A'isha and Susanna are women falsely accused of adultery. Both finally appeal to God to vindicate them when the people closest to them doubt their innocence. However, for each woman, God works through male prophets to achieve a classic deus ex machina resolution to their personal crises. The fate of both women is ultimately determined by men: in Susanna's case, through Daniel in his role as judge, in `A'isha's case, through Muhammad in his role as prophet.The resolution of these accusations of adultery is both a divine and legal judgment. The link between God and his law, notably the penalties for the Hebrews in Deuteronomy for false witness are, at last, justly applied with the help of Daniel. In the Islamic context illustrated by `A'isha's accusation, the penalties for the false accusation of adultery are established in the fledgling religious community for the first time. Daniel's task as a true judge is to destroy the corruption of the faith represented by the elders in a preestablished system of divinely inspired legal codes and to restore the sanctity, not just of the law, but of the principles of its just application. Muhammad, the recipient of direct revelation from Allah, founds the first penalties for the Islamic community for false witness to the charge of adultery.

The specifics of the cases of Susanna and `A'isha bear comparative scrutiny because they are both examples of deus ex machina. Each details the nature of female chastity as the object of communal shame and male dishonor. Susanna, like `A'isha, is defined primarily as a daughter and a wife. She, like her Islamic counterpart, is noted for her beauty. It is not surprising that she is also described as linked to a male genealogy of high lineage and honor.

There was a man living in Babylon whose name was Joakim. And he took a wife named Susanna, the daughter of Hilkiah, a very beautiful woman and one who feared the Lord. Her parents were righteous, and had taught their daughter according to the law of Moses. Joakim was very rich, and had a spacious garden adjoining his house; and the Jews used to come to him because he was the most honored of them all.

Defined in relation to male eminence within the community, Susanna like ʿAʾisha, is married to the most honored man in her community. Her status, despite her innate qualities of belief and beauty, is irrevocably linked to the honor of her husband.

It is with malicious and lustful intent that the elders plot the seduction of Susanna. The backdrop of the encounter between the elders, who were also appointed as judges in the community, and Susanna is set by detailing her established habit of walking alone in her husband's garden.

Susanna would go into her husband's garden to walk. The two elders used to see her every day, going in and walking about, and they began to desire her. And they perverted their minds and turned away their eyes from looking to Heaven or remembering righteous judgments. Both were overwhelmed with passion for her.

Conspiring together to seduce Susanna, the elders watch for the opportunity to approach her with their indecent proposition when she is alone. The scene of the attempted seduction of Susanna in the Apocrypha developed into a popular Renaissance subject within the European pictorial tradition.[39] The implications of this scene fueled numerous treatments in Western Christian literature and theology.[40] Alone, the elders approach Susanna. They bluntly state their lascivious intent to their intended victim:

Look, the garden doors are shut, no one sees us, and we are in love with you; so give your consent, and lie with us. If you refuse, we will testify against you that a young man was with you, and this was why you sent your maids away.[41]

The incident is problematic for Susanna because she is alone when she is approached by the elders. ʿAʾisha too had been alone in the desert except for her young male rescuer in the incident precipitating the rumors about her. Both Susanna and `A'isha are without witnesses to testify to their conduct. Their word is pitted against their accusers. Their solitary states provide the context for the accusations made against each woman and force the moment when they must verbally defend their reputations. Each false accusation reduces both women to sexual ciphers, symbols of lost marital chastity.

Confronted by the elders' proposition Susanna realizes that no matter what her response, she cannot prove her innocence against the testimony of the two threatening male witnesses.

Susanna sighed deeply and said, "I am hemmed in on every side. For if I do this thing, it is death for me; and if I do not, I shall not escape your hands. I choose not to do it and to fall into your hands, rather than to sin in the sight of the Lord."

Susanna understood that death was the penalty for adultery, already pre-scribed in Leviticus 20:10: "If a man commits adultery with the wife of his neighbor, both the adulterer and the adulteress shall be put to death." The words of Deuteronomy 22:22 confirm the punishment for men and women caught in the act of adultery: "If a man is found lying with the wife of another man, both of them shall die, the man who lay with the woman, and the woman; so you shall purge the evil from Israel." The accusation of adultery could only be proved by two or more witnesses, which is why the two elders appeared, initially, to prevail in their threats as witnesses over Susanna. Susanna realized that although she had not committed adultery she would still be falsely accused of the crime. Despite the futility of her situation, she chooses to reaffirm her innocence in terms of faith. The wages of the sin attributed to her by the elders will be death, but she chooses death rather than the loss of her chastity. Appealing to God as her witness, she alone continues to tell the truth in the face of those who disbelieve.

The assembly believed them, because they were elders of the people and judges; and they condemned her to death.
Then Susanna cried out with a loud voice and said, "O eternal God, who dost discern what is secret, who art aware of all things before they come to be,

thou knowest that these men have borne false witness against me. And now I am to die!Yet I have done none of these things that they have wickedly invented against me!"

The Lord heard her cry. And as she was being led away to be put to death, God aroused the holy spirit of a young lad named Daniel.[42]

Daniel tests the accounts of the two elders and in their contradictions proves their lies. The penalty found in Deuteronomy 19:16–21 as an attempt to prevent personal motives from prompting false accusations illuminates the gravity of the elders' charge against Susanna.

If a malicious witness rise up against any man to accuse him of wrongdoing, then both parties to the dispute shall appear before the Lord, before the priests and judges who are in office in those days; the judges shall inquire diligently, and if the witness is a false witness and has accused his brother falsely, then you shall do to him as he had meant to do to his brother; . . .Your eye shall not pity; it shall be life for life, eye for eye, tooth for tooth, hand for hand, foot for foot.

The concept of lex talionis, the law of exact vengeance, was indeed carried out against the elders whose failed seduction and accusation of the innocent Susanna had originally condemned her to death. The death sentence meted out for the elders, with Daniel's intervention as inspired by God, proved the just application of preestablished communal laws. Daniel, inspired by God, acts to save Susanna's life. Her innocence is thus publicly confirmed and the honor of her family vindicated "because nothing shameful was found in her."

Both Susanna and ʿAʾisha were accused of adultery and vindicated of this charge in ways which reaffirmed or established a legal status quo. The accusations leveled against both women threatened the honor of the men to whom they were tied, which in turn threatened their lives. Ultimately, neither woman had the power to vindicate herself. Only God, acting through his male agents on Earth could do this, saving them, but ultimately reserving the highest accolades, not for the women whose innocence he had confirmed, but for his most exalted male servants: Daniel and Muhammad. Daniel acts through divinely inspired wisdom as a judge;

the Prophet Muhammad through the direct verbal revelation of the Qur'an proves that 'A'isha's true judge is Allah. Both Susanna and 'A'isha are, in fact, the objects not the subjects of their respective tales of divine vindication. Although each woman is successfully defended against the accusation of adultery, neither had the power to exonerate herself. By the sixteenth century, a Western Christian source had aptly, but incorrectly, linked these two women. The author Pascual San Pedro alleges in his work *Sobre el seta mahometana*, "Concerning the Muslim Sect," that "the Muslims . . . read the story of the rehabilitation of 'A'isha in their Lent, as Christians do Susannah in theirs."[43] Clearly, the reference to the Muslim "Lent" was to Ramadan, the ninth month of the Islamic calendar during which Muslims fast from sunrise to sunset and celebrate in prayer the initial revelation of the Qur'an.

While Susanna remained exemplary by stasis in the Apocrypha, 'A'isha's exoneration was destined to continue as the object of an evolving medieval Islamic polemic. Although Muslim sources never utilized the example of Susanna for comparison with 'A'isha, they did make frequent reference to the Qur'anic figure of Maryam, the mother of Jesus. As outlined in the previous chapter, third/ninth-century Sunni hadith and fourth/tenth-century chronicle and exegesis often refer to the connection between 'A'isha and Maryam. This tenuous linkage is not made explicit until quite late in the medieval period when the Egyptian Sunni author al-Zarkashi (d. 794/1392) stated that Allah had vindicated only four people: the prophets Joseph and Moses, as well as Maryam the mother of Jesus, and 'A'isha.[44] Maryam was charged with adultery when she returned to her people with the child Jesus in her arms. Al-Zarkashi explains that Maryam was exonerated by her infant son. Maryam did not defend her unmarried maternity, but as recorded in the Qur'an 19:29-32, instead motioned to her child who miraculously spoke on her behalf. However, while the prophet Jesus spoke in vindication of his mother's reputation, al-Zarkashi states that 'A'isha was exonerated by "glorious verses" of the Qur'an which "will be read until judgement day" and "were transformed into law" as a "blessing not just on her, but on all Muslims." In both cases the accused women are successfully defended by male prophets, but in 'A'isha's case alone, Allah is the source of her vindication. The tremendous importance of the comparison between Maryam and

`A'isha binds the two women together in their mutual need for a defense of their chastity.[45] The aspersions against both women emphasize their female sexuality and their unique proximity to male prophets. In `A'isha's case, her connection to Maryam will be detailed in chapter 5 as a positive, but ineffective, Sunni attempt at her idealization. The linkage of the hadith al-ifk with Maryam as a Qur'anic female model served to remind even Sunni Muslims not simply of `A'isha's vindication, but of the initial accusation, an emphasis that left her vulnerable to Shi`i Muslim attack.

Shi`i Interpretations: The Medieval Politics of Slander

The wife of the Prophet Muhammad became part of a communal debate over the interpretation of the past through her presence in the hadith al-ifk. The remembrance of the accusation of adultery prompted very different interpretations by medieval Sunni and Shi`i Muslim authors. Every repetition of the account of the lie was rendering both religious and historical record. In each context, the initial slanderous accusation against `A'isha could be neither ignored nor forgotten. In post third/ninth-century sources, the account of the lie handed `A'isha's Shi`i detractors ready-made ammunition with which to attack her reputation and, through her, the Sunni majority. Staunch Sunni supporters were forced to temper their praise of `A'isha in the medieval period with a defense of her memory. Despite the divine exoneration of `A'isha to which most Muslims would attest, her historical depiction would continue to face the negative implications of the affair of the lie.

Through Shi`i–Sunni debate about `A'isha's meaning for the Muslim community, scholars would also come to define themselves and their religiopolitical differences. The initial accusation of adultery was directed against a specific woman, `A'isha, and was intended to damage Muhammad's honor and the religious prestige of the entire community. References to the hadith al-ifk in the medieval period became a barometer for definitions of political allegiance to Sunni authority or the competing claims of Shi`i affiliation. At the doctrinal level, the Muslim community began to determine communal identity and difference according to the interpretation of a shared past and the importance of the most prominent members of the Muslim community. At a personal level, increasingly detailed declarations of faith also served to determine whether, in terms of the Sunni majority, the believer was a Muslim or a heretic.

If Shi'i Muslims were to reject 'A'isha's vindication from the charge of adultery, they still had to reckon with those verses in the Qur'an which Sunni Muslims believed were revealed in her honor. In the fourth/tenth-century exegesis of the Shi'i author al-Qummi (d. 307/919) the verses of the Qur'an Sunnis applied to 'A'isha found a distinctly different interpretation, context, and subject. Al-Qummi cites the Qur'an 24:11: "Those who spread the lie are a gang among you. Do not regard it as a bad thing for you; no, it is good for you."[46] He says of these verses that while *al-'amma*, the Shi'i designation for the general population synonymous with Sunni Muslims, "relate that this verse was revealed about 'A'isha" on the raid against the Banu Mustaliq, *al-khassa*, "the select," the term used by Twelver Shi'is for themselves, relate that these verses were instead revealed about Muhammad's concubine Maryam the Copt. Thus, al-Qummi's commentary reveals that while the Shi'i population knew of 'A'isha's involvement in the hadith al-ifk as defined by the majority of Muslims, the Twelver Shi'i minority themselves did not accept this interpretation of the event. Al-Qummi's commentary emphasizes the potential problematic of the verses as a testimony to divine intervention on 'A'isha's part. Since the revelation does not name 'A'isha specifically, its application to her became a potential object of dispute. Shi'i Muslims could thus suggest that the verses were not meant for 'A'isha at all, but for Muhammad's concubine Maryam. They argued that Maryam the Copt had been the object of slander from the women among the hypocrites in Medina, those who had only nominally accepted Islam. Indeed, in other verses of the Qur'an al-Qummi argues that 'A'isha herself slandered Maryam the Copt.[47] Thus, the implication of the verses applied to Maryam by Shi'i Muslims is that they refer to 'A'isha not as the object of lies, but as a source of the slander against the Prophet's concubine. As proposed by Sunni sources, the revelation took place after the raid against the Banu Mustaliq, but Shi'i Muslims did not accept this context for the verses, placing them after a different raid, that of Tabuk, which took place five years after the campaign against the Banu Mustaliq.[48]

The contested points in the interpretation of these verses of the Qur'an also underscored the partisan divide in the matter of its preservation. Whereas all the Sunni accounts relied upon ʿAʾisha and other members of her family to attest to the object, context, and interpretation of the incident, Shiʿi Muslims believed these same individuals to be suspect sources, people so partisan that they could not be relied upon to relate the truth of the Islamic past or the meaning of Qurʾanic revelation. By relying upon their own select chain of authorities in the interpretation of the Qurʾan, Shiʿi Muslims found themselves able to explain past events differently from the Sunni majority. As a demonstration of Shiʿi polemic, the incident termed by Sunni Muslims "the affair of the lie," demonstrated for Shiʿi Muslims a different kind of falsehood, a lie promoted by the majority of Muslims which depicted ʿAʾisha as the object of divine intervention. Thus, the Sunni exegete al-Tabari (d. 310/923) would interpret Qurʾanic verses 24:11–20 based on the same chain of authorities that had supported the tale of ʿAʾisha's vindication found in the earlier account of Ibn Hisham.[49] His detailed explanation of these verses and ʿAʾisha's part in them stands in stark contradiction to the contemporary interpretation of the Shiʿi al-Qummi. Al-Tabari implicitly acknowledges the basic distinction between the Sunni and Shiʿi readings of ʿAʾisha's role in the revelation by stressing that Muslims "do not think that it [the revelation] revealed adultery." Rather, he declares, "The people of Islam, all of them, are unified on this position. They are the people of one religious community." Al-Tabari surely understood that his declaration of a unified doctrinal front flew in the face of rather different Shiʿi evidence. However, not all Shiʿi Muslim commentators interpreted the hadith al-ifk differently from the Sunni majority. The interpretation of the Shiʿi author al-Tabarsi (d. 548/1153) represents a case in point. Drawing upon the Medinan school of relaters including al-Zuhri, ʿUrwa ibn al-Zubayr and ʿAʾisha herself as the originator, al-Tabarsi departed from his coreligionists and adopted a Sunni position in the interpretation of these verses.[50] His stance was contingent on the acceptance of a chain of Sunni authorities, a position inconsistent with the usual Shiʿi emphasis on the authority of the imams. Most Shiʿi scholars did not accept these individual relaters of the hadith al-ifk, especially ʿAʾisha, whom they did not consider a source of religious authority. Al-Qummi's commentary represented the more standard Shiʿi route in determining the meaning of these verses. His doctrinal definition of this part of the Qurʾan also clarified the medieval Sunni defense of `A'isha, a defense that was geared to a consistently negative Shi`i reading of her reputation.

The Shi`i rejection of the verses attributed to `A'isha left open-ended the accusations made against `A'isha's chastity. Shi`i Muslims accepted the accusation of adultery made against `A'isha, but not her divine exoneration from the charges. If she had not been vindicated by a heaven-sent missive recorded in the Qur'an, clearly, this defined her overall reputation as vulnerable to Shi`i Muslim slander. `A'isha's sexual conduct would remain an explosive but effective political tool for Shi`i Muslim propaganda. She could be termed by Shi`i Muslims both an adulteress and, due to her slander of Maryam the Copt, a liar. Now the object of sectarian definitional differences, `A'isha's reputation allowed the Shi`i minority a highly visible target for new insinuations about the values of the majority of Muslim believers who praised `A'isha as a virtuous female example for their community. As the hypocrites in Medina had sought to wound the Prophet's honor through the suggestion of `A'isha's infidelity, Shi`i Muslims of the medieval period could articulate their polemic against Sunni Muslims through the remembrance of this same incident by taking a similar position in regard to the reputation of the wife of the Prophet. In the contest for the maintenance of communal honor, Sunni Muslims would find themselves beset by definitions of the past in which their notions of truth and falsehood and their own definitions of Islamic beliefs were challenged through the controversial persona of `A'isha.

The religiopolitical ramifications of the hadith al-ifk were exploited actively by Shi`i Muslims. Motivated by opposition not just to `A'isha but to all Sunni claims to moral superiority, Shi`i Muslims referred to the accusation as a reminder of the illegitimacy lurking at the core of all Sunni governments. In this way Shi`i Muslims utilized their negative interpretation of `A'isha's historical legacy to promote a debate within the Islamic community employing `A'isha's persona as a part of their very different reading of a shared past. Shi`i interpretations of `A'isha's sexuality were intended to strike at the Sunni ability to project and claim the collective supremacy demonstrated by the order of succession to Muhammad. `Ali had been supplanted by `A'isha's father, the first caliph Abu Bakr and later threatened as the fourth caliph by `A'isha herself at the Battle of the Camel. By undermining `A'isha's reputation, Shi`i Muslims sought to vitiate the standing of Abu Bakr, the most important male example for the majority of Muslims after the Prophet Muhammad. Although the initial lie had been intended to hurt Muhammad's prestige, later Shi`i manipulation of the incident would be utilized to attack the first caliph, Abu Bakr. Once more, the honor of the father would be challenged through the example of the daughter. Sunni Muslims defended `A'isha by praising her as al-mubarra'a, "the vindicated," the woman cleared of the charge of adultery. In contrast, Shi`i sources represented `A'isha as al-fahisha, "the whore," or al-zaniya, "the adulteress."The Sunni honorific, pitted against the blasphemous Shi`i apellation, succinctly captures the conflicting perception of `A'isha in medieval sources.[51]

The Sunni Defense: The Accusation As a Component in Definitions of Belief

The Sunni need to respond to Shi`i Muslim polemic about `A'isha is most clearly demonstrated in professions of faith from the fourth/tenth century. In the middle of this century, the Sunni majority had found increased doctrinal cohesion through explicit professions of faith. However, just as theologians of the Muslim majority began to fully define themselves as Sunni Muslims, they were beset from within and without by Shi`i political threat and invective. In the year 334/945, the Shi`i Buyid dynasty took effective political control of `Abbasid Baghdad. Although the Sunni `Abbasid caliph remained as the nominal head of state, for the first time in Islamic history, an effective Shi`i regime had seized control of an Islamic government. Although the Buyids had originally been Zaydi or Fiver Shi`i Muslims, there is strong evidence that they embraced Twelver Shi`ism with the consolidation of their dynasty. Their support for Shi`ism allowed Twelver Shi`i authors to flourish during their hundred year reign. The Buyids also sanctioned public celebrations of Shi`i holidays in Baghdad such as the commemoration of the martyrdom of the third Imam Husayn.[52] In the year 351/962 in Baghdad, Shi`i Muslims reportedly scrawled curses against the first three caliphs Abu Bakr, `Umar, and `Uthman on the walls of a city mosque. Greater Shi`i freedom in the urban centers of Iraq led to greater sectarian tensions among Muslims and resulted in civil unrest in Baghdad during this period. In Egypt, the Isma`ili or Sevener Shi`i dynasty named after the Prophet's daughter Fatima gained control of Egypt in 358/969. The Fatimid dynasty proved both a political and ideological threat as it consolidated control over Syria and threatened the `Abbasid heartland of Iraq.

In such turbulent times, Sunni Muslims began to profess their faith and define their differences from the Shi`i minority within and without. Confessions of faith suggest that by the fourth/tenth century Sunni Muslims were increasingly proclaiming their differences from Shi`i Muslims through the order of merit which designated the strict order of the first four caliphs: Abu Bakr, `Umar, `Uthman and `Ali. Such definitions of the status quo not only committed the believer to a religiopolitical male order, but to a defense of `A'isha's reputation. In the Sunni Muslim profession of faith of Ibn Batta (d. 387/997), a member of the Hanbali legal school, reverence for the companions of the Prophet and his wives figures prominently. Ibn Batta's testimony has been described as "on the forefront" of the Sunni defense of the faith during a time of religious upheaval.[53] He dedicates a section of this document to `A'isha, whom he defines as the daughter of Abu Bakr, as-siddiq, "the truthful," referring to her by the feminine form of the same epithet.[54] In addition in this treatise, `A'isha is defined as *al-tahira*, "the pure," a term which refers to purity in the sense of chastity or, in Islamic ritual practice, the state of a non-menstruating woman.[55] The term in `A'isha's case appears to promote her chastity in defense of the charge of adultery. Such an assertion is born out by Ibn Batta's linkage of this epithet with the one that immediately follows: al-mubarra'a, "the vindicated."[56] `A'isha's chastity and vindication from the charge of adultery are described by the author as "transmitted from Allah by the tongue of Gabriel." The assertion of `A'isha's innocence is, in Ibn Batta's profession of faith, a test for believers. Those who doubt the Qur'anic revelation concerning her innocence, in essence, suggest that the Qur'an is lying and thus "doubt the message of the Prophet of Allah," claiming that his revelation "comes from a source other than God." `A'isha's reputation as "the mother of believers in this world and the next" and the Prophet's wife "in heaven" was under attack by Shi`i Muslims for whom the accusation of adultery, clearly, did not conclude with a Qur'anic vindication. In Ibn Batta's profession of faith, support for `A'isha's innocence was part of a communal Sunni definition of belief.

A profession of faith attributed to Abu Hanifa (d. 150/767), founder of the Hanafi legal school of Sunni Muslims, but recorded by a disciple in the fourth/tenth century raises a similar defense of ʿAʾisha's reputation. There is a strong suggestion that ʿAʾisha's historical persona continued to merit a necessary defense by the Sunni faithful:

> . . . she is the mother of the believers, purified from [the charge] of adultery and vindicated from whatever the rejectors [Twelver Shiʿis] testify to against her regarding fornication. Whoever slanders her regarding this, he is a child of fornication. He is a an unbeliever who denies the bold verses about the exoneration which acquitted her . . . Whoever denies a verse of the Qurʾan, he is an infidel.[57]

In the fifth/eleventh century, opponents of the Sunni Seljuk regime in Iran and Iraq referred to ʿAʾisha as a "whore."[58] The vizier Nizam al-Mulk (d. 485/1092) cites this blasphemous usage in his story about the "Robbers of Kuch Baluch." His work, designed as a manual of admonitory yet practical instruction for his Sunni sovereign, maintains that the robbers in question were Ismaʿili, or Sevener Shiʿi Muslims connected to the Fatimid regime. Their rejection of ʿAʾisha's innocence in the matter of the hadith al-ifk identified them at once as political enemies of the Sunni Seljuk state. Nizam al-Mulk is quick to distinguish himself from these brigands by referring to ʿAʾisha by her honorary epithet al-siddiqa, "the truthful," a clear indication of his respect and reverence for the Prophet's wife. In this context, his approbation for ʿAʾisha is also a doctrinal statement which allows him to condemn these Shiʿi Muslims as both heretics and enemies of the state.

Ibn Taymiyya (d. 728/1328), a Sunni Muslim theologian and jurist of the Hanbali school, in his own defense of the faith, made clear the importance of the hadith al-ifk in the defense of ʿAʾisha's reputation. Written in response to the Twelver Shiʿi Muslim theologian al-ʿAllama al-Hilli (d. 726/1325), Ibn Taymiyya's treatise chastises Shiʿis who

> . . . accuse ʿAʾisha of terrible things, among them they call her an adulteress even though Allah vindicated her from that [charge] by sending down a Qurʾanic revelation about the matter. They enhance their ignorance by

naming someone other than her [to whom the verses apply] among the wives of the Prophet.[59]

Ibn Taymiyya emphasizes both the Shi`i invective about `A'isha's chastity and its root in a different interpretation of the meaning of the Qur'anic verses. He also notes the Shi`i linkage of `A'isha as an adulteress in the description of the Qur'anic wives of Lot and Noah. These two women are cited in the Qur'an 66:10 as examples for those who disbelieve and their ultimate destination is hell. Each wife, in betraying her husband, also committed sins of sexual excess. Thus, the wives of Lot and Noah are both compared with `A'isha as adulteresses.[60] Such a description of the wives of Lot and Noah may be found in the earliest fourth/tenth-century Shi`i Qur'anic commentary of al-Qummi where `A'isha is described in regard to slightly earlier verses of the same chapter, but not as an adulteress.[61] Ibn Taymiyya's rebuttal of this Shi`i polemic against `A'isha's chastity compares her medieval opponents to the original "hypocrites" and "sinners" who "slandered `A'isha with a lie" by calling her an adulteress and not repenting.[62] In comparing medieval Shi`i polemic to the offenses of the original source of the slander against `A'isha in Medina, Ibn Taymiyya also argues that such an attack contradicts the Qur'an and the basic interpretation of the faith of Islam.

During this period of the eighth/fourteenth century in Mamluk Egypt it was also possible for Sunni Muslim scholars to find themselves accused of insufficient reverence in their treatment of `A'isha's legacy. The scholar Mughultai ibn Qilij al-Hukri who was a member of the Hanafi legal school may have been the victim of an academic power struggle in Cairo.

. . . in 745 [A.D. 1342] . . . a Shafi`i traditionist and son of a Turkish soldier came to Cairo, Mughultai's book came to his attention one day in the book market, whether by accident or someone's design it is not clear. When he learned that it contained a story unfavorable to `A'isha, the Prophet's wife, he took offense and brought a case against Mughultai. . . . As a result Mughultai was rebuked and imprisoned for a time. It is reported that local book dealers took the book off the market after that incident.[63]

The exploitation of something Mughultai had written about `A'isha to persecute him is indicative of the power of such an accusation. Unfortunately, the specifics of Mughultai's allegedly offensive work have not been preserved. It is clear, however, that the penalty for insulting `A'isha was harsh, for Mughultai was not just rebuked, he was imprisoned and his books, in effect, were banned. This incident suggests that insults against `A'isha, the most common being related to the hadith al-ifk, could serve personal as well as political ends. It may have been a combination of the two which prompted the scrutiny of Mughultai's work by his rival within the scholarly hierarchy of Mamluk Cairo. `A'isha's reputation in the medieval Sunni community was a serious matter which could serve many ends in defining who was a true member of the Sunni faithful and what was acceptable in Sunni Muslim scholarship.

In the year 999/1590, the victorious Sunni Ottoman government concluded a treaty with the Shi`i Safavid regime of Iran in which they dictated terms concerning territory as well as the definition of the faith. The treaty with the Safavids contains statements which make the Sunni defense of `A'isha regarding the hadith al-ifk a component of their agreement. The establishment of peace was proposed by the Ottomans with specific provisions about the Shi`i attacks against the Prophet's companions, specifically Abu Bakr and `A'isha, "the chaste . . . whose chastity is attested by a divine communication."[64] Further, states the treaty, "There will be no further dissimulation about `A'isha because the revelation does not apply to any other woman." As part of a defense of Sunni Islam, the Ottomans ostensibly manipulated these sectarian divisions to impose their vision of the faith. However, it is more likely that the Sunni Ottomans did not expect compliance, but rather employed these irreconcilable doctrinal differences to provide a future pretext for war against their Shi`i Muslim neighbors.

Praise of the Hadith al-Ifk As A Defense of `A'isha and the Sunni Community

Sunni Muslims defined themselves in defense of `A'isha's reputation in contradistinction to their Shi`i coreligionists. The majority of the faithful, particularly in the seventh/thirteenth and eighth/fourteenth centuries also chose to celebrate the hadith al-ifk as a tribute to `A'isha's memory and a demonstration of their own communal identity. The celebration of the account of the lie as a source of praise for the Prophet's wife allowed the incident to receive treatment in separate Sunni texts during this period. After the third/ninth century, biographical accounts of `A'isha's life in Sunni sources continued to include references to the hadith al-ifk. In one biography, the scholar Ibn al-Athir (d. 632/1233) defined `A'isha's singular importance through her participation in the event: "Even if `A'isha possessed no excellent qualities except those found in the account of the lie, then that would still be sufficient excellence and honor for her."There is no extended reference to the event, although the author does refer to `A'isha elsewhere in his biographical entry as al-mubarra'a, "the vindicated."[65] Roughly one hundred years later, al-Dhahabi (d. 749/1348) details the hadith al-ifk in his biography of `A'isha. His version of the incident, though condensed, is not substantially different from that of Ibn Hisham.[66]

During this same period, the hadith al-ifk began to appear in separate manuscripts unattached to `A'isha's biography. Unlike the biography of the Prophet which had Muhammad's life story as its subject and which served as the initial setting for the tale, the separation of this incident was inspired by a need to celebrate the incident as a positive aspect of `A'isha's reputation and the honor of the Sunni community. Two examples of this phenomenon parallel aspects of praise found in the biographical accounts cited. The seventh/thirteenth-century work of Ibn al-Haytham (d. 609/1212) represents a faithful rendition of the Sunni version of this event.[67] The author of the manuscript wrote in Syria. His work follows the basic event, but deviates slightly in the matter of `Ali's interrogation of the servant girl Barira as a character witness for `A'isha. In Ibn Hisham, the servant states, even after a sound beating, that she knows nothing but good of her mistress.[68] In Ibn al-Haytham's account, the servant swears that `A'isha "is better than the good [people]."[69] Such an enhanced declaration may have been directed at those latter day partisans of `Ali's family who continued to refuse to believe that `A'isha's character was beyond reproach. The progression from knowing nothing but good of `A'isha to her being among the best of all people in her community, a response prompted by a question from `Ali himself, suggests that the account may have been strengthened in its Sunni praise of `A'isha in response to Shi`i attack. The work of Ibn al-Haytham may have been separated from the Prophet's biography in order for Sunni scholars to utilize it as a vehicle of sectarian praise.

In the eighth/fourteenth century, the unique poem of the Sunni preacher al-Andalusi made explicit the potential of the hadith al-ifk as a Sunni response to Shi`i criticism of `A'isha. Ibn al-Haytham had separated the text from biographical accounts of `A'isha, but al-Andalusi appears to have been the first and only medieval poet to have linked his panegyric about the Prophet's wife to the matter. Al-Andalusi's poem of praise made explicit the Sunni defense of `A'isha and, in so doing, celebrated the account of the lie as a remembrance of divine revelation and a communal triumph. Al-Andalusi used his poem as an attack upon the Shi`i Muslims who contradicted the Sunni interpretation of the event. In this way, al-Andalusi transformed the implications of the hadith al-ifk into a Sunni reaffirmation of faith.

We know very little about the poet or the original date or circumstances of his composition, except that al-Andalusi wrote his work on commission for local patrons described variously as a military commander or prime minister. The poet was paid for his work in gold with one hundred dinars.[70] One of the extant manuscripts suggests that the original was composed during the Fatimid period (297-567/909-1171), a time when such a paen of praise for `A'isha would have provided a suitable Sunni response to those Isma`ili Shi`is whose love of the Prophet's daughter Fatima was evident in the name they gave their Egyptian-based dynasty.[71] Initially, the poem may have been designed as Sunni polemic aimed at a specific, politically and ideologically threatening Shi`i dynasty, but the earliest extant copies date from nearly two hundred years later during the rule of the Sunni Mamluk regime and most, except for two manuscripts in Western collections, remain in Egypt and Syria. The earliest copy is dated 745/1344. A total of four copies are preserved from the eighth/fourteenth century and three of them date from after the onset of the Black Death in 749/1348, a communal crisis during which `A'isha's words would be invoked.[72] Two subsequent copies were made during the tenth/sixteenth and eleventh/seventeenth centuries.[73]

The popularity of this unusual poem is attested by the frequency with which it was reproduced and the number of extant copies. Yet the reason for the poem's appeal during a time of stable Sunni rule in Egypt and Syria remains a question. Only one of the manuscripts suggests the environment in which `A'isha and the hadith al-ifk became an object of celebration. Those who recited the poem and recorded it were not members of the populous at large, but Sunni scholars and judges who are described as hearing and transmitting the verses.[74] The scholarly promotion of the poem may be explained as a manifestation of ʾAʾisha's practical importance to these men as a source of hadith. Through ʾAʾisha, a revered source for their communal past, these same scholars gained access to the words and deeds of the Prophet, materials critical to the Sunni edifice of theology and law to which they had dedicated their lives. The Shiʾi rejection of ʾAʾisha signalled for Sunni scholars an attack upon the very sources of their beliefs and social practice. ʾAʾisha's vindication from the charge of adultery could be celebrated as the exoneration of one woman and the divine proof of her truthfulness. In celebrating ʾAʾisha's innocence, Sunni scholars both defended the Prophet's wife and defined their communal honor as an extension of their role as the defenders of her legacy as a truthful source of their faith.

In one of the eighth/fourteenth-century manuscripts, the poem is prefaced by an account of the hadith al-ifk. The coupling of the account of the lie with al-Andalusi's verses occurs only once in a version dating from 776/1374: "These pages include the account of the hadith al-ifk which is [the tale of] the vindication of ʾAʾisha, the mother of the believers, together with verses of poetry which unite the matter of her noble lineage with her excellence."[75]

However, the internal evidence of the poem suggests that it was originally conceived as a defense of ʾAʾisha prompted by Shiʾi allegations that termed her an adulteress. The opening verses of the poem signal that their author created it as a response to criticism concerning the scandal surrounding the accusation of adultery. The poem consists of fifty-six verses, with minor variations and organizational differences between versions.[76] In the first line, the poet uses his own voice to set up the main body of the poem, "What is the affair of the mother of the believers? That is my subject."[77] The word used for "affair," is *shaʾn*, meaning also "matter" or "concern." The term is synonymous with the hadith al-ifk where it is used in the contemporary work of al-Dhahabi as a caption for the accusation of adultery.[78]

In the second line, al-Andalusi introduces the reader to his role as someone who will clarify ʾAʾisha's merits by "translating her words into my language."[79] As poet, al-Andalusi allows `A'isha to speak in the first person throughout the rest of the work. This device animates the argument and lends immediacy to many of `A'isha's standard claims about her own precedence in the Islamic community. Moreover, the use of the first person in this late medieval poem is consistent with many traditions narrated on `A'isha's authority in early hadith, one of which was Ibn Hisham's third/ninth-century version of the hadith al-ifk. Again, `A'isha appears to maintain narrative control in the depiction of her legacy, but such power remains illusory. The force of the poet's ire, directed through `A'isha's address, is clearly directed by al-Andalusi himself who arranges her first words to challenge a specific audience of "hateful ones." These anonymous detractors become the focus of `A'isha's words and her warning about the consequences of their behavior. The poem, in this regard, represents a practical admission of how entrenched the points of conflict about `A'isha's historical legacy had become in the medieval period. Seven hundred years after her death, the poet allows the Prophet's wife to address at once her original and her medieval detractors as a historical persona. Thus, she warns: "Do not perpetrate [a sin] upon the tomb of Muhammad; for the house [he was buried in] is my house and the place, my place." She reminds those who would dishonor the memory of the Prophet that she was an integral part of his life. In death, he was buried beneath her house. The line emphasizes that `A'isha shared not just a hut with the Prophet, but a marital bond which gives her precedence and unshakeable authority in the Islamic community. Moreover, her words remind the reader that attacks against `A'isha are also directed against her husband. His honor remains linked to her legacy. She continues to elaborate her position as the wife preferred by the Prophet above all others in lines four through nine. The proofs provided are ones which differ little from the earliest hadith in which she is the source for the ten qualities which made her Muhammad's favorite wife. Among these she specifically mentions that the Prophet died in her arms on a day turned over to her. She states that she was his only virgin bride and that the angel Gabriel himself arranged the marriage.

The key issue of her vindication from the charge of adultery is discussed explicitly in verses ten through nineteen, with special emphasis placed upon the punishment meted out for those in Medina who falsely accused her of adultery. Those addressed in the eighth/fourteenth-century poem are equated with the people in Medina who started the slanderous rumors about the Prophet's wife. The true object of `A'isha's spirited address, as scripted by al-Andalusi, are those medieval Shi`i detractors who persist in their willful misinterpretation of the Sunni vision of the past. Thus, `A'isha rails in lines ten through thirteen:

> Allah, the greatest, voiced my proof and my vindication in the perfection of the Qur'an.
> Allah protected me and enhanced my virtue, for my vindication was upon the tongue of the Prophet.
> And in the Qur'an, Allah damned those shameful ones after my innocence [was proved].
> Allah rebuked those who wanted to harm me through a lie and he honored himself in my concern.[80]

In addition to being described in the poem as *muhsina*, "a woman of unblemished reputation," with the the help of Allah, she has been proven "chaste." In contrast, the ahl al-ifk, "the people of the lie . . . were humiliated." The remaining lines dealing with the accusation explain that `A'isha was present when the revelation from Allah descended, through the angel Gabriel, to Muhammad. The majority of the initial sixteen lines of the poem's praise for `A'isha are devoted to the hadith al-ifk.

Verses eighteen to thirty focus on `A'isha's father Abu Bakr, his devotion to the Prophet, and his leadership. The remaining twenty lines of the poem, build upon the praise for the Sunni father-daughter ideals `A'isha and Abu Bakr, by dealing directly with their Shi`i Muslim opponents: "Woe to those who are disloyal to the family of Muhammad through their hostility to his wives."[81] Stated in the following lines is the idea that between Abu Bakr and the Sunni Muslims and `Ali and his Shi`i followers "is a friendship which cannot be changed by the insinuation of the devil."[82] In line thirty-six the doctrinal conflict within the medieval Islamic community alluded to by al-Andalusi as the devil's work is further elaborated. `Ali and Fatima make their appearance in the poem anonymously, but effectively in a verse in which the Prophet's daughter Fatima is referred to by her epithet al-batul, "the virgin." In reference to the Prophet's family, al-Andalusi takes a conciliatory approach and one which reduces `A'isha's alleged narration to anachronism: "The love of al-batul and her husband is not different in the two communities of Islam." Quite skillfully, the poet has implied that since Sunni Muslims revere and respect Fatima and `Ali, Shi`i Muslims ought to extend the same inclusive generosity toward `A'isha and Abu Bakr. The suggestions, as a Sunni demonstration of good will, remained doctrinally impractical. Even within the context of the poem, such a placatory attitude was not consistent with the tone of disgust which al-Andalusi permits `A'isha in her concluding lines. She warns her detractors that "the wives of the Prophet are the best of [all] women." Ultimately, the wife of the Prophet reaffirms that "Allah honors those who desire my honor and my Lord humiliates those who desire my shame."[83]

Al-Andalusi had expressed the passion of the Sunni medieval defense of `A'isha, but it was his focus on the hadith al-ifk which provided the perfect vehicle with which to strike back at Shi`i polemic. The parallel between the original accusers of the Prophet's wife and the medieval Shi`i Muslims who blasphemed against `A'isha over the same event seven hundred years later proved apt. In both sources, `A'isha directs her own defense with words which narrate her virtues and reiterate her divinely designated vindication. The debate which had begun with the honor of the Prophet and the potential shame of his wife as recorded in the earliest third/ninth-century accounts had evolved from its initial context and become a demonstration of political allegiance and religious definition within a much later Islamic community. Partisans of `A'isha and family members had solidified the version of events at Medina recorded in Ibn Hisham and other third/ninth-century Sunni sources. More than five hundred years later, new scholarly supporters in Egypt and Syria closely identified their own concerns with a defense of `A'isha. They promoted a poem whose polemical intent reflected their communal identity. Her legacy for them had been transformed into a Sunni symbol of their collective identity and honor. Her image as a chaste and truthful source for their interpretation of the past demanded that she be defended as a representative of their collective honor, a reputable source for their transmitted understanding and true interpretation of the past.

The precedent for poetic praise of `A'isha had begun with the hadith al-ifk of Ibn Hisham and the verses in that account by Hasan ibn Thabit which defend and celebrate `A'isha.[84] Once punished for slander, Hasan ibn Thabit's references to `A'isha's reputation were deployed as praise, but were, in fact, a defense. In al-Andalusi's work this method had been employed and improved upon by merging praise of `A'isha with polemic. Unlike Hasan ibn Thabit, al-Andalusi's task was to celebrate `A'isha's exoneration and, in so doing, vindicate the entire medieval Sunni community for whom she had come to symbolize a vital aspect of their collective honor: the definition of their faith and political dominance. The poem of al-Andalusi is hardly a panegyric in the purest sense, for it is was first designed as a polemical defense designed to rally the Sunni faithful and rebuke Shi`i opponents.

The hadith al-ifk had begun as an attack upon the Prophet Muhammad through his wife, but its resolution determined that male honor would be welded to a divine demonstration of the Prophet's mission and `A'isha's innocence. Muslims never ceased to recall the lessons of the incident no matter how differently they might be applied in an increasingly sectarian context. `A'isha's historical legacy consistently refracted crucial elements of the dispute between Shi`i and Sunni Muslims. Her centrality as a focal point of disagreement in communal debate gave al-Andalusi the impetus to allow `A'isha to poetically defend not just herself, but all Sunni Muslims. Her defense and theirs had become inextricably linked in medieval Islamic communal debate.

Medieval Western and Modern Islamic Versions of the Accusation of Adultery

Sunni and Shi`i Muslims were not the only medieval believers to manipulate the hadith al-ifk for their own ends. The Western Christian perception of the accusation of adultery, not surprisingly, emphasized Muhammad's ability to fake or create revelation at will. The accusation made against `A'isha was utilized in Christian medieval polemic to define Islam as a heresy based on the revelations of a false prophet.

. . . one Latin author adopted the attitude of Muhammad's contemporary enemies. San Pedro saw nothing worse in the episode than the manufacture of revelations, which was evidence of hypocrisy, or diabolical possession, or both; he also thought that Muhammad's fondness for `A'isha unworthy of a prophet. This last was `Ali's own argument at the time.[85]

According to Norman Daniel, Peter of Toledo described `A'isha as the "beloved of Safwan ibn al-Mu`attal al-Sulami" with whom, the medieval author charged, she had indeed had adulterous relations. The implication that `A'isha was not only unfaithful to her husband, but that Muhammad was aware and consented to her adultery with Safwan is pure polemical Christian fiction. The odd Western twist given the hadith al-ifk may be perceived as part of the broader program of Christian propaganda aimed at discrediting the Prophet Muhammad through `A'isha. In this instance, the Prophet and his wife were enlisted to personify, for Christian condemnation, the decadent sexuality of Islam. As Daniel correctly suggests about this slanderous Christian version of the affair of the lie: "The credit for this absurd, nasty and gratuitous invention (the final point in which would make nonsense of the entire story) must go to Peter of Toledo in whose translation alone it occurs."

More recently, the retelling of the account of the lie in Salman Rushdie's novel *The Satanic Verses* contains a deft, if cynical, paraphrase of the earliest account of the incident given in Ibn Hisham.

Ayesha and the Prophet had gone on an expedition to a far-flung village, and on the way back to Yathrib their party had camped in the dunes for the night. Camp was struck in the dark before the dawn. At the last moment Ayesha was obliged by a call of nature to rush out of sight into a hollow. While she was away her litter-bearers picked up her palanquin and marched off. She was a light woman, and failing to notice much difference in the weight of the heavy palanquin, they assumed she was inside. Ayesha returned after relieving herself to find herself alone, and who knows what might have befallen if a young man, a certain Safwan, had not chanced to pass by on his camel. . . . Safwan brought Ayesha back to Yathrib safe and sound; at which point tongues began to wag, not least in his harem, where opportunities to weaken Ayesha's power were eagerly seized by her opponents. The two young people had been alone in the desert for many hours, and it was hinted, more and more loudly, that Safwan was a dashingly handsome fellow, and the Prophet was much older than the young woman, after all, and might she not therefore have been attracted to someone closer to her own age? "Quite a scandal," Salman commented, happily.[86]

Rushdie maintains the details of the earliest Islamic accounts of the texts. He repeats nearly verbatim the third/ninth-century rationale for `A'isha's separation from the caravan. He adds, of his own accord, an excursus on Safwan as a "dashingly handsome fellow" whose youth he defines as a probable aspect of the alleged adulterous actions. However, Rushdie's overarching fictional purpose in recounting this incident is to question the very source of the Prophet's revelation. The circumstances of `A'isha's vindication from the charge of adultery afford him the same opportunity seized upon by medieval Christian theologians. Rushdie's suggestion that Muhammad's revelation was not inspired by God provoked most of the controversy, Islamic censure, and threats associated with the novel.

"O, he's done it," Salman replied. "Same as ever. He saw his pet, the archangel, and then informed one and all that Gibreel had exonerated Ayesha." Salman spread his arms in worldly resignation. "And this time, mister, the lady didn't complain about the convenience of the verses."

The reference to `A'isha and the "convenience" of the verses is Rushdie's nod to a different revelation which allowed Muhammad to marry Zaynab, the former wife of his adopted son.[87] In the earliest Islamic accounts, as Rushdie also fictionally reminds the reader, `A'isha had been rather caustic about the benefit of this revelation for the Prophet.

Rushdie's treatment of Muhammad's wives has been criticized by certain Muslim clerics, particularly Iranian Shi`is, for his creation of a brothel environment in which prostitutes took the names and characteristics of the Prophet's wives thus, apparently, making them more alluring to their customers. However, Rushdie's treatment of the hadith al-ifk has not been singled out for rebuke. Ironically, since the medieval period, Shi`i Muslims had referred to `A'isha as an adulteress long before Rushdie's provocative modern novel.[88]

Medieval Western Christian polemicists and modern Western-educated novelists like Rushdie questioned the divine inspiration of the Islamic faith in their readings of the account of the lie. However, a modern Iranian version told by a village woman presents a rather different resolution to the Prophet's dilemma. As recorded by Erika Friedl, the Shi`i female narrator has paraphrased the accusation of adultery made against `A'isha although neither her name nor the original title of the incident appear. The details of the lost necklace remain in this modern telling, but the role of Safwan has been replaced by an anonymous carvanserai owner, an Iranian rather than an Arabian travel convention.

For better or for worse, the wagging of tongues is inescapable. The Prophet himself was once going somewhere in a caravan. They stopped to eat at a caravanserai, and his wife went outside to relieve herself. There she lost her necklace. Afraid to tell her husband, she looked around everywhere. Meanwhile, the caravan moved on without her. After a while the Prophet missed her and the people told him she had stayed behind to have an affair with the owner of the caravanserai, that they had seen her talk to him and move about outside the gate. But the Prophet, who could see everything if he wanted to, said that no, she only had lost her beads and was looking for them. But the people would not stop talking, and everybody had still more to tell about her and the owner of the caravanserai. In the end the Prophet said that not even he, a prophet, could contain the tongues of the people, and he divorced her.[89]

The emphasis in this Shi`i version of the accusation of adultery reflects the original suggestion of `Ali ibn Abi Talib recorded in Ibn Hisham. In one sense it projects the logical outcome of the first Shi`i imam's opinion that the Prophet simply divest himself of his troublesome wife. What is interesting is that the story's emphasis clearly distinguishes between the social reality of the slander that prompts the Prophet's divorce and the truth that is warped by the "wagging of tongues." The moral of the story does not mention the Qur'anic revelation that exonerates `A'isha according to Sunni Muslims, most probably because these verses are not thought by Shi`i Muslims to apply to the Prophet's wife. Instead, the modern Iranian version uncompromisingly points to the power of the scandal to take on a life of its own even for Shi`i Muslims. The debate between truth and falsehood is less important than the human reality that prevails, which suggests that not even the Prophet Muhammad "could contain the tongues of the people." Indeed, the Iranian version suggests that over time `A'isha's

Figure 1. `A'isha exclaims:"Allah has vindicated me."
—From the Turkish newspaper *Hurriyet*, June 19, 1985.

dilemma could not be separated from historical interpretation, the very human relativity of the truth.

Thus, contemporary with this Iranian Shi`i interpretation, the Turkish Sunni newspaper Hurriyet published a popularized version of the accusation made against `A'isha which ran during Ramadan with a picture of the Prophet's wife and the caption: "Allah has vindicated me"[90] (figure 1).

four *gender and the politics*
of succession

Humble thyself, ambitious woman that thou
art! Now thou ridest on a mule, now on a
camel! Why dost thou not abandon this thy
unjust contention?

The Martyrdom of Hasan

isha bint Abi Bakr's legacy in medieval Islamic historiography affixed her memory for all time to the politics of succession. Her example would be cited by Sunni and Shi'i Muslims alike when the issue of female involvement in government arose. Her depiction, most particularly with reference to the first civil war in the Muslim community, reflected the crystallization of Islamic definitions of gender and politics. Sunni Muslims recognized the tension between 'A'isha's exemplary status as the acknowledged favorite wife of the Prophet and her political actions as his widow. Their task, collectively, was to assess her problematic political participation without complete condemnation. Shi'i Muslims faced no such dilemma in their representation of the past. 'A'isha had opposed and fought 'Ali ibn Abi Talib their male political and spiritual ideal. Her involvement in the first civil war provoked Shi'i scorn and censure. Once again, Sunni authors had the more difficult task of defending 'A'isha. Their praise of her, already qualified by the defense of her reputation as a wife

after the accusation of adultery, would be tested again due to her controversial political actions as a widow.

`A'isha's presence and participation in the Battle of the Camel in
A.H. 36/A.D. 656, the major military conflict of the first civil war,
reflects her prestige within the Islamic community. Her proximity to
the Prophet and his preference for her promoted her symbolic significance for believers. Identified as part of the new Islamic female elite, the
mothers of the believers, `A'isha's political importance was not
achieved, but ascribed. Without her primary marital tie to the Prophet,
`A'isha would have had no foundation for her political involvement. Sec-
ondarily, her father Abu Bakr, the Prophet's close companion and his
first successor as caliph, solidified the male axis of her political prestige.
Yet while this doubly powerful linkage made possible `A'isha's part in
the affairs of the Islamic community, it did not sanction such a role. In
the quest for political power in the Islamic community after Muhammad's death, marital ties to the Prophet had quite different implications
for males and females.

Marriage conferred upon Muhammad's many wives a prestige at once
separate and singularly potent. The number of wives taken by the Prophet
Muhammad has been the subject of much speculation by non-Muslim
scholars who have often cynically judged these marriages as a form of self-
indulgence. However, the motives of the Prophet, generated in a world
where polygyny was common, may be perceived not merely as a personal act, but as part of a social and political program. The Prophet Muhammad changed the institution of marriage from more flexible pre-Islamic
options through the Qur'anic injunction that all men, with the exception
of himself, take no more than four wives.[1] In the pre-Islamic period, tribal alliances were cemented through matrimony.[2] In binding significant
Muslim families together the Prophet Muhammad also employed the
Islamic institution of marriage to insure the unity of the new community
of faith.

All of Muhammad's wives were widows except `A'isha. Marriage to
the Prophet Muhammad in many cases provided these widows with their
sole means of economic support after the death of their husbands. However, Muhammad's marriages were not merely a means of providing simple social welfare for the widows of his fledgling religious community. The

Prophet utilized marriage to forge major political alliances, the strength of which would be demonstrated even after his death. Marriage, the giving and taking of women by men, in both the pre-Islamic and Islamic periods provided the social glue of Arabian society. Beginning with Abu Bakr, each of the first four political successors to the Prophet was linked to him through marriage. These men, Muhammad's close companions, either gave their daughters to the Prophet in marriage or married Muhammad's own daughters. It has been suggested that "the Muslim community used Muhammad's decision making concerning political alliances solidified through marriage as a guide to which men were worthy to rule."[3] The marriage of ʿAʾisha bint Abi Bakr serves as the first case in point, linking her father, the first caliph of Islam, to the Prophet. ʿAʾisha's political access derived from the prestige of her father and her husband, the two most prominent men of their time. Indeed, the Battle of the Camel and the tale of the first civil war in Islamic society exemplifies not just a dispute over the leadership of the community, but the attempt by Muslims to define their loyalty to those who could demonstrate the closest relationship to the Prophet Muhammad through the newly defined criterion of *sabiqa*, "Islamic priority."

ʿAʾisha took the field as a representative of a political marriage alliance, one enhanced by the Prophet's preference for her during his lifetime. ʿAʾisha, mother of the believers, daughter of the first caliph Abu Bakr opposed the fourth caliph ʿAli, the representative of a marital union with the Prophet's daughter Fatima. After the death of the Prophet, the Islamic community would be directed for forty-eight years (11–60/632–680) by individuals connected to the Prophet through marriage. All of them would be male. Indeed, both of the dynasties which followed the first four caliphs were also tied to the Prophet by marital alliances. In the case of the Umayyads, the Prophet's wife Umm Habiba was the sister of the dynasty's founder Muʿawiya (d. 60/680). The dynasty of the ʿAbbasids (132–656/750–1258) who traced their descent from the Prophet's paternal uncle ʿAbbas were also linked to Muhammad through marriage. The Prophet's wife Maymuna was the sister-in-law of ʿAbbas. Thus, while political power was determined by primarily patrilineal demonstrations, the connective foundations of Islamic political structure were enhanced by distinctly feminine familial bonds.

There has been much scholarly debate concerning the position of women in Arabia before and after the advent of Islam and the effect of the new religion on female participation in politics. Even a brief survey of these varied writings concerning women during this transitional period reflects more division than consensus. The politics of the present intrude everywhere on arguments concerning a limited body of materials linked to the period Muslims call the *jahiliyya*, the time of ignorance before the advent of Islam. Indeed, these works suggest that from the same body of limited early material, scholars may draw quite opposite conclusions about the status of women before and after the advent of Islam. Such discussions, no matter what their conclusions, inevitably include references to ʾAʾisha's pivotal political role in the first Muslim community. One leading scholar has gone so far as to suggest that ʾAʾisha's defeat at the Battle of the Camel effectively excluded all Muslim women from participation in Islamic political life.[4] Although after the first civil war ʾAʾisha never again joined in the struggle over political succession, it is unlikely that her defeat alone blocked the access of all other Muslim women. Women in general faced a more complex environment in first/seventh-century Arabia with regard to religious and political authority. ʾAʾisha in specific seems to have tested the boundaries of political participation during this crucial period of transition for the Muslim community.

Pre-Islamic Arabian society was once thought to be matrilineal, a notion that has been successfully challenged in this century.[5] More recent analyses suggest three quite different interpretations of the impact of Islam on women and their ability to participate in society. One scholar argues that before Islam "the majority of pre-Islamic women appear to have lived in a male dominated society in which their status was low and their rights were negligible."[6] Her overall assessment of the transition from the jahiliyya to the Islamic period underscores a perception of the more positive standing women found in the new Muslim community: "When studied against the background of the jahiliyya, both social status and the legal rights of Muslim women were much improved." In contrast, the Prophet Muhammad has been depicted as a reformer who "strove successfully for the improvement of the economic and legal status of all Moslem women," while at the same time leaving "woman forever inferior to man, placing her one step below him."[7] Cited as evidence in this argument is the Qur'anic injunction of 4:34: "Men are in charge of women, because Allah has made one of them to excel the other." The divine definition of such a gendered social hierarchy was further strengthened by injunctions directed specifically to the wives of the Prophet which secluded them from the rest of early Muslim society. It has been argued that this combination of Qur'anic stipulations restructured the role of all Muslim women "into one of passivity and submissiveness comparable to that already imposed" on contemporary Jewish and Christian women. The notion that later misinterpretation by Muslim scholars resulted in a closure of female social options has been challenged by more negative readings of the initial Islamic impact.[8] In this analysis of the past, the assertion is made that "those elements of activeness and independence which were to be found in the women of the first Muslim society" were inexorably eradicated by Islamic norms.[9] Such an argument posits a discernible dichotomy between pre-Islamic and Islamic society. Women are revealed to have had more opportunity to participate before rather than after Islam.[10]

The examination of the earliest written Arabic sources about `A'isha's participation in politics suggests that her actions at the Battle of the Camel reflect a fusion of pre-Islamic and Islamic components. However, whether one argues that the new Islamic environment of the first/seventh century opened or closed options for women, `A'isha's example alone was not responsible for keeping other Muslim women out of political affairs. After `A'isha's defeat at the Battle of the Camel other women participated in the second civil war, taking part in battle as they had before and after the advent of Islam.[11] `A'isha's political actions represent at once a convergence and a clash of pre-Islamic practice and Islamic strictures. `A'isha derived her influence as a political participant and symbol from her relationship to two men, her husband and her father. `A'isha's unique position was derivative of a new, truly Islamic prestige. The Qur'an does not explicitly forbid women from exercising direct political rule. In the one instance in the Qur'an where a woman rules her society she is faulted not for her inability to govern, but for her ignorance of monotheism. The Queen of Sheba is described in the Qur'an 27:23 as a commanding figure who consults men, but retains the ultimate right to govern according to her own final judgment. As a divine precedent, this positive association between women and government would be neutralized by Sheba's initial ignorance of monotheism. The Qur'anic revelation with the greatest impact on the assessment of `A'isha's political participation was directed specifically to the wives of the Prophet who in 33:33 are enjoined to stay in their homes. Retrospectively, the citation of this verse would be utilized to censure `A'isha's political participation as a member of the new Muslim female elite, the wives of the Prophet. `A'isha gained access to the politics of succession through her Islamic marital ties and status, but that same prestige served to demonstrate the practical limits of her highly visible membership among the mothers of the believers.

`A'isha's political participation was symbolically charged in Islamic historiography, not just because she was a Muslim woman, but because she was the most highly visible member of the mothers of the believers. By taking the battlefield and assuming a role as a political figure after the death of her husband, `A'isha challenged the restrictions placed only upon Muhammad's widows, restrictions which did not apply to the actions of any other first/seventh-century Arab woman. In the short term, `A'isha's defeat in the first civil war assured that the mothers of the believers, the most prominent group of women in the first Islamic community, remained outside the political arena. Thus, while the men linked to the Prophet through marital alliances vied for political control, the very women who embodied those ties were obstructed from similar actions by divine revelation and the defeat of the Prophet's favorite wife.

`A'isha's posthumous medieval depiction transformed her political defeat into an object lesson for both Sunni and Shi`i scholars on the inevitable disasters of female participation in politics. Her example would be utilized consistently by male authors of the medieval communal record to prove their retrospective rule: all women, by definition of their gender, were a threat to political order. The manipulation of `A'isha's example provided a platform for debate about her role in politics. Although Sunni and Shi`i authors disagreed about the essential nature of `A'isha's persona, they found significant similarities in the derivative, negative rules which her singular example implied for all Muslim women in the matter of political participation. `A'isha's legacy would prompt both Sunni and Shi`i scholars to refract broader issues of gender and politics through the controversial legacy of the wife of the Prophet.

`A'isha's Motivations

The Battle of the Camel was the major military conflict in the first *fitna*, "civil war," in Islamic society. The fitna was precipitated by the murder of the third caliph `Uthman (d. 35/656), a man who like his predecessors was linked to the Prophet Muhammad through marriage. The motivation for `A'isha's involvement in the political trials leading to `Uthman's assassination is documented in early chronicles as the object of debate.[12] In one account, `A'isha is depicted as not wanting bloodshed, but as a supporter of the provincial opposition that perpetrated `Uthman's murder.[13] In contrast, both al-Baladhuri and al-Tabari suggest that `A'isha hoped `Uthman would be killed and that Talha would assume control.[14] Al-Tabari suggests that `A'isha did nothing to aid `Uthman while he was besieged by those men who would eventually kill him and some verses of poetry in the chronicle even attribute to her responsibility for the murder.[15] `A'isha's relationship to `Uthman is depicted as suspect. `Ali's supporter `Ammar ibn Yasir plays a prominent role in relating `A'isha's mixed motives in suddenly demanding blood vengeance for `Uthman's murder. He effectively questions the sincerity of her motivation in raising the cry to avenge the caliph's death, the basis for `A'isha's opposition to `Ali.

Then `A'isha came out mourning [for `Uthman], saying that he was murdered. `Ammar ibn Yasir said to her, "Yesterday you agitated against him, but today you are mourning for him."[16]

The account suggests that `A'isha's response to `Uthman's death represents a purely political rather than a sincere personal stance. The motivation for her participation in the first civil war is thus implicitly criticized.

Nowhere is there evidence that `A'isha herself sought to rule the Islamic community. The civil war in which `A'isha would urge revenge for the slain `Uthman and opposition to the fourth caliph `Ali would end in Iraq in a battle near Basra. Together with her male allies Talha ibn `Ubayd Allah (d. 36/656) and al-Zubayr ibn al-`Awwam (d. 36/656), `A'isha was defeated by `Ali ibn Abi Talib. Her two male conspirators lost their lives in the military encounter. The battle, referred to in written sources by the pre-Islamic phrase *yawm al-jamal*, "the Day of the Camel," immortalized

`A'isha's presence in a closed litter atop her camel. The Battle of the Camel would forever remain synonymous with `A'isha's participation in the first internecine Islamic military and political conflict. Even her troops would be referred to by the opposition as *ashab al-jamal*, "the companions of the camel."[17] The heaviest fighting in the Battle of the Camel took place around `A'isha's camel. In the pre-Islamic era Arabs exposed their women to danger in battle as a final incentive to achieve victory.[18] It was the risk to `A'isha's life which precipitated the bloody last stand of her partisans. Indeed, one of the accusations lodged by `Ali's supporters against `A'isha's male companions is that they had exposed the wife of the Prophet to the threat of death in battle.[19]

The first civil war provided `A'isha with an opportunity to participate directly in the determination of Islamic succession. Her closeness to the Prophet during his lifetime, the result of her preferred status among his wives, had given her a tremendous amount of prestige within the Muslim community, a factor which even her husband's death did not obliterate. Men followed her, a woman, into battle together with two other male companions of the Prophet, a phenomenon which suggests not just her prestige, but her power. The question of `A'isha's responsibility for the course of events which took place after the murder of `Uthman varies. Her participation cannot be denied, but her role as a director of events is questioned in Sunni sources. While Sunni historiography sought to invalidate `A'isha's participation without making her completely responsible for the carnage of the first civil war, Shi`i authorities would not hesitate to define `A'isha as a full and responsible participant in the opposition to `Ali. Early Shi`i sources selected many Sunni motifs for development in their own rendition of `A'isha's historical persona. Many of their most effective forms of censure are drawn from non-Shi`i sources. Unlike the Sunni majority, Shi`i Muslims would trace their origins as a community to their initial support for `Ali in his struggle against `A'isha in the first civil war. In this military and political conflict, those who fought for `Ali first identified themselves as his *shi`a*, or partisans. In both Sunni and Shi`i sources `A'isha speaks, but she is not cited as the originating authority for the great majority of the words attributed to her. Her defense against the charge of adultery had depended on her apparent first person narration and the transmission of her words through a partisan chain of relaters. However, in the first civil war, ʿAʾisha's depiction and heavily qualified defense are placed solidly in the hands of other, more critical authorities.

The Definition of ʿAʾisha's Political Persona

The range of reactions to ʿAʾisha's role in the first civil war begins in the third/ninth century and evolves dramatically over the next two hundred years. The earliest written responses to ʿAʾisha's role in the first fitna may be divided into five general thematic categories including slander, humor, regret, predictions of doom and negative definitions of the feminine.[20] Often in the same account, ʿAʾisha is the object of both praise and blame, praise as the wife of the Prophet and blame for her political actions as his widow. In this precarious Sunni balancing act, ʿAʾisha's reputation would be salvaged even as her supporters found ways to censure her. Ultimately, ʿAʾisha's political legacy was transformed into a convenient component of the medieval cultural construct which defined all women as threats to the maintenance of Islamic political order.

Slander

The majority of references found in the third/ninth-century biographies of Ibn Saʿd and al-Baladhuri that include the Battle of the Camel depict a similar incident: an unnamed man slanders ʿAʾisha on the day of the Battle and is publicly rebuked by ʿAmmar ibn Yasir, a companion of the Prophet and a supporter of ʿAli. ʿAʾisha's prestige within the community is enhanced by the defense articulated by her opponent. Many versions of this incident exist in the third/ninth century, but all of them feature ʿAli's supporter as a primary player in the defense of ʿAʾisha's reputation. Ibn Saʿd's biographical dictionary includes one account.

A man slandered ʿAʾisha on the Day of the Camel. The people agreed with him. Then ʿAmmar said, "What is this?" They replied, "A man slandered ʿAʾisha." ʿAmmar said to him, "Silence your disgraceful clamor. Are you reviling the *habiba*, beloved, of the Prophet of Allah? She is his wife in heaven."[21]

This tradition reflects ʿAʾisha's prestige as the favorite wife of the

Prophet. Her marital reputation is defended, but the political actions for which she is reviled as a widow are implicitly separated. She is praised as a wife and blamed as a widow. Her defense by `Ammar reminds those who would slander `A'isha that her place in heaven is assured despite her dubious actions on earth. The incident preserved for Sunni Muslim audiences the notion that `A'isha's reputation was vulnerable to attack due to her actions in the first civil war. However, while as a widow she might be censured, the solidity of the Prophet's preference for her as a wife could not obliterate her primacy of place in Muslim memory. The reference to `A'isha's place in heaven reveals a dimension of her religious prestige, but in no way suggests she was blameless. Rather, reference to her status as the Prophet's wife in heaven reveals the centrality of her marital bond with him as a fundamental Sunni line of defense. The account, implicitly, also preserved a current of ridicule and derision regarding `A'isha's involvement in the Battle of the Camel.

The version found in Ibn Sa`d's biography of `A'isha appears to be included because of its reference to her place in heaven. The account is flanked by other references to `A'isha as "the wife of the Prophet in heaven," a theme of praise which appears to be an organizing principle for the pages surrounding this single mention of the Battle of the Camel. In the same section there are reiterations of `A'isha's place in heaven which make no mention of the first civil war.[22] Moreover, in one, `Ali's supporter `Ammar narrates a truncated version in praise of `A'isha without any allusion to the provocation or context of his utterance: "We know that she [`A'isha] is the wife of the Prophet in this world and the next."[23]

A variation of this theme occurs in al-Baladhuri who provides a more detailed context for an essentially similar core of content. In this version, an anonymous man at the Battle of the Camel slanders `A'isha and `Ammar again defends the wife of the Prophet by rebuking him. There is no crowd in this tradition. Once more, `Ammar's defense of `A'isha rests on her prestigious relationship to Muhammad. She is still the Prophet's beloved, but in this tradition remains his wife in this world only.[24] Her marital prestige is recalled by her ostensible opponent as her defense. The reputation of `A'isha as the Prophet's wife must be maintained despite the independent actions of his widow. The man who slanders `A'isha is rebuked, but none of the specifics of his assault on her reputation are detailed. Her political persona remains vulnerable and, by extension, worthy of critique.

The broader implications of `A'isha's direct involvement in the political contests of the early Islamic community are more detailed in al-Bukhari's hadith. It is significant that this tradition is found under the chapter on `A'isha's excellence. As in Ibn Sa`d, the element of praise appears to be the paramount organizing principle in situating this hadith in al-Bukhari's compilation. Yet while the theme offers `A'isha her due in prestige as the wife of the Prophet in this world and the next, al-Bukhari's version provides a new setting and motivation for `Ammar's loyalty to `Ali and his political opposition to `A'isha in the first civil war.

When `Ali sent `Ammar and [his son] Hasan to Kufa to call upon them [the inhabitants] to fight [against `A'isha] `Ammar made a speech. He said, "I know that she is his [the Prophet's] wife in this world and the next, but Allah puts you to the test [whether] to be His followers or hers."[25]

The Kufans were urged to support `Ali by the partisan `Ammar who, in deference to the Prophet, gives `A'isha her prestigious due. However, there appears little doubt in `Ammar's plea about whose cause is the righteous one. `Ali's followers are also the supporters of the divine will. This idea finds its logical extension in one fourth/tenth-century Shi`i hadith which records that the angel Gabriel endowed `Ali with extra strength at the Battle of the Camel.[26] `A'isha, while praised is thus faintly but distinctly damned, despite her future access to heaven for to follow her is to fail Allah's test, the moral definition of fitna, the word also synonymous with civil war. A nearly identical rendition of this hadith is found in Khalifa ibn Khayyat al-`Usfuri's (d. 240/854) history.[27]

Each of these four accounts which refer to `A'isha and the Battle of the Camel features `A'isha as the object with `Ammar as the true protagonist. It is `Ammar who twice implicitly and once explicitly supports the side he defines as the only divinely determined, just military force. The subtlety of each account rests on the balance of blame and praise directed at `A'isha. Each compiler emphasized the positive component of this account in his placement of the tradition in Sunni sources. However, the

Battle of the Camel is also recalled as a divisive, bloody defeat for the wife of the Prophet. Her political involvement summoned a slanderous response. In such a context her praise was not unadulterated for it rested upon the need for a Sunni Muslim defense of her reputation.

The theme of a mixed perception of `A'isha as a historical persona may be illustrated by another selection from al-Baladhuri's third/ninth-century biography of the Prophet's wife. In this instance, the Battle of the Camel becomes a point of departure for observations about the components of her character.

They were talking about the journey of `A'isha to Basra [that is, to the Battle of the Camel]. Then he said, "That isn't included in the teaching that refers to her distinguished excellence . . . And in spite of that, she is preferred by the Prophet to other women and he loved her more than the others."[28]

This account, recorded after the event, registered more directly the conflict between `A'isha's prestige as a wife and her actions as a widow. The Battle of the Camel is never named, nor are those discussing the components of her reputation. `A'isha's participation in the Battle is not described as belonging to the other qualities which compose her multiple merits. Yet the speaker admits that despite this less than positive aspect of `A'isha's biography, her place in the Prophet's life remained her primary asset in the communal memory. Her inherited status, though positive, here confronts her achieved status, the negative reaction to the Battle of the Camel. These elements in al-Baladhuri's account are depicted as conflicting characteristics which must be reconciled to form a vision of `A'isha as a woman central to the representation of the Islamic past. The complexities of `A'isha's controversial legacy became part of the communal record of the first civil war.

The five examples previously cited emphasize a process of coping with a gamut of positive and negative reflections about `A'isha's reputation. There were also more bluntly partisan maneuvers found in third/ninth-century sources. One tactic recorded by al-Baladhuri defends `A'isha through a frontal assault on her enemies. The tradition, cast as a predictive dream of the Prophet, foretells that there will emerge two evil groups from among those who had embraced Islam. He mentions specifically *al-*

Rawafid, a later Sunni designation for Twelver Shi`i Muslims, which liter-
ally means those who rejected the first three caliphs in favor of the primacy of `Ali. The Prophet signals in his dream that the second evil group
of Muslims are *al-Khawarij*, those Muslims who deserted `Ali in the sec-
ond phase of the civil war. Unlike Shi`i Muslims, the Khawarij rejected
genealogy or Islamic priority as a guide to the selection of the leader of
the Islamic community. They argued for equality among men in the Muslim community and the collective choice of a leader based upon the communal determination of individual excellence. As examples of the evil
deeds of both groups, the Prophet states that a member of the Khawarij
assassinated `Ali and that `Ali's partisans killed `A'isha's male allies, Talha
and al-Zubayr at the Battle of the Camel. In this selection, `A'isha's name
is not used, but she is instead referred to by the Prophet's pet name for
her, *al-humayra*, "the little ruddy one." These anachronisms represent a
later Sunni mode of defense for `A'isha's political persona. Convenient
prophetic castigation of groups opposed to the Sunni vision of the past
serve as an effective, but transparent form of defense for the memory of
the Prophet's wife.

Fourth/tenth-century sources emphasize a continuation of earlier
themes of slander and defense, praise and blame. In al-Tabari's chronicle a new incident of slander is presented in the context of a confrontation between the supporters of `A'isha and those of `Ali in Basra.
A man named Hukaym ibn Jabala slanders `A'isha.[29] As in third/ninth-
century accounts Hukaym's utterances are nowhere specified. However, the reaction to his words by the people who hear them is detailed. A
woman rebukes the slanderer for abusing `A'isha and calls him the son
of an evil mother. Hukaym's response is to kill the woman. It is `A'isha's
status as the mother of the believers with which her supporters defend
her reputation, not the righteousness of her political cause. The incident which begins with the vilification of `A'isha ends in a riot which
engulfs the population of Basra. In the conflict, Hukaym is said to have
struck three hundred people with his sword. `A'isha's persona and the
controversy which her participation in politics provoked are portrayed
as a source of danger to the Muslim community demonstrated by the
violence that ensues even before the actual military confrontation of
the Battle of the Camel.

Humor as a Weapon of Censure

A unique type of reference to `A'isha's role in the Battle of the Camel utilized humor to underscore criticism of the Prophet's wife. Al-Baladhuri offers the following account of the tradition:

`A'isha needed something so she sent to Ibn [Abi] `Atiq saying, "Send your mule," so that she could ride it on an errand. He replied to her messenger, and he [Ibn Abi `Atiq] was an idle joker, "Say to the Mother of the Believers, `By Allah, we have not yet recovered from the shame of the Day of the Camel. Are you not too exhausted to give us the Day of the Mule?' "[30]

The point of the jest relies on the play of words and images. When the mule is substituted for the camel, the idea of a new battle so-named becomes ludicrous.[31] The sting of this idle joker's words is emphasized by his true identity as Abu Bakr's great grandson `Abd Allah.[32] However, it seems doubtful that even a relative reputed to be an idle joker would address his great aunt with such scorn and sarcasm. The word shame when attached to the Battle of the Camel was not directed at `A'isha in any other ninth-century biographical account and was, despite its ostensibly humorous intent, a pointed accusation of `A'isha's wrongdoing made all the more powerful because of its placement in the mouth of a family member.

A variation of this incident is found in a work of belles-lettres by al-Jahiz (d. 255/868). In his treatise on mules, he cites a similar account and explains why he, as an avid supporter of `A'isha, believed it to be forged.

The story goes that once when a dispute had broken out between two clans of the Quraysh, `A'isha, the mother of the believers, left her home on a mule. Ibn Abi `Atiq met her and asked, "Where are you going?" "To reconcile the two clans." "By Allah," he said, "We have hardly gotten over the Day of the Camel and now we shall have to start talking of the Day of the Mule!" She laughed and went on her way.[33]

Again the jokester Ibn Abi `Atiq regales `A'isha with the verbal jest substituting the word mule for the word camel. Unlike the version found in al-Baladhuri, al-Jahiz's example defines `A'isha's errand as a dispute between two clans. This detail combined with the dubious presence of Ibn Abi `Atiq sets up al-Jahiz's scathingly thorough critique of the forgery that he attributes to the imagination of Shi`i Muslims whom he refers to from his Sunni perspective as "the rejectors."

. . . its inventor must have supposed that if he brought in Ibn Abi `Atiq's name and made an amusing story out if it, it would gain currency and become as popular as traditions recorded by Umm Habiba and Safiyya [two other wives of the Prophet]. If the forger had known the respect in which `A'isha was held, he would not have tried to gain acceptance for this story.[34]

It is clearly a measure of al-Jahiz's own respect for `A'isha that he used what he perceived as a Shi`i attack upon her to launch his own counteroffensive. In this process, he cited a very different tradition which he places in the mouth of `Ali, `A'isha's chief opponent at the Battle of the Camel. Thus he states:

For `Ali ibn Abi Talib said: "I had four people against me: The bravest of people, that is al-Zubayr; the most generous of people, Talha; the richest of people, Ya`la ibn Munabbih; and the most influential of people, `A'isha."[35]

Al-Jahiz does not invoke the chain of transmission for the tradition he considers the offensive forgery, nor does he provide one of his own for his more laudatory version of `A'isha's reputation. His mode of argument subjects what he considers blatantly false, partisan evidence to a rebuttal which, by definition, is equally partisan. Ironically, one of al-Jahiz's criticisms of the tradition emphasizes that it is not accompanied by a chain of transmission. Although according to a fourth/tenth-century account, `Ali referred to `A'isha as "the wife of the Prophet in this world and the next" at the Battle of the Camel, there appears to be no third/ninth-century written evidence to support al-Jahiz's contention that the fourth caliph ever referred to the Prophet's wife as "the most influential of people."[36] Al-Jahiz's final condemnation of the hadith as a forgery rested upon `A'isha's overall stature in the communal memory of the Islamic community. Al-Jahiz claimed that her status was "too exalted," her station "too august in the eyes of all men" for this uncomplimentary tradition to gain acceptance.[37] The terminology applied by al-Jahiz as praise refers to `A'isha's position and prestige. Each term is prefaced by superlatives which express al-Jahiz's personal support for `A'isha. His defense, by extension, is presented as a reflection of communal support for her. However, the need for this defense of her character mutes intended praise and reveals an acrimonious dispute in the third/ninth-century Islamic community about `A'isha's role in the first/seventh-century civil war.

The presence of this incident in the Sunni communal record in the later medieval period is attested in the work of the Sunni biographer Ibn Khallikan (d. 681/1282). In his account of `A'isha's life he is consistent with earlier Sunni sources in his reference to Ibn Abi `Atiq who warns the Prophet's wife about her intended intervention in a vague dispute between two clans of the Quraysh. He then contributes the line about the Battle of the Camel and the mule. This version, although cited without a chain of authorities, appears quite close to that critiqued by al-Jahiz because it concludes with `A'isha laughing and proceeding on her way.[38] Despite the objections of al-Jahiz in the third/ninth century, Ibn Khallikan's inclusion of the anecdote suggests that not all Sunni authors rejected the recollection of this rather scathing vision of `A'isha's political persona.

In a different version of the same event recorded in the chronicle of the Shi`i author al-Ya`qubi (d. 284/897), an even more politicized backdrop is provided for `A'isha's foray. Unlike the contemporary accounts found in al-Baladhuri and al-Jahiz, al-Ya`qubi provides a specific context for this observation about `A'isha's role in the Battle of the Camel. He places the scene at the funeral of `Ali's eldest son Hasan. Hasan had, apparently, wanted to be buried with his grandfather the Prophet Muhammad. The problem was that since the Prophet was buried beneath `A'isha's house permission would have been needed from her to grant Hasan's request. According to al-Ya`qubi, `A'isha, riding a gray she-mule, met Hasan's funeral procession protesting that she had not given permission for his burial under her house.[39] At this juncture, the tension between `A'isha and Hasan's burial party is enhanced by the presence of her nephew Qasim, the son of `A'isha's brother Muhammad ibn Abi Bakr, a partisan of `Ali who had fought against her at the Battle of the Camel. In this Shi`i version it is `A'isha's nephew Qasim, not `Abd Allah, the idle joker known as Ibn Abi `Atiq and featured in Sunni sources, who condemns his great aunt.[40] In al-Ya`qubi's version, the original confrontation between `A'isha and `Ali is rekindled by the confrontation with the burial party of Hasan, `Ali's son. Critiqued by her own nephew, a partisan of `Ali's cause and family, the humorous tone of the anecdote gives way to a more overt political intent. One wonders how al-Jahiz, who had seized upon the dubious authenticity of a less pointedly political version of this incident, would have reacted to al-Ya`qubi's account.

The instincts of al-Jahiz about the propagandistic power of this incident for Shi`i Muslims are ultimately confirmed by the presence of variations of this account in the works of two fifth/eleventh-century Shi`i works, neither of which provides chains of transmission. In the work of al-Mufid (d. 413/1022), Ibn `Abbas, the Prophet's companion and nephew, first takes the verbal offensive with `A'isha. In this setting a new political detail is provided. `A'isha has allied herself with the clan of Umayya, the founders of the Umayyad dynasty and the arch enemies of the family of `Ali and, thus, all Shi`i Muslims. Ibn `Abbas, as a representative of the family of `Abbas, whose descendants will come to power and found a dynasty after overthrowing the Umayyads, speaks.

What calamities you have caused, one day on a mule and one day on a camel! Do you want to extinguish the light of Allah and to fight the friends of God? Go away! . . . By Allah, the people of this House will have victory, even if it comes after some time.[41]

At this juncture, Husayn, the son of `Ali and the third Shi`i imam, rebukes `A'isha for her behavior in not allowing Hasan to be buried under her house. He then threatens her with violence, but states that he had promised his dead brother not to shed blood. This is the only reason, he claims, why `A'isha was spared the knowledge of "what the swords of Allah would have done" to her.

The dynastic, highly politicized frame for this event remains in the slightly later Shi`i account of Ibn `Abd al-Wahhab who wrote around the middle of the fifth/eleventh century. `A'isha has once more allied herself with the clan of Umayya, but in this version, she is described as the person who actually incites the people against Husayn. Thus, she is portrayed as ready to fight the son, just as she had fought his father `Ali at the Battle of the Camel, an indication of her unrepentant and staunchly anti-Shi'i posture. Ibn 'Abbas addresses 'A'isha as "the little ruddy one" and asks her if after the day of the camel, there will also be a day of the mule.[42] Both of these Shi'i examples suggest that although the core of content may have originated in Sunni sources, its most logical extension was displayed in its appropriation by Shi'i Muslims who understood and embellished the charged political ramifications of the confrontation.

The same altercation is transformed into Shi'i public remembrance in the form of a much later *ta'ziyeh*, the ritual drama or passion play which commemorates the martyrdom of Husayn and the general sufferings of 'Ali's family. In the play, *The Martyrdom of Hasan*, the drama of the burial scene emphasizes the confluence of politics and gender. 'A'isha's opposition to the burial of Hasan beneath her house transforms her, finally, into the archetypal evil woman. As variously addressed by members of 'Ali's family, 'A'isha is described as a "mischievous," "worthless," and "ambitious" woman. Her role in the Battle of the Camel is signalled once again by the mule on which she rides during the altercation with Hasan's funeral procession: "Humble thyself, ambitious woman that thou art! Now thou ridest on a mule, now on a camel! Why dost thou not abandon this thy unjust contention?"[43] The nexus of gender and power is here summoned in this Shi'i ritual drama to confirm 'A'isha's illegitimate and destructive political presence in the Islamic community.

Shi'i Muslims were not the first to mention the event in their ta'ziyeh. In fourth/tenth-century Baghdad, Sunni Muslims reportedly tried to commemorate the Battle of the Camel with what may have been the first and last dramatic reenactment of the conflict in the year 363/973.[44] Sunni Muslims placed a woman on a camel to reenact 'A'isha's part in the Battle. She was accompanied on her ride by two men taking the roles of Talha and al-Zubayr. The staged procession provoked civil strife between Sunni and Shi'i Muslims. The chronicler even uses the word fitna, the term for civil war first applied to the original Battle of the Camel, to describe the event. Whether the incident was designed as a Sunni taunt aimed at Shi'is during their traditional month of mourning or an attempt to start a public Sunni form of religiopolitical drama is unclear.[45] The fact that the Shi'i Buyid dynasty encouraged Shi'i demonstrations in Baghdad may also have incited a provocative Sunni Muslim response during this period. However, the Battle of the Camel never became a centerpiece of Sunni remembrance as ritual drama.

Regret

Third/ninth-century sources depict `A'isha expressing regret for her actions in the Battle of the Camel. Ibn Qutayba (d. 276/889) included an account in which `A'isha apparently overheard unidentified men glorifying the Battle of the Camel, though whose role or what side they supported was not revealed. The wife of the Prophet urged them to desist, stating that there had been enough "outcry" regarding that "fiasco."[46] `A'isha's feelings as they are represented in this statement nowhere signify repentance. The account may be read as regret defined in the light of a desire to disassociate herself from the defeat rather than participation in the first civil war. In short, the passage is suggestive, but not conclusive regarding `A'isha's purported retrospective reaction to her political activities.

Ibn Sa`d's biographical dictionary contains many references to `A'isha's regret for her actions in the Battle of the Camel. The majority of these traditions depict `A'isha's despair. Remembering her actions during the first civil war, `A'isha wishes that she were "completely forgotten," that she did not exist. One variation actually includes the word "repentance," although nowhere is the Battle of the Camel specifically mentioned. The majority of the traditions in which `A'isha expresses regret for her political role in the first civil war reveal her depression. The reader must fill in the context of these utterances, some of which may be provided by the clues contained in the surrounding accounts which suggest that `A'isha may have had most of these regrets near the end of her life. The one example in Ibn Sa`d which comes closest to an outright confession by `A'isha is supposed to have occurred just before her death: "I caused wrongdoing after the Prophet. So they should bury me with the [other] wives of the Prophet."[47] The implications of her own feelings about her behavior after Muhammad's death result in the implicit admission that her burial site should not be special. Instead of being buried with the Prophet beneath her own house, she denies herself any privileged status and asserts that she is to be buried among the other wives of Muhammad. The striking nature of such an utterance lies in the great detail with which she lists in contemporary sources the multiple factors which made her superior to her co-wives. Such depictions of ʿAʾisha allow her to acknowledge her wrongdoing in the political affairs of the Islamic community. Indeed, ʿAʾisha's presentation in these accounts allows her to acknowledge her presumably misguided behavior and, implicitly, to ask forgiveness for it from her community. The topic of ʿAʾisha's regret for her part in the Battle of the Camel surfaces only twice in the fourth/tenth-century chronicle of al-Tabari. In the first incident, years after the event, she encounters the cousin of a man who died defending her on the day of the Battle and she weeps. In the second incident, ʿAʾisha, in the midst of the defeat and carnage resulting from the Battle of the Camel, says "How I wish I had died twenty years before this day."[48]

Predictions of Doom

The portrayal of ʿAʾisha's participation in the Battle of the Camel, as predicted and condemned by the Prophet before his death, forms the core of a major motif of censure in medieval Islamic historiography. As in the case of the anecdotes concerning the camel and the mule, these references to ʿAʾisha also begin in Sunni sources, but become part of later Shiʿi Muslim representations of the first civil war. The earliest written references to this anecdote are found in the third/ninth-century collection of Sunni hadith by Ibn Hanbal (d. 241/855).[49] Unlike other references to ʿAʾisha's participation in the first civil war, these statements originate with ʿAʾisha herself. She is the first authority to transmit them, which implies a tacit support for the content of the report. As recorded succinctly by Ibn Hanbal, ʿAʾisha en route to the Battle of the Camel hears the howling of dogs at a spring called al-Hawʾab. The noise prompted her to instantly recall the rather vague words that had been uttered by the Prophet more than twenty years before in the presence of all of his wives: "At which of you will the dogs of al-Hawʾab howl?"[50] In both recorded traditions, ʿAʾisha hears the dogs, finds out the name of the place, and immediately recalls the Prophet's words which she interprets as a sign that she should desist from her role in the first civil war and turn back. The incident demonstrates the power of the Prophet's foresight and possibly the traditionist's hindsight. A version of this incident is found in the third/ninth-century Shiʿi history of al-Yaʿqubi. In this account, the Prophet warns ʿAʾisha directly, "Do not be the one at whom the dogs of al-Haw'ab howl." Only when forty men falsely swore to `A'isha that the place at which she heard the dogs was not the spring of al-Haw'ab did the force move on with her to Basra and battle.[51]

Al-Jahiz, the staunch Sunni defender of `A'isha's reputation, condemns this anecdote as a fallacious Shi`i invention.[52] Western scholars have also sensed that this incident represents a contrived and convenient way to account for `A'isha's disastrous participation in the Battle of the Camel.[53] Depending on the emphasis of the anecdote, the content also suggests `A'isha's understanding that she was acting against her husband's wishes, a reading of her political actions that clearly appealed to both Sunni and Shi`i authors. Indeed, despite the suspicious nature of this motif, it became quite popular in the medieval period in both Muslim communities as a succinct way of both condemning `A'isha and, in the Sunni community, allowing a pointed emphasis on her wrongdoing while stressing that the direction of the opposition to `Ali was not controlled by the Prophet's wife, but by the male leaders who were her allies in this endeavor.

The predictions of doom associated with the Dogs of al-Haw'ab expand in scope and detail in the fourth/tenth and eleventh/fifth centuries. Both Sunni and Shi`i chronicles feature a proliferation of embellishments which continued to promote the incident as a powerful indictment of `A'isha and her cause. In al-Tabari the story is prefaced by the words of warning: "The evils of the [Battle of] the Camel and the tidings of the Dogs of al-Haw'ab belong to `A'isha alone."[54] These lines of poetic prophecy are transformed into a retrospective Sunni affirmation of the fourth caliph `Ali's cause. Such an application is prefigured in the third/ninth-century sources, but only in the fourth/tenth century do its political possiblities begin to be overtly displayed.

Al-Tabari's chronicle links the incident of the Dogs of al-Haw'ab with the actual purchase of `A'isha's camel on the way to Basra. In this scene between seller and buyer the first question which arises is price. When `A'isha's supporter declares one thousand silver dirhams far too much for the camel in question, the seller asks for whom the animal is intended.[55] The response from the prospective buyer is "Your mother."[56] The camel-owner replies, "I left my mother sitting in her house." The confusion ends with the clarification, "Rather, the camel is wanted for the mother of the believers." The account provides a subtle, but pointed critique of the place `A'isha should have occupied. She too should have been sitting at home, not going off to battle. The exchange appears to invoke the Qur'anic injunction 33:33 that specifically enjoins the wives of the Prophet to remain in their houses. It is doubly ironic that the purchase for `A'isha of the camel in question will aid and abet her, not just in ignoring her role as the mother of the believers, but in facilitating the first civil war and the military conflict which will become synonymous with the image of `A'isha's mount.

`A'isha's encounter with the Dogs of al-Haw'ab in al-Tabari's chronicle occurs because the man who sells her the camel guides her to that spring on the way to Basra. When `A'isha hears the dogs, she strikes her mount and, reportedly, urges her companions three times to turn back. Ibn al-Zubayr, the son of `A'isha's ally and her own nephew, a man destined to be a rebel in his own right after her death, puts an end to her hesitancy by urging the troops to hurry onward since, he claimed, `Ali's forces were almost upon them. Thus, said `A'isha, ". . . so I departed and my anxiety left me a little." Without the false alarm given by Ibn al-Zubayr, `A'isha would not have continued on to Basra and conflict, but would have turned for home. The question of responsibility for her not heeding the Prophet's words at al-Haw'ab is thus raised in conjunction with the culpability of her male supporters in the first civil war. In the second account of the incident found in al-Tabari Ibn al-Zubayr once more induces `A'isha to ignore the prophecy of doom and march on toward Basra. In this version, he convinces `A'isha that whoever had claimed the place where they had stopped was called al-Haw'ab had lied. Once more, the premonitions of `A'isha, prompted by the Prophet's original warning, nearly save her from disaster, but the insistence of her male companions ultimately prevails.

In the Shi`i al-Mas`udi's (d. 354/956) account of the incident, `A'isha hears the dogs, learns that the spring is that of al-Haw'ab, states that she wants to return home, and suddenly declares that she no longer had the need to make the journey. It is at this point that al-Zubayr claims that whoever told `A'isha the place was al-Haw'ab lied.[57] Along with him, Talha and fifty other men, swear the same falsehood to `A'isha. At this point in the narrative, al-Mas`udi editorializes that this "was the first false testimony given in Islam."[58] Al-Tabari, the Sunni chronicler and the Shi`i history of al-Mas`udi treat this motif in the same way, although they assign the task of misleading `A'isha to different men. In al-Tabari, Ibn al-Zubayr performs the task while in al-Mas`udi, both al-Zubayr and Talha indulge in duplicity. In both accounts `A'isha's recollection of the Dogs of al-Haw'ab produces the same effect and outcome. Both versions of the incident suggest the beginning of a more direct condemnation of `A'isha's male companions.

The Sunni Muslim Ibn `Abd Rabbih (d. 328/940) describes the Prophet speaking of his dire prophecy directly to `A'isha. In his version, Muhammad's vision not only predicts, but condemns. In Ibn `Abd Rabbih, the Prophet addresses `A'isha by her pet name: "O little ruddy one, it is as though I can see the Dogs of al-Haw'ab barking at you, and you fighting against `Ali unjustly."[59] These words take the political implications of the prophecy one step further than either al-Tabari or al-Mas`udi, for they use the Prophet himself to condemn `A'isha's involvement in the first civil war. Much later in the medieval period, they would be condemned by a Sunni theologian on the grounds that the supporting chain of authorities for such a statement was weak. Yet the damaging definition of `A'isha's opposition to `Ali as caliph was a position which appealed retrospectively to both Sunni and Shi`i Muslims. The suggestion that `A'isha's actions should be further separated from those of her male allies Talha and al-Zubayr is implied when she declares that she "is guiltless of the actions of al-Zubayr and Talha and of the matter about which the Dogs of al-Haw'ab howled."[60] As a defense of `A'isha, the pronouncement remains rather weak. However, the notion that al-Zubayr and Talha tricked her, an inflection that suggests that `A'isha as a woman was not in complete control, would certainly have appealed to a Sunni Muslim audience who might utilize such an anecdote to both condemn and, finally, forgive her. Shi`i Muslims would not allow any latitude for a defense of `A'isha's actions or for a shift of blame away from her and onto her male companions.

The Shi`i adoption of the Dogs of al-Haw'ab incident for their own remembrance of the first civil war allows `Ali to reflect on the journey of `A'isha, Talha, and al-Zubayr and to link them in condemnation. In the fifth/eleventh-century work of the Shi`i author al-Mufid, the mention of the canine noises at the spring in question is recalled by `Ali in order to predict disaster for the enterprise in political opportunism that has prompted all three to journey to Basra.

When he [`Ali] learned of the journey of `A'isha and Talha and al-Zubayr from Mecca to Basra, he praised Allah and said: "`A'isha and Talha and al-Zubayr have begun their journey. Each of the two men claims the caliphate separately from the other. Talha claims the position of caliph because he is the paternal cousin of `A'isha and al-Zubayr because he is the son-in-law of her father [Abu Bakr]. By Allah, if they are victorious in what they want, then al-Zubayr will kill Talha or Talha will execute al-Zubayr, each in dispute over [the right] to the kingship. By Allah, I know that she is the one who rides the camel. She will not stop at any pasture, nor follow any steep path and she will not stop anywhere except in rebellion against Allah until her soul and [the souls of] those who are with her come to an end."[61]

`Ali does not cite the particulars of the Prophet's prediction about the Dogs of al-Haw'ab which suggests that al-Mufid's readers already knew the import of the anecdote. Instead, he makes prognostications of his own in which he foresees the outcome of the Battle of the Camel. In this context, the barking dogs allow `Ali to interpret `A'isha's actions as resolutely wrong and sinful.

A third [of those with her] will be killed, a third will flee and a third will return . . . By Allah, the Dogs of al-Haw'ab bark at her, but does one who has been warned take warning and does one who remembers recall? The unjust faction has arisen. Where are the good?[62]

In this version of events surrounding the Dogs of al-Haw'ab, there is no attempt made to portray Talha and al-Zubayr as more culpable because they tricked `A'isha. Rather, `A'isha is portrayed as a full member of the opposition to `Ali who is equally responsible for the disasters of the first civil war. In a separate work dedicated by al-Mufid to the remembrance of the first civil war, another favorite Shi`i figure, the Prophet's wife Umm Salama, cites the example of the Dogs of al-Haw'ab for `A'isha in order to keep her from making her journey to Basra.

Figure 2. `A'isha and the Dogs of al-Haw'ab.
—OR MS 2936, fol. 313b. By permission of the British Library,
London.

"I implore you by Allah to remember what the Prophet said to you: 'Fear Allah
and beware should the Dogs of al-Haw'ab bark at you.'" `A'isha replied that
she did remember and this prevented her a little, but then she returned to her
former opinion about the journey.[63]

The sixth/eleventh-century Shi`i author Ibn Shahrashub also details several versions of the Dogs of al-Haw'ab in his work on the virtues of the family of `Ali ibn Abi Talib. In his discussion of this anecdote he cites its presence in the works of earlier Sunni authorities including al-Baladhuri and al-Tabari, a tactic that suggests shared communal condemnation.[64]

The evolution of the Dogs of al-Haw'ab motif in Shi`i sources is transformed to reflect the victor's vision of the political conflict and its resolution. In this trajectory, `A'isha's association with politics and disaster becomes synonymous to her opposition to the rule of `Ali. Retrospectively, the Dogs of al-Haw'ab incident is transformed into the prelude for `A'isha's inevitable defeat and `Ali's predictable victory. Shi`i Muslims aptly perceived the potent symbolism of the Dogs of al-Haw'ab as part of their hero's story because it lends prophetic credence to `Ali's ultimate triumph at the Battle of the Camel. In a nineteenth-century Kashmiri manuscript, based on an eighteenth-century Shi`i poem, the Dogs of al-Haw'ab are painted with open, presumably barking mouths in a miniature which details the story of `Ali's life, not `A'isha's (figure 2). Present upon her famed camel, yet invisible behind the curtains of her palanquin, the wife of the Prophet plays only a bit part in the trials of the Shi`i hero. The Kashmiri miniature utilizes the famed dogs to reduce `A'isha to a visual cipher synonymous with political opposition to just rule.

Sunni and Shi`i Assessments of `A'isha's Culpability

One of the events of the Islamic past over which Muslims first began to argue, retrospectively, was the first civil war. Various groups determined their doctrinal positions in regard to their determinations of the religiopolitical status of `A'isha, Talha, al-Zubayr, and `Ali.[65] Both Sunni and Shi`i Muslims also wrote some of their earliest, no longer preserved treatises on the conflict.[66] At stake in this communal effort to come to terms with a traumatic past event was the need to ascertain the relative culpability of all parties, not just as an historical exercise, but also as a moral determination of culpability and future salvation.

The question of `A'isha's culpability in Sunni sources would be effectively linked to the actions of Talha and al-Zubayr. As these two male companions of the Prophet were presented in fourth/tenth and fifth/

eleventh-century sources, they are made to assume the ultimate burden for `A'isha's presence at the Battle of the Camel. If the two male leaders were responsible for her presence at the Battle of the Camel, `A'isha's political legacy could be condemned even as her reputation as the Prophet's wife could be salvaged. Thus, what begins as a series of accusations against `A'isha in al-Tabari concerning her leaving the house and thus breaking a Qur'anic injunction concludes with harsh criticism for Talha and al-Zubayr. The essence of the tirade launched against the two males once again emphasizes their failure to protect the wife of the Prophet from danger on the battlefield. Their ambitions thus dishonor the memory of Muhammad and the divinely decreed position of his widow.

A young man of the Banu Sa`d went to Talha and al-Zubayr saying, "As for you, O Zubayr, companion of the Prophet of Allah, and as for you Talha, you offered the Prophet the protection of your hand. Look at your mother [`A'isha] there with the two of you! Did you bring your wives?" They said, "No." He replied, "I will not support you in any way," and he withdrew.[67]

The account is then followed by a poem about `A'isha at the Battle of the Camel and the danger of her being exposed to arrows and swords.

These accusations against Talha and al-Zubayr make `A'isha a passive player in the political conflict. The charges suggest that `A'isha is not in control of her own actions. She is perceived as a mere symbol being manipulated by these men to rally support for their opposition to `Ali. The blame attributed here to both men in allowing `A'isha to be present at the Battle parallels the earlier part they had played in coercing her to move on to Basra after the omen at the spring of al-Haw'ab. Their influence and duplicity there motivated her to proceed against her instinct and thus it follows that once at the Battle, those who oppose her presence also assume that Talha and al-Zubayr are responsible for her. `A'isha in these two scenarios cannot be completely culpable for her actions because she is presumed to be passive, the object of male decisions and overall control in political situations. The irony of these accounts is that `A'isha is censured for breaking Qur'anic injunctions, even though the same sources suggest that she may not have been able to do so without encouragement, support or coercion by men. In essence, the elaboration of Talha and al-Zubayr as faithless companions of the Prophet is also an assertion of the consistency of the Islamic political model of male control.

The Sunni philologist al-Mubarrad (d. 286/900) captured the speculation of one of ʿAʾisha's supporters about the effect that her death in the conflict might have had. His suggestion, though morbid, outlines the political possibilities her demise might have provided for further opposition to ʿAli ibn Abi Talib and his supporters. The speaker is ʿAmr ibn al-ʿAs (d. 42 /663), who allied himself late in the first civil war with ʿAli's opponents, the founders of the Umayyad dynasty. In this anecdote he addresses ʿAʾisha directly:

"I wish that you had been killed on the Day of the Camel." "Why?" she said. He replied, "Had you died, you would have quickly entered heaven and we would have used your death as the best way to condemn ʿAli."[68]

Such reflections suggest one overtly partisan, anti-Shiʿi vision of the possibilities of the past. These words also suggest the potential force of ʿAʾisha's remembrance as a Sunni martyr. However, since ʿAʾisha survived the Battle of the Camel, such observations remained firmly in the realm of historical speculation.

Sunni heresiologies of the fifth/eleventh and sixth/twelfth centuries detailed doctrine about the Battle of the Camel and its protagonists as a matter of faith as well as politics. In the Sunni author al-Baghdadi's (d. 429/1037) treatise on the schisms within Islam, it is clear that the majority of Muslims condemned both Shiʿis and groups like the Khawarij because they believed Talha, al-Zubayr, and ʿAʾisha sinned by fighting against ʿAli and were therefore destined for hell.[69] Unlike the Shiʿis, however, the Khawarij also condemned ʿAli to a similar judgment and eventual destination. The Sunni response to these condemnations of Talha, ʿAʾisha and al-Zubayr was, on the one hand, to affirm that ʿAli was rightfully caliph, but that all the participants in the Battle of the Camel had sinned against other Muslims and that whoever called another Muslim an unbeliever was a heretic. In terms of faith, Sunni Muslims did not allow ʿAʾisha or her male allies to be perpetually condemned as unbelievers or inhabitants of hell.

In the sixth/twelfth-century Sunni heresiology of al-Shahrastani (d. 548/1153) the Sunni position on the Battle of the Camel and the roles of Talha, al-Zubayr, and `A'isha are defined in ways which make the evolution of the themes of responsibility and culpability concrete. The author describes the Battle of the Camel as part of the tenth dispute in Islam.[70] He holds Talha and al-Zubayr responsible for inducing `A'isha to accompany them to Basra, a choice which she later regretted and repented.[71] Her culpability is transferred to Talha and al-Zubayr and forms part of the Sunni defense of her political actions. As projected by al-Shahrastani, `A'isha is not perceived to be a fully responsible participant in the first civil war. Early emphasis on her feelings of regret after the Battle of the Camel allowed her to repent and be forgiven in communal memory. Unlike the heterodox Shi`i Muslims and the Khawarij, Sunni Muslims affirmed the reputations of Talha, al-Zubayr, and `A'isha as true Muslims, destined for a place in heaven.[72] However, despite Sunni arguments, Shi`i Muslims persisted in condemning `A'isha as a serious political player. Indeed, in one fourth/tenth-century Shi`i chronicle the only way in which she was misled in her political mission was in her own desire to become caliph.[73] This very different vision of the wife of the Prophet continued to merit the need for a Sunni defense of her political persona throughout the medieval period.[74]

The sixth/twelfth-century Shi`i author Ibn Shahrashub (d. 588/1192) depicts `A'isha as an active, determined, and independent political persona. The wife of the Prophet is defined by him as fully responsible and culpable for her actions at the Battle of the Camel. The Prophet predicts `A'isha's role in the first civil war in words which link the issue of her sexuality to her future political involvement: "There is an obvious whore among you for whom punishment will be doubled."[75] The reference to the anonymous whore reveals once more the Shi`i interpretation of the accusation of adultery made against the Prophet's wife. The author then confirms that these words were directed to `A'isha "concerning her war with `Ali."

In another inflammatory anecdote, `A'isha is described in verse during her march to Basra:

She came in a palanquin with the two villains; She pressed her army onto Basra;

And it was as if she, in this action, was a cat who wanted to devour her male offspring.

The active, predatory nature of her political mission points to the Shi'i belief in 'A'isha's responsibility for the slaughter of her own forces and those of 'Ali at the Battle. Indeed, the association of 'A'isha with a mother who devours her children cites at once her position as a mother of the believers and her unnatural, literally inhuman, female behavior. Nowhere are Talha and al-Zubayr accused in Ibn Shahrashub's account of responsibility for inducing or coercing her into going to Basra. Instead, 'A'isha appears to lead her two male companions who are described by the Shi'i author as villains. In a prophetic mode, Muhammad confides to 'Ali, as 'A'isha demonstrates her intractability by laughing at her husband, that "If I could command her in anything, it would help her." Once again it is implied that her behavior is consistently contrary to the wishes of the Prophet and beyond anyone's ability to control. Even in her married life, she is thus defined as a wife whose behavior merited censure and signalled further future problems.

Ultimately, in the Shi'i Muslim representation of the past, 'A'isha's political participation is condemned as the result of purely personal motives. In al-Mufid's description of the Battle of the Camel, 'A'isha's opposition to 'Ali is cited in a series of grievances which are placed under the heading, "the reasons for 'A'isha's hatred." All of 'A'isha's reputed reasons for her hatred of 'Ali are personal, none are accorded any religious merit.[76] Jealousy is a consistent theme in this enumeration of 'A'isha's grudges. She is jealous of the many times the Prophet demonstrated his preference for 'Ali over her father Abu Bakr. The implications of such actions in the matter of the initial succession to the caliphate are clear. Further, she hates the Prophet's first wife Khadija and her memory. According to al-Mufid, 'A'isha transferred this resentment to 'Ali's wife and the Prophet's daughter Fatima. Finally, in the matter of the accusation of adultery, it is stated that she could not forget that 'Ali had suggested to the Prophet that he divorce 'A'isha since there were many other women to choose from. 'Ali vows that in this instance he meant 'A'isha no harm.[77]

'A'isha's political participation is also condemned in Ibn Shahrashub's work as an enterprise inspired by personal ambition, not loyalty to 'Uthman or regard for divine commands.

`Ali wrote to `A'isha: "You went out from your home in disobedience to Allah and his Prophet . . . Then you pretend that you want peace between Muslims . . . So tell me how can a woman incite armies and the establishment of peace between people?"[78]

`Ali then asserts that `A'isha had no genealogical basis for raising the cry of blood revenge for the third caliph `Uthman, since she was not considered a close relation. `Ali's address to `A'isha concludes: "Fear Allah, O `A'isha and return to your dwelling and cover yourself with your veil." It is a criticism launched at both the viability of her politics and her gender.

The dichotomy between the Sunni defense of `A'isha and the Shi`i condemnation of her in the medieval period reveals the construction of two different characterizations of the same historical figure. The Sunni apologists ultimately define `A'isha as passive, a woman either coerced or induced to participate in the final slaughter of the Battle of the Camel. Her repentance for her actions is part of an attempt to maintain her place, however flawed, in Muslim communal memory. Sunni Muslims admit that `A'isha erred, in part, because as a woman she had no right to interfere in the politics of the Islamic community. Her actions are excused because she acted as a widow against her husband's wishes and because other men encouraged her to do so. Her husband's prophetic words about the Dogs of al-Haw'ab affirm to the community that had he been alive he would have prevented her political foray. `A'isha ignored the Qur'anic injunction 33:33 that ordered her as a wife of the Prophet to stay in her house. Her repentance allows for both communal critique and forgiveness.

In Shi`i versions of the first civil war, `A'isha assumes full and prime responsibility for breaching the rules of the Qur'an and for taking the field against Allah's designated caliph `Ali, the ultimate male representative of divine and temporal authority. As Ibn Shahrashub's example brilliantly emphasizes, `A'isha opposed the fourth caliph "in disobedience." Shi`i Muslims, desiring `A'isha's denigration in the communal memory, directly attribute to her blame for the very political authority and decisiveness denied her by her Sunni supporters. Indeed, the implication of the Shi`i accounts is that `A'isha is the true leader of the opposition to `Ali.

These divergent accounts reveal that in the process of writing about the first civil war the Sunni and Shi`i communities formulated very different strategies in their representation of a shared past. In the Sunni historical record, `A'isha had been transformed from an active subject to a passive participant. The woman who is described as inciting the crowd against `Uthman can hardly be recognized as the one who, due to the howling of a pack of dogs, is too terrified to march to Basra and must be duped to continue. An opinionated and intelligent woman such as `A'isha would not easily have been coerced to continue. These variations in her historical persona may be attributed to her defenders who sought to rationalize her actions after a disastrous military encounter in terms consistent with their notions of appropriate female behavior. The Sunni historiographical dilemma may, in part, explain the contradictions of fourth/ tenth and fifth/eleventh-century accounts. Sunni historians created a political legacy for `A'isha which by the sixth/twelfth century didn't fully exonerate her actions, but sought to shift the critical burden of blame to her male counterparts. Such a qualified defense continued to leave the wife of the Prophet open to attack from Shi`i Muslims who consistently condemned `A'isha as an active political player.

Female Obedience and Transgression

The conflict between Sunni and Shi`i interpretations concerning `A'isha's persona in the Battle of the Camel points to a larger point of consensus concerning appropriate female behavior. Nowhere is this shared vision more fully articulated with regard to the first civil war than in the adversarial exchanges recorded between Umm Salama and `A'isha. Umm Salama, a wife of the Prophet and a staunch supporter of `Ali, was considered to be the Prophet's favorite wife after Khadija by Shi`i Muslims. They denied this privileged status to `A'isha. The antagonism between Umm Salama and `A'isha personifies the clash of politics and gender in medieval Islamic debate. The specifics of the heated exchange between these two wives of the Prophet contained important referents to the more general limitations placed upon all Muslim women in the matter of politics.

The first reference to the dispute between Umm Salama and `A'isha about the Battle of the Camel is found in the Shi`i author al-Ya`qubi. On `A'isha's departure, Umm Salama reminded `A'isha in a censorious way that "the support of the religion does not depend upon the exertions of women."[79] The antagonism between ʿAʾisha and Umm Salama reflects not just their differing personalities, but the political divisions rife within the Prophet's own household after his death. This exchange evolves from al-Yaʿqubi's third/ninth-century version in the fourth/tenth-century Sunni works of al-Tabari and Ibn ʿAbd Rabbih. The exchange between Umm Salama and ʿAʾisha is both personal and political. ʿAʾisha is reminded by her co-wife and past rival Umm Salama that she is disobeying the command of Allah in setting off for Basra. However, Umm Salama adds in al-Tabari's chronicle that she too would march if Allah had not forbidden the wives of the Prophet such actions in the Qurʾan. She would have marched with ʿAli against ʿAʾisha. Instead, Umm Salama sent her son by a previous marriage to fight for ʿAli's cause.[80] The remainder of Muhammad's wives appear not to have taken a stand in supporting ʿAʾisha, with the exception of Hafsa, the daughter of the second caliph ʿUmar. Hafsa had been asked by ʿAʾisha to accompany her and would have gone except for her brother's opposition. The day ʿAʾisha took leave of the rest of her co-wives is described by al-Tabari as a scene of highly charged emotion, known ever after as the Day of Weeping.

The account of the friction between Umm Salama and ʿAʾisha over the latter's role in the Battle of the Camel escalates in Ibn ʿAbd Rabbih's account and is described as a series of written communications. In the first version of the exchange in the third/ninth-century account of al-Yaʿqubi the two women speak to each other. By the fourth/tenth century, Umm Salama is writing her critique of ʿAʾisha in a letter. However, her major objections while expanded have not changed in their essentials. ʿAʾisha is wrong to leave her house, an act forbidden all the wives of the Prophet in the Qurʾan. She is also criticized for thinking that women should play a role in political life, for Umm Salama alleges: "If the Prophet knew that women were permitted to engage in battle, then he would have authorized you."[81] The statement is an important amplification of the Qurʾanic argument which had been the sole Islamic doctrinal opposition to ʿAʾisha's role in the Battle of the Camel. Umm Salama also accuses ʿAʾisha of being an obstruction between Muhammad and his community. Finally, Umm Salama reiterates that the supports of the faith do not rest upon women, an echo of the phrase found earlier in al-Yaʿqubi. However, with this admonition Ibn ʾAbd Rabbih includes the words, "You know that he had prohibited you from taking a prominent place in the land."

ʾAʾisha is allowed a written response to Umm Salama. She sarcastically reminds Umm Salama that her involvement in the problems of the community is her own business and that she needs no words of counsel from anyone. ʾAʾisha begins the letter by implicitly addressing her co-wife as her inferior. The missive is written from ʾAʾisha, the Mother of the Believers, to Umm Salama. ʾAʾisha does not accord her co-wife her requisite honorary title. ʾAʾisha then caustically thanks Umm Salama for her "sermon" and remarks on her presumed right to counsel her. About her departure ʾAʾisha states:

I make a distinction between two parties of disputing Muslims. If I stay, then it will not be because of any restriction [on your part]. If I leave, it will be concerning something about which I need explain no further.[82]

ʾAʾisha here demonstrates that no remonstrances from a co-wife are enough to direct or redirect her course of political action. However, it would be naive to take this exchange as a confirmed piece of historical altercation. In tracing the evolution of the dispute about ʾAʾisha's participation in politics, it becomes clear that Ibn ʾAbd Rabbih's elaborate expression of the debate between Umm Salama and ʾAʾisha represents a contrived version of an earlier, less detailed argument. Moreover, with time, accretions have added the significant factor of the Prophet's express disapproval. According to Umm Salama, ʾAʾisha was not acting as the Prophet would have wished, but she is hard pressed, apart from her reference to the Qurʾan 33:33 to define more clearly in what words he defined the directives which would prevent ʾAʾisha from political involvement. Indeed, Umm Salama articulates a rather weak argument when she states that if the Prophet had made it permissible for women to go into battle he would have authorized the action. The statement represents a contradiction of military realities for women in both the jahiliyya and early Islamic periods.

Umm Salama also takes the offensive in a critique of ʾAʾisha's involvement in politics in the fifth/eleventh-century work of the Shiʾi author al-Mufid. In this account, Umm Salama reprimands ʾAʾisha with an outline of the need for her obedience to a proper Islamic standard of female behavior as represented by both the Qur'an and the Prophet. These pronouncements include veiling and not expecting any woman to think of herself as critical to the support of the community of the faithful.[83] Umm Salama elaborates that if `A'isha were to act in obedience to the Prophet's mandate she would keep her eyes averted and remain in her tent. Further, Umm Salama asks `A'isha, "What would you do if the Prophet of Allah met you on your journey?" In this Shi`i source, Umm Salama's critique of `A'isha presents a general code of behavior for all women, a communal standard which `A'isha knowingly transgresses in the first civil war.

An explicit defense and explanation of `A'isha's place on the battlefield occurs in Ibn `Abd Rabbih. In Basra `A'isha addresses the inhabitants and emphasizes her "sanctity of motherhood," the special place she held in the community as a mother of the believers.[84] She claims no restrictions apply to her as the wife of the Prophet. Instead, she argues, it is this very status that allows her the right to deliver a public speech. In response to the charge that she is disobeying Allah and his Prophet she exclaims: "Do not suspect me of disobeying Allah. The prophet of Allah died in my arms. I am the first of his wives in heaven." From this point on her narrative becomes a recitation of her special qualities including her virginity at the time of her marriage and her blessedness in the receipt of the revelation in the Qur'an which exonerated her from the charge of adultery. It is ironic that her role as a member of the mother of the believers which in the Qur'an separates her from other women as exemplary and which is cited frequently by her detractors as the reason for her culpability in the first civil war, ultimately made her political access and presence possible. One wonders if the Battle had gone the way of `A'isha's forces if her status as mother of the believers would not have been elaborated in an argument designed to counter the Qur'anic injunction and justify her political participation.

The emphasis on `A'isha's transgression of the Qur'an 33:33 is re-echoed in medieval sources as the basis for censure in both Sunni and Shi`i medieval works. The shared assumption being that if `A'isha had not left her house, if she had followed the revealed word of the Qur'an, the carnage of the Battle of the Camel would not have occurred. Ibn Sa`d concludes his third/ninth-century biography of `A'isha with a citation of these critical Qur'anic verses which reveals that the wife of the Prophet understood their application too late. It is reported that when she recited them, she wept until she wet her veil.[85] Al-Mas'udi's fourth/tenth-century Shi'i chronicle emphasizes the significance of this contention by including a scene in which 'Ali, at the end of the Battle, confronts 'A'isha with her wrongdoing: "O little ruddy one, is this what the Prophet of Allah commanded you to do? Did he not order you to remain in your house?" This rhetorical question focuses on her transgression in the midst of 'A'isha's great defeat at the Battle of the Camel. Al-Mas'udi emphasizes the loss of human life which is blamed upon 'A'isha's role in the first civil war. He does this dramatically by including a poem of lament by a woman who claims to have had two sons, two brothers and her husband killed in the confrontation. Her reaction, narrated in the first person, is a lyrical indictment of 'A'isha's participation. The final line underscores the perceived causal relationship between 'A'isha's transgression of the Qur'anic injunction and the human suffering occasioned by the Battle.

> I have seen many combats and my hair is now white, but I never saw a day like the Day of the Camel.
> The most damaging civil war fought among believers killed the foremost warriors.
> If only *al-za'ina* [the woman on the camel, i.e., 'A'isha] had stayed in her house! And you 'Askar, [her camel] if you too had not left![86]

The Qur'anic verses which are cited in the fourth/tenth century to censure 'A'isha are not discussed in contemporary exegesis with direct reference to 'A'isha or the Battle of the Camel.[87] In Sunni definitions of heresy and defenses of the faith, attempts are made to suggest that 'A'isha's departure from her house in the first civil war was undertaken on her part in order to restore peace between the two parties. Such assertions occur in both the fifth/eleventh and the eighth/fourteenth century.[88] Ibn Taymiyya's late medieval defense of the faith from Shi'i polemic suggests that the use of such verses to condemn 'A'isha are invalid and represent only a selective application of the divine word. He argues that they did not forbid her absolutely from going out. Thus, he mentions that 'A'isha left her house many times with her husband on raids and just prior to the first civil war to perform the lesser pilgrimage for which she travelled, without comment, from Medina to Mecca.[89] These attempts to place `A'isha's political mission in a positive light seem not to have prevailed in medieval chronicle, but instead appear to represent the strongest possible Sunni response to Shi`i attacks on `A'isha's motives and character.

The Shi`i Muslim medieval use of the Qur'an to condemn `A'isha was both consistent and forceful. It formed the basis for a renewed debate about politics and gender mediated through `A'isha's example. In al-Mufid's fifth/eleventh-century treatise on the first civil war, `A'isha is reminded that according to the Qur'an, she along with Muhammad's other wives is not like other women.[90] Closely following this reminder is the citation of the Qur'an verses 33:33 which command the wives of the Prophet to stay in their houses. The inference drawn by the Shi`i author from `A'isha's perceived disregard for this revelation is that she went out, not as some Sunni defenders might argue to establish peace between Muslims, but rather to wage war against `Ali. The Shi`i author Ibn Shahrashub also utilizes these verses to condemn `A'isha in his work.[91]

The debate between Umm Salama and `A'isha with regard to the first civil war resonates with definitions of female obedience and transgression. Umm Salama serves to articulate for both Sunni and Shi`i authors the centrality of the Qur'an in the debate about `A'isha's political actions. Ultimately, both communities agreed that `A'isha had contravened the import of the verses found in 33:33. Her participation in the Battle of the Camel thus has a negative universal application for all women who are, through `A'isha's censure, warned not to involve themselves in political matters. Retrospectively cast in the historical record as the defeated political activist, `A'isha is scripted to defend an untenable legacy as a woman already defined by the errors of female transgression. The results of her political involvement ultimately bear out the warnings of her antagonist. It is the voice of Umm Salama that is meant to echo through time with admonitions for all Muslim women to be obedient, forsake `A'isha's example and stay in their homes. As `A'isha's critic, Umm Salama also assumes the tacit role of directing the religiopolitical interpretations of both Sunni and Shi`i male Muslim scholars.

The success of Umm Salama's articulation of the merits of female obedience and political inactivity, found expression in the choice of Zubayda, the wife of the Abbasid caliph Harun al-Rashid (d. 193/809). Zubayda lost her son Amin in a civil war over the politics of succession. Amin was killed by his half-brother in his quest to become the sole Abbasid caliph. When Zubayda heard the news of her son's death, she was urged to follow ʿAʾisha's example and seek vengeance on the battlefield for her son. Her rejection of ʿAʾisha's political legacy is a near paraphrase of Umm Salama's speeches. Zubayda asks rhetorically:

"What do women from among the believers have to do with seeking vengeance and taking the field against warriors?" Then she withdrew and went into deep mourning.[92]

The lessons of the Battle of the Camel are cited as the reason that prevented Zubayda from marching to war. Zubayda states that as a good Muslim woman she should have nothing to do with political or military ventures. Unlike the wives of the Prophet, Zubayda was not explicitly prohibited in the Qurʾan from taking up arms or leaving her house. However, the anecdote suggests that her rejection of revenge as a motive for her participation in the politics of succession at the ʿAbbasid court was based upon her understanding of the negative precedent set by ʿAʾisha's political legacy. The lessons of the first civil war would not inspire any Muslim woman to take political action.

Fitna: Civil War and Female Sexuality

ʿAʾisha's involvement in the politics of succession made her historical persona central to the debate in Islamic medieval sources over the relationship of all women to Islamic government. The discussion of women and government in third/ninth-century Sunni sources may be best introduced by traditions which present the defects of women as the greatest *fitna*, a term which in this context refers to all females as a source of temptation or chaos.[93] This usage of the term is a direct reference to male assumptions about the dangers of female sexuality. Fitna also denotes a moral trial whereby an individual must choose between good and evil which is how the word is used in the Qurʾan, 10:85. The Prophet Muhammad describes women as synonymous with the greatest fitna confronting the community after his death as recorded in many third/ninth-century Sunni hadith collections.[94] The term fitna was also used as the word for civil war. Although ʾAʾisha is never defined directly as a female linked to fitna, she implicitly participates in the connotations of the term as applied to all women in third/ninth-century sources by virtue of her gender. Thus, when the definition of women as fitna is coupled with ʾAʾisha's participation in the first fitna or civil war, Islamic gender and politics collide in discussions of the Battle of the Camel.

As defined in third/ninth-century hadith, women are implicitly perceived as flawed and prone to err. Women are described as the majority of the people in hell.[95] The same sources also imply that the cause of female over representation in the fire is their characteristic lack of ʾaql, or reason. This serious defect is assumedly one from which no woman is exempt. These early, powerful definitions of the feminine as dangerous, sinful, and irrational set the stage for projections about the outcome of any potential female involvement in politics. Since all women were similarly flawed, the consequences of female rule are depicted as demonstrably dire. Such is the framework articulated in early traditions which cite ʾAʾisha's political legacy as mere confirmation of this misogynist argument.

The promotion of negative definitions of the feminine in affairs of state were often cast through the words of the Prophet himself as predictions. On hearing that a woman ruled Sasanian Iran (A.D. 224–651), the Prophet said: "A people who place women in charge of their affairs will never prosper."[96] Al-Bukhari records the same phrase with an implicit reference to ʾAʾisha's role in the first civil war in his section dedicated to the missives sent by the Prophet to the ruler of the Sasanian empire of Iran.[97] The narrator of the hadith confirms that the Prophet made his prediction about women who rule over men, but he states that later, presumably after Muhammad's death, he understood these words not as a reflection about the specific woman who ruled Iran, but as the truth about the Battle of the Camel. A woman named Boranduxt did in fact rule pre-Islamic Iran during the years 629–630, but we know little of her short reign for good or ill, except that she ruled long enough to be immortalized with a remarkably intricate hair style on coins. The Prophet had been twice right in "predicting" disaster for those men ruled by women. The Sasanian empire would be conquered by invading Arab Islamic armies shortly after his death in the first/seventh century and `A'isha would be remembered for her prominent presence in the disastrous Battle of the Camel later in that same century. The connection between the import of this hadith and `A'isha's role in the first civil war is stated once again in these early sources. In a stronger prediction found in Ibn Hanbal, the Prophet warns: "Men perish if they obey women." Enhancing the impact of his words was the fact that they were spoken "while his head rested on `A'isha's breast."[98] Such a hadith condemned in silent eloquence, for the outcome of the Battle of the Camel and the role of `A'isha in the conflagration was at once seemingly predicted, but still more pointedly recalled. In the context of this tradition, `A'isha's political legacy could not even be defended for she had as yet done nothing to bear out the Prophet's prognostications. The same hadith would be utilized in later medieval Islamic political theory to exclude women from government positions such as that of prime minister.[99] The popularity of these observations continue to be attested in the modern Islamic world. Even when they are paraphrased without reference to these specific early sources, they represent a powerful precedent. Thus, Afghanistan's interim President Sibjatullah Mojadedi, when asked why a woman should not lead an Islamic government, could respond in 1992:

The weakest nations in the world are those that had a woman as a leader. It doesn't mean that Islam is against women. On the contrary, it respects them and says that they are equal to men. But [history shows] that weak nations are led by women.[100]

`A'isha's Legacy in Islamic Political Theory

The prime minister and author Nizam al-Mulk (d. 485/1092) dedicated an entire chapter of his *Book of Government* or *Rules for Kings* to the issue of women and government.[101] Nizam al-Mulk was a practical politician dedicated to the promotion of Sunni Islam and the protection of his patron, the Seljuk Sultan Malikshah. In offering advice to a particular ruler Nizam al-Mulk sought a wide range of examples from pre-Islamic and Islamic history to make his point. In the chapter titled "On the Subject of Those Who Wear the Veil," Nizam al-Mulk refers to a series of famous females, beginning with Eve, to confirm the consistently disastrous effects of women who, through their husbands, gain access to political power. His premise reflects his negative view of the entire gender and their threat to the stability of the state.

Their [women's] commands are mostly the opposite of what is right. In all the ages when the king's wife has dominated the king, nothing but infamy, evil, chaos, and corruption has resulted.[102]

It is clear from this introductory statement that the prime minister was attempting to warn rulers against permitting their wives any influence in matters of state. One of the terms utilized by Nizam al-Mulk to describe the deleterious effects of women upon the natural perfection of the male-dominated state is *fetna*, the Persian equivalent of the Arabic term fitna. In Persian as in Arabic the word denotes chaos in political affairs, but carries with it earlier, specifically feminine implications of uncontrolled sexuality, a different kind of threat to male authority. By using the term fitna in conjunction with the words infamy, evil and corruption, the prime minister confirmed previously established Islamic assumptions about all women as a source of trouble, turmoil, and temptation.

Nizam al-Mulk's chapter on women may be read as a succinct treatise on medieval Islamic conceptions of gender and politics. His pronouncements on the matter of female inferiority were not novel in the Islamic context. He merely restated in the fifth/eleventh century a series of observations first documented in third/ninth-century traditions. What made his counsel for kings a unique document was his ability to effectively link a general condemnation of all women with a mythological, historical or religious specific in female form. His selective examples helped fortify observations which may otherwise have failed to impress his elite male audience. The examples were chosen to hammer home the applicability of his collection of object lessons in unsuccessful government. Overall, his intent in his section on women was to distinguish the female gender as part of the dual threat that confronted the Sunni Muslim Seljuk state: "the infidel without and the woman within."[103] The Seljuks had come to power in the `Abbasid territories of Iraq and Iran by defeating the Shi`i Buyid dynasty. The `Abbasid caliph remained the nominal head of state, but true political power belonged to the Turkish Sunni Seljuk dynasty. The ideological threat of the infidel without and within remained for the Seljuks in the form of the Sevener or Isma'ili power of the Egyptian Fatimid dynasty and their more extreme branch who came to be called the Assassins.

Nizam al-Mulk's anxiety about the influence of women in matters of succession was not purely theoretical. As vizier, his great enemy and opponent at the Seljuk court was Turkhan (d. 487/1094), the wife of the reigning sultan Malikshah (d. 485/1092).[104] His chapter devoted to those who wear the veil was thus not merely a foray into political theory, but appears to have been an evocation of the prime minister's immediate problem with the one woman who had influence over her husband in the matter of succession. Turkhan wanted her son Mahmud to succeed her husband as sultan. Nizam al-Mulk opposed her choice and supported the son of a rival wife.[105] Not only did Turkhan "oppose what was right" in the vizier's choice of a successor, but she threatened Nizam al-Mulk's own position in the Seljuk government. She wanted to replace the vizier with her own choice for the post.

Nizam al-Mulk's definition of women reiterated earlier Islamic traditions which concluded that women do not have complete intelligence. The passage in the treatise which conveys this idea is rendered as literally an imperfection in reason or intelligence.[106] The argument for female inferiority was thus founded on the concept of the entire gender being innately defective. Nizam al-Mulk offered a standard caveat to male rulers about their wives' damaging effects on government. He argues that female influence in government, literally since the beginning of history, results in nothing but disaster. Indeed, the argument itself is not even uniquely Islamic. The position that exclusively female biological defects prohibit women's inclusion in public life was first suggested in Aristotle's *Politics* and the Greek philosopher's conclusions were re-echoed in both Christian and Islamic medieval treatises.[107]

Nizam al-Mulk selected 'A'isha bint Abi Bakr as his single Islamic female example. As a champion of the Sunni revival, he was compelled to strike a delicate balance between portraying the favorite wife of the Prophet as an exalted personage and detailing her exemplary failings as the predictable consequences of her gender. As in the case of the third/ninth-century traditions about women and government, 'A'isha's application in Nizam al-Mulk's fifth/eleventh-century text fit the frame of a prevalent medieval Islamic model of women as dangerous and destructive to political order. Although the idea of female opposition to that which was right was amply illustrated in the *Book of Government* through the citation of select pre-Islamic examples, it was the hadith featuring `A'isha which would have captured the attention of many Sunni Muslims. The tradition in question sought to illustrate a terse saying attributed to the Prophet Muhammad himself: "Consult them and oppose them."[108] By quoting the Arabic sentence in which the feminine plural pronominal suffix *hunna* clearly indicated that women were the objects of Muhammad's statement, the Seljuk prime minister utilized the Prophet's own words to discredit all women. Next, Nizam al-Mulk introduced a hadith in which `A'isha, the favorite wife, is said to have opposed a directive of her husband the Prophet. During Muhammad's last illness he was apparently so weak that he could not lead Muslim believers in prayer. The question of which male companion should lead the prayer in the Prophet's place was perceived by Sunni Muslims as a tacit indication of who should succeed Muhammad as caliph after his death. `A'isha thus becomes linked to an episode in which she, as a wife, had critical proximity and potential influence over her husband's political decision-making.

`A'isha said to the Prophet, "O Prophet of Allah, it is time for prayer and you are not strong enough to go to the mosque. Whom do you command to lead the prayer?" He said: "Tell Abu Bakr to conduct the prayer." `A'isha replied, "O Prophet of Allah, Abu Bakr is a tender-hearted man and cannot stand in your place." The Prophet said: "Tell Abu Bakr to conduct the prayer." Then `A'isha said yet again: "He is a weak and tender-hearted man." Then the Prophet replied, "Tell Abu Bakr to conduct the prayer." Whereupon `A'isha said to Hafsa, "You tell [him] that I said many times that Abu Bakr is tender-hearted and loves you more than all your companions. If he stands at prayer and sees your place empty, he will be overcome with weeping and he will spoil [both] his and the people's prayers. `Umar is a hard man and has a strong heart. If you command him [to conduct the prayer] there will be no harm." Then Hafsa spoke in this manner [to the Prophet]. The Prophet of Allah became angry and said, "You are like Yusuf and Kirsuf. I do not want what you desire. I will command that [which is in] the interest of the Muslims. Go and tell Abu Bakr to conduct the prayers of the congregation."[109]

In selecting this tradition, Nizam al-Mulk as author and statesman consciously chose to combine the two components necessary for his own political point to be made. His intent was to illustrate how the wives of political and religious leaders often seek to use their influence to do the opposite of what is right and, most significantly, how this perverse female tendency may disrupt the order of political succession.

The Prophet Muhammad is believed by Sunni Muslims to have appointed no successor at the time of his death. However, this hadith serves to illustrate that the Prophet acknowledged ʿAʾisha's father Abu Bakr by designating him prayer leader during his illness. The tradition may also be regarded as a later Sunni affirmation of the choice of Abu Bakr as the first caliph. At such a politically sensitive juncture, Nizam al-Mulk implies that ʿAʾisha's opposition to the Prophet ran counter to the already proven right course of early Islamic history. ʿAʾisha's preference for ʿUmar, Hafsa's father, in such a scenario not only sought to abrogate the Prophet's directive, but by extension would have disrupted the proper order of Sunni succession among the first four caliphs, a critical point in the determination of the majority's communal identity.

Nizam al-Mulk's citation of ʿAʾisha's attempt to undermine her own father's succession to the Prophet is an incident repeatedly recounted in third/ninth-century sources. The tradition finally chosen by Nizam al-Mulk was only one of many versions of the incident recorded in this period. Ibn Hisham's biography of the Prophet and the biographical dictionary of Ibn Saʿd together contain more than ten variations of the hadith. However, only one of the accounts in Ibn Hisham's work refers to ʿAʾisha. There is no trace of Hafsa, but ʿAʾisha's rationale for opposing the Prophet enlarges upon her father as too weak of voice and prone to weeping to lead the prayers. The tradition, narrated on ʿAʾisha's authority, renders a more politically astute vision of her, for as she explains:

I wouldn't have said that except that I wanted to spare Abu Bakr. I knew that the people would never love any man who stood in the Prophet's place [in the mosque]. The people would blame him for everything and I wanted Abu Bakr to be spared that.[110]

The second and third accounts featured in Ibn Hisham do not involve

`A'isha at all. Instead, `Umar is mistakenly told to lead the prayers by a male companion, and the Prophet, on hearing `Umar's voice, objects, saying, "Allah and Muhammad forbid this." In another version of the event, Abu Bakr prays and the Prophet enters the mosque and motions for him to continue and prays with him.

Ibn Sa`d's work contains ten variations on the hadith included in Nizam al-Mulk's handbook. Out of these, only three, less than one third of the total, refer to `A'isha. Two of these traditions include Hafsa, but those involving `A'isha make reference to Abu Bakr's weakness and follow Ibn Hisham's variation in mentioning `A'isha's fear that any man who replaced the Prophet in leading the prayers would be met with a challenge from the Muslim community.[111] Almost half of these traditions are related on `A'isha's authority. In Ibn Hanbal, ten more variations of this theme are presented, all on `A'isha's authority, three of which feature Hafsa.[112]

Nizam al-Mulk manipulated the Islamic past and `A'isha's political persona for his own purposes. Unlike Hafsa with whom she had been mentioned in many of these traditions, `A'isha had by far the highest historical profile. She had become by the fifth/eleventh century a figure to be reckoned with for Sunni as well as Shi`i believers. Not only did she hold the undisputed title of favorite wife for the majority of believers, but reference to her provoked a spectrum of responses in which praise and censure had already been coupled. `A'isha alone among the mothers of the believers represented an Islamic female historical figure already explicitly associated with political controversy in the communal record. Nizam al-Mulk was aware of `A'isha's heady symbolic valence. He did not mention the Battle of the Camel, `A'isha's one direct foray into the politics of Islamic succession because he knew that she was a widow at the time, not a wife wielding influence over her husband. Therefore, her actions in the first civil war could not enhance his own treatise on the dangers of female involvement in Islamic government. Instead, he selected a tradition in which `A'isha in her role as a wife could personify the evils of her gender.

The vizier's version of the past which featured `A'isha also consciously summoned images of another negative feminine Qur'anic precedent. Nizam al-Mulk's brief reference to `A'isha and Hafsa as comparable to Yusuf and Kirsuf reflects a subtheme which originates in chapter 12 of the

Qur'an. Third/ninth-century hadith are more revealing than Nizam al-Mulk's gloss, for they capture the Prophet angrily comparing his two wives to *sawahib Yusuf*, "the female companions of [the prophet] Joseph."[113] Joseph's story in the Qur'an is a narrative of many trials and temptations. Bought by al-'Aziz, the vizier of Pharaoh, Joseph is nearly seduced by his master's wife. She remains nameless in the Qur'an, but in her post-Qur'anic evolution assumes the name of Zulaykha'. In the Qur'an, Zulaykha' succumbs to Joseph's beauty and unsuccessfully tries to seduce him. The female companions of Joseph referred to in third/ninth-century traditions represent the women of the city. In the Qur'anic tale these flighty females gossiped about Zulaykha's passion for her slave boy Joseph. Zulaykha' then invited these women to her house and gave them each a knife. According to Qur'an 12: 31, she commanded Joseph to enter the room and his beauty so stunned the women that they cut themselves with their knives.

In the Qur'an, third/ninth-century traditions and the treatise of Nizam al-Mulk, the particular precedent of Zulaykha' is extended to encompass the behavior of all women. When Zulaykha' first attempted and failed to seduce Joseph the young prophet tried to prove his innocence in the Qur'an 12:28: "This is the guile of you women. Your guile is very great!" Later Joseph, threatened with imprisonment because he would neither submit to Zulaykha's sinful intent nor lie, prays to God to save him from the wiles of women, a reference made in the feminine plural in Qur'an 12:33:

He [Joseph] said: "O my Lord! Prison is more dear to me than that into which they urge me, and if You do not fend off their wiles from me I shall incline unto them and become foolish."

The word used throughout chapter 12 of the Qur'an is *kayd*, which may be translated as "wile" or "guile," but which also implies deceit and trickery as a means to an end. Although the word kayd is also applied in the story of Joseph to his deceitful brothers, it is the association of this term with specifically feminine artifice that resonates in the depiction of Zulaykha', the Qur'anic women of the city, and 'A'isha. In the confluence of feminine guile, 'A'isha's actions as described by the Prophet, are both clarified and condemned through her association with specific negative precedents found in the Qur'an. The examples of `A'isha and Zulaykha' exemplify the construction of a universal definition of the feminine in medieval Islamic sources. `A'isha, who had been compared to the positive Qur'anic images of Maryam and the wife of pharaoh, would also be associated with the negative aspects of Zulaykha' featured in the sacred text. Just as `A'isha's political involvement in the first civil war combined the sexual and political definitions of fitna, her association with the feminine wiles of kayd first exemplified by Zulaykha' further emphasized the nexus between female sexuality and danger. Nizam al-Mulk assumes that just as Zulaykha' sought to practice her feminine tricks upon the prophet Joseph, so too did `A'isha seek influence over the Prophet Muhammad. In both cases, the triumph of the feminine force over male prophets would have produced moral and political disaster. In the Shi`i application of the Qur'anic reference to Zulaykha', `A'isha's meddling in the politics of succession represents an overt attempt to promote her father at `Ali ibn Abi Talib's expense. The Prophet said:

"Let one of my people pray for them, for I am too ill." Then `A'isha said, "Call Abu Bakr." Hafsa said, "Call `Umar." The Prophet heard their words and saw the desire of each one to exalt her own father . . . And the Prophet said: "You are like the female companions of Joseph."[114]

In another Shi`i version of the incident in which the Prophet tries to summon his successor without naming him, `A'isha again calls Abu Bakr, Hafsa summons `Umar, but Umm Salama in vain attempts to indicate that the Prophet really meant `Ali ibn Abi Talib.[115] The message about `A'isha's feminine guile remains the same in the Shi`i version, even if the favorite contenders for the caliphate differ.

The implicit tie between Zulaykha' and `A'isha at the symbolic level has been more recently emphasized by Abdelwahab Bouhdiba. He describes Zulaykha' as "the archetype of the eternal feminine." He argues for the association of `A'isha and Zulaykha' implicitly as different manifestations of his vision of Islamic female sexuality.

Despite the extreme variety of the feminine myths and of the poetic fascination they exert, two types of women have assumed symbolic value in Islam: Aysha the 'virtuous' coquette, and Zuleikha, Joseph's enigmatic temptress: Aysha so much a woman but always without reproach, and Zuleikha, driven mad by desire![116]

According to Bouhdiba, the only difference between the two images of the Islamic feminine is that `A'isha, as the Prophet's wife, exerts her sexuality in the legitimated framework of marriage and so is beyond reproach while Zulaykha', in her role as temptress, has no control over her primarily sexual nature.

It was `A'isha's collective reputation, her historically constructed persona, on which Nizam al-Mulk capitalized when he chose a particular version of the hadith which combined both the issue of succession and the import of the Qur'anic Zulaykha' for his work. Only `A'isha could accommodate the vizier's postscript to the observation with which he concluded his chapter on women:

And with all the greatness, knowledge, asceticism and piety of `A'isha, the Prophet still did the opposite of what `A'isha wanted. Therefore, of what worth are the opinions of other women?[117]

It was only about `A'isha that he could so easily couple praise and blame in order to make his point about an entire gender. Even as he extolled her as a symbol of excellence, `A'isha became an object of censure: an example of the capacity of all women to destroy political order.

In theory, Nizam al-Mulk might try to manipulate the past in order to direct the future by selectively utilizing third/ninth-century tradition in his *Book of Government*. There he could point the way for the ruler Malikshah not to be influenced by his wife Turkhan, just as the Prophet Muhammad persevered in what was right over and against his wife `A'isha. In practice, however, despite the vizier's efforts his untimely assassination helped to assure that Turkhan's female influence triumphed in the matter of Seljuk succession.[118]

The perception of `A'isha in the politics of Islamic succession, whether inspired by the depiction of the first civil war or the problematic of the order of the designation of the first caliph as cited by Nizam al-Mulk, reflects the Sunni concept of her as a flawed ideal. `A'isha's multivalent historical persona inspired praise and blame, defense and censure. The first civil war marked the beginning of an enduring conflict in the community for both power and religiopolitical identity. In the midst of communal fragmentation, `A'isha's medieval political persona became a central, contested part of the representation of the past. Although Sunni and Shi`i Muslims disagreed about `A'isha's responsiblity and culpability in the first civil war, they agreed fundamentally about her potential as a negative political example for all women. Thus, while the Sunni vizier Nizam al-Mulk wrote his chapter "On the Subject of Those Who Wear the Veil," the Shi`i author al-Mufid could also include a similarly titled chapter in his work on the Battle of the Camel. Seventy years before Nizam al-Mulk, al-Mufid would also make an argument about the exclusion of all women from politics based on `A'isha's example. [119]

Although `A'isha's direct participation in the politics of succession ended after the Battle of the Camel, she alone cannot be assigned responsibility for the exclusion of all women from Islamic government. Neither `A'isha's defeat, nor the Qur'anic injunction directed only at the wives of the Prophet to stay in their houses affected all Muslim women as profoundly as the universal application of negative Islamic definitions of the feminine. In this didactic, retrospective process of writing history, the revealing application of the terms fitna and kayd to `A'isha and all women signalled that the wife of the Prophet could be conveniently and consistently promoted by male authorities in both Sunni and Shi`i communities as a particularly powerful example of what they chose to define as a general phenomenon. Whether or not the fate of modern Muslim women in politics hangs on the continuing negative construction of `A'isha as a model, her centrality in the current debate remains. A limit to the future application of `A'isha's acknowledged negative political persona has recently been suggested by the author Ghassan Ascha:

If these societies must qualify the participation of Muslim women in politics on the pretext that `A'isha, one of the wives of the Prophet, once became entangled in the political quarrels of the seventh century, then what reason will we find, for example, to send a Muslim woman to the moon when `A'isha never made such a voyage? [120]

five   *the politics of praise:* `A'isha and the development of Islamic female ideals

> *"There are many perfect men, but there are no perfect women except . . ."*
>
> —From a third/ninth-century hadith

`A'isha's unique legacy as a female historical persona did not develop in a vacuum. There were other women close to the Prophet Muhammad who were promoted and exalted in the earliest Islamic sources. The Prophet's first wife, Khadija bint Khuwaylid (d. A.D. 619), and his daughter Fatima bint Muhammad (d. A.H. 11/A.D. 633) were the two women who together with `A'isha became the earliest and most visible sources of emulation for women in the Muslim community. The reverence accorded each of them in titles and honorifics due largely to their distinct personal ties to the Prophet became by the third Islamic century an attempt to demonstrate their individual excellence over other women within the Muslim community. An ongoing debate within the Muslim community about the nature of female idealization and the feminine is revealed by the selectivity employed in their distinct depictions. The first evidence of an implicit debate arises in the earliest materials devoted to tradition and biography. Its culmination and logical extensions are found in the earliest *tafsir*, Qur'anic exegesis, and subsequent professions and defenses of Sunni Islam.

Degrees and Attributes of Excellence

Praise for each woman was predicated on a foundation of Qur'anic precedent. Not only are Khadija, Fatima, and `A'isha joined in unique ways to the Prophet Muhammad, they are also linked explicitly to specific women extolled in the Qur'an. The figures of Maryam, the mother of Jesus, and the wife of pharaoh are mentioned in the Qur'an in ways which make them natural ideals for Muslim women. Maryam, the only woman actually named in the Qur'an, is mentioned frequently. Sura 19 is named after her. The wife of pharaoh, who in post-Qur'anic sources is referred to as Asiya, is mentioned only twice in the Qur'an. In sura 28: 9, she saves the life of Moses. In sura 66 the mother of Jesus and the wife of pharaoh are introduced together as examples for the Muslim community:

And Allah cites an example for those who believe: The wife of Pharaoh when she said: "My Lord! Build for me a home with you in paradise and deliver me from Pharaoh and his work and deliver me from evil folk." (Qur'an 66: 11) And Maryam, daughter of `Imran, whose body was chaste. We breathed therein something of Our spirit. And she put her faith in the word of her Lord and His scriptures, and was of the obedient. (66:12)[1]

In this continuum of praise, the association of the Qur'anic Maryam and Asiya enhances and reinforces an emerging Islamic vision of the most exalted women of the Islamic community as devout, chaste, and obedient to the will of Allah. However, it is Maryam whose presence is most prominent in the Qur'an, where she is described as "chosen," "made pure," and "preferred" by Allah "above [all] the women of the worlds" (3: 42).[2] The critical notion of preference associated with Maryam alone provides the most consistent precedent for the linkage of Khadija, Fatima, and `A'isha with a Qur'anic archetype. In Islamic historiography Muhammad's supremacy would be enhanced by comparison to the male prophets from Adam through Jesus, who are acknowledged in the Qur'an as his predecessors. The symbolism associated with Khadija, Fatima, and `A'isha would develop in a separate, but parallel female continuum, based upon the lives of the women mentioned in the Qur'an in conjunction with prior male prophets.[3] The precedence of Qur'anic female ideals and their evolution had a demonstrable impact on Islamic historiography. Medieval Muslim authors fleshed out Qur'anic female ideals and, in so doing, transformed the depiction of the women closest to the Prophet Muhammad. The titles used to extol the prominent women of the first Muslim community in the earliest written Arabic sources emphasize particular characteristics and aspects of their lives. The praise accorded Khadija, Fatima, and 'A'isha, when examined in relation to one another, reveals their centrality and significance in the early Islamic communal record. The nuanced presentation of each woman in the process of their idealization ultimately reflects an implicit debate about which of these three women should occupy the position of the most exalted female figure in Islamic memory. Examination of the honorifics applied to the figures of Khadija, Fatima, and 'A'isha in early Muslim scholarly discussions of their excellence ultimately separates and distinguishes them as representatives of differing political and confessional loyalties.

Khadija

Khadija bint Khuwaylid is depicted in the earliest biographical dictionaries not just as the Prophet's first wife, but also as the first convert to Islam.[4] Khadija had been twice-widowed when, according to most sources, at the age of forty she hired the twenty-five-year-old Muhammad to assist her in her trading business and then married him.[5] She is described consistently as a woman of wealth and honor within Meccan society.[6] Khadija lived monogamously with Muhammad during her lifetime and was the mother, with one exception, of all his children, including Fatima, the longest-lived.[7] Khadija died in A.D. 619, three years before the emigration of Muhammad and his followers from Mecca to Medina in 622, the first year of the Islamic calendar. Khadija thus departs from Muhammad's life at a critical juncture in the turbulent story of the nascent Islamic community before its true religiopolitical foundation and triumph at Medina.

Despite Khadija's early demise she was accorded many titles posthumously that convey the esteem in which she would continue to be held by the Prophet and his followers. Khadija was counted among the *ummahat al-mu'minin*, "the mothers of the believers," a title conferred after her death upon all the wives of the Prophet. The phrase originates in the Qur'an and refers to the exemplary status of the Prophet and his wives within the Islamic community: "The Prophet is closer to the believers than themselves and his wives are [as] their mothers."[8] Although posthumously attributed, the title "mother of the believers" represents an affirmation of Khadija's status as the Prophet's first wife and supporter.[9]

The most famous of honorary titles bestowed upon the most elite women of the first Muslim community is, not surprisingly, an allusion to a basic female biological role. `A'isha is reported to have taken exception to the title when a Muslim woman addressed her as "mother," meaning "mother of the believers." `A'isha replied, "I am not your mother, I am the mother of your men," an observation which does not suggest her disaffection for women, but rather her grammatical savvy since the masculine, not the feminine plural is employed for the Arabic word "believers."[10] Although the masculine plural implicitly includes women, `A'isha was no doubt aware of the instructions proffered in the Qur'an that are explicitly addressed to both male and female believers. Such an anecdote also unintentionally suggests the power of `A'isha's exclusively male children to interpret her import for all believers.

Khadija's legacy to the Muslim community is founded on her presentation as a steadfast supporter of her husband's mission at a time when he was rejected by other Arabs. Her role as wife and mother is augmented by Muhammad's attachment to her memory even after her death. `A'isha's own selection as a marriage partner is described, in part, as Allah's way of distracting the Prophet from his grief after the death of Khadija.[11] Such a description promoted the theme of `A'isha as a successor to Khadija, a role which was true figuratively as well as literally, for both women played prominent roles in Muhammad's life at different stages and in different ways.

Khadija's virtues were often mentioned by the Prophet. As reported, they emphasize `A'isha's jealousy. She is said to have admitted, "I wasn't jealous of any of the wives of the Prophet except Khadija even though I came [after] her death."[12] The fact that Khadija was beyond `A'isha's criticism was also confirmed by Muhammad. Once in an angry mood, `A'isha referred to Khadija as that "toothless old woman whom Allah has replaced with a better," meaning herself.[13] Muhammad quickly retorted in the negative, confirming Khadija's irreproachable legacy:

No indeed, Allah has not replaced her with a better. She believed in me when I was rejected. When they called me a liar, she proclaimed me truthful. When I was poor, she shared with me her wealth and Allah granted her children though withholding those of other women.

The fact that several accounts concerning `A'isha's jealousy are found in Khadija's biography, related on `A'isha's authority, raises clear questions about the attribution and placement of these traditions. Since Khadija predeceased `A'isha, it is logical that `A'isha should appear to have the last word over her predecessor. `A'isha's role in these accounts is that of an instigator. She provides the jealous impetus for the Prophet's glowing memory of his first wife. Her words simultaneously exalt the memory of Khadija while serving to emphasize `A'isha herself in a less than positive perspective. Such a frame effect appears to empower `A'isha with a voice in order to elevate her silent, deceased rival and adds, implicitly, to the promotion of an alternative female ideal. Thus `A'isha praises Khadija while, in effect, undermining her own detailed claims for superiority of place among Muhammad's wives. Later Shi`i sources capitalize on these very traditions to emphasize `A'isha's jealousy as part of her pronounced antipathy for both mother and daughter.[14]

The honorifics bestowed upon Khadija are found in the earliest Arabic sources mainly in collections of hadith, not biographical dictionaries. The majority, nine in all, refer to Khadija as "the best of her women," together with Maryam, the mother of Jesus.[15] Khadija's comparison to Maryam thus binds the two women together as superior even as it separates them, presumably, by chronology. Khadija and Maryam are superior not to all women, but the women of their time. Khadija would by definition appear to be the best of Muslim women while Maryam would be similarly defined for the period of time preceding the revelation of Islam. All of the traditions originate with `Ali ibn Abi Talib, Muhammad's cousin, Khadija's son-in-law, and the husband of her daughter Fatima. `Ali's attributed support for Khadija's excellence cannot be noted without a nod to his documented antipathy toward `A'isha as the Prophet's wife and widow. Support for Khadija did not necessarily promote opposition to `A'isha as an exemplary woman, but those who supported `Ali would, by extension, be more inclined to praise Khadija as the wife of the Prophet and the mother of `Ali's spouse, the Prophet's daughter Fatima. Praise and preference for Khadija as mother would be quite easily extended to promote the qualities of Fatima as daughter.

In six additional hadith, Khadija is linked to Qur'anic figures in honorifics shared by her daughter Fatima. Together, Khadija and Fatima are bound to both Maryam and Asiya, the wife of pharaoh: "You shall reckon among the women of the worlds Maryam, Khadija, Fatima, and Asiya."[16] The linkage of the four women is particularly important because it includes the Qur'anic phrase "women of the worlds," first applied in relation to Maryam in sura 3:42. Although there are only three instances that bind Khadija and Fatima in relation to this Qur'anic reference, the phrase will eventually lead to the inclusion of both women in the earliest Qur'anic commentary, a critical juncture in their written idealization.[17]

The notion of heaven as the ultimate destination for women of faith and religious fortitude is reflected in the third honorific shared by Khadija and Fatima. Both are described as "the most excellent" of the female inhabitants of heaven along with Maryam and Asiya.[18] Khadija alone is described as having a luxurious dwelling in paradise where there will be neither "clamor nor toil."[19] It is possible that the notion of a such a heavenly abode subtly parallels the wife of pharaoh's request in the Qur'an for Allah to build for her a house in heaven (66: 11). Once again, the presence of Maryam and Asiya in the Islamic communal record creates a religiohistoric continuity of women whose excellence, while relative to one another, remains absolute in relation to all other women.

Fatima

Information about Fatima in the earliest sources is sparse compared with the tremendous elaboration of detail about her life in later sources, particularly among Shi`i authors.[20] As depicted in early biographical dictionaries and hadith collections, Fatima's world is captured primarily as one defined by her marital and maternal functions.[21] The exemplary nature of Fatima, her specialness among her female contemporaries is, in part, an extension of her descent from Muhammad and Khadija as their longest surviving child. The fact that Fatima outlived her siblings accidentally guaranteed her exalted position among the Prophet's female children. Had the Prophet produced male heirs, Fatima's uniqueness would, perhaps, have been severely qualified in regard to the more standard emphasis on a direct patriline. Fatima's superior status was derived primarily in early sources from her father, but increasingly in later accounts from her husband `Ali ibn Abi Talib. Together with `Ali, Fatima had two male children. As the mother of Hasan and Husayn, the grandsons of the Prophet Muhammad, Fatima insured that her father's male genealogical line would continue. After her exceptional participation as a female link in this important Islamic genealogical chain, Shi`i Muslims would consistently trace the descendants of `Ali only through the male line.[22] For those who supported `Ali's preeminent claim to the caliphate, Fatima would be remembered as the spouse of the first imam, the Shi`i Muslim spiritual and political authority, as well as the mother of the second and third imams. Nowhere is the genealogical and generational connection more obvious than in the early hadith concerning the *ahl al-bayt*, "the people of the house," a phrase taken from the Qur'an that is interpreted, with some debate, as synonymous with the Prophet Muhammad and his family: Fatima, `Ali, Hasan, and Husayn.[23] Early accounts of the family of the Prophet as unique and superior to other Muslims are often recounted on the authority of Umm Salama, one of the Prophet's wives who describes an incident featuring the *kisa'*, the cloak with which Muhammad covered his family.[24] Umm Salama's support for Muhammad's family would eventually prompt Shi`i authors to consider her, not `A'isha, as the Prophet's favorite wife after Khadija.

Fatima's bond with her father is depicted as particularly affectionate and strong in the early sources. Muhammad defines Fatima as "the best" of his family.[25] Muhammad described his daughter as "part of me," adding that "what hurts her, hurts me."[26] These words were often addressed to Fatima's husband `Ali at the time of his request to take a second wife while still married to the Prophet's daughter. The Prophet, who himself had more than one wife, denied his son-in-law's request as an offense against both father and daughter.[27]

A cluster of early honorifics attributed to Fatima emphasizes the special nature of her relationship with her father. These titles are bestowed upon Fatima while Muhammad is on his deathbed. Most reports of the exchange between father and daughter hinge on the presence of `A'isha. The questions posed by `A'isha concern Fatima's very private conversation with her dying father and her seemingly contradictory emotional responses. As prompted by `A'isha's curiosity, Fatima explains:

The Prophet told me that he would die of the illness with which he was then afflicted. Then I cried. He whispered that I would be the first of his family to follow him [in death]. Then I laughed.[28]

In two other versions of this tradition, `A'isha relates the same encounter, but Fatima adds that she laughed when the Prophet told her that she would be the "mistress of the women of the believers" and the "mistress of the women of this community."[29] A more laudatory version of the encounter exists, narrated by the Prophet's wife Umm Salama. Her account recreates the same context, but includes titles which predict Fatima's place in heaven and tie her status there to Maryam the mother of Jesus. In Umm Salama's account, Fatima is designated by the Prophet as "the mistress of the women inhabitants of heaven, except for Maryam." Such a hadith, again, cements Umm Salama's connection to Fatima and her family even as it demonstrates the basis for the special reverence in which Shi`i Muslims would come to hold her.

`A'isha narrates four of the earliest recorded encounters between Fatima and the Prophet, but in only two are Fatima's epithets mentioned. Moreover, the titles which originate with `A'isha give Fatima a preeminence limited to this world and the Islamic community. Nevertheless, `A'isha's role in the tradition frames Fatima's encounter with her father and emphasizes the position and privileges of the Prophet's daughter. `A'isha is not part of the intimate father-daughter conversation, but her queries are the reason for its revelation, the impetus for Fatima's explanation of her status. `A'isha's marginality is thus contrasted with the special knowledge and position imparted to Fatima by her father. Just as `A'isha's jealousy of Khadija's memory enhances the Prophet's praise of his first wife, so too `A'isha's curiosity about Fatima's reaction to her father promotes a similar negative comparison between the two women.

Only two other early references in works of tradition link Fatima with Maryam. In their depiction of Fatima as the "mistress of the female inhabitants of heaven, except for Maryam," they echo the father-daughter exchange narrated by Umm Salama.[30] Both, however, are related without reference to that context. In light of the nine traditions which link Khadija and Maryam together exclusively in the early hadith material, the three references to Fatima and the mother of Jesus seem unusually slight. Six additional early accounts, previously mentioned, feature Fatima and Qur'anic archetypes, but they promote a female quartet and do not place singular emphasis on the Prophet's daughter. The absence of a pronounced early linkage between Fatima and Maryam is all the more remarkable in retrospect, for it will be Fatima not Khadija whose life will be elaborated in succeeding centuries to parallel and, eventually, transcend the image of Maryam.[31]

As early as the fourth/tenth century, the Shi'i collection of hadith compiled by al-Kulayni (d. 329/941) includes key references connecting Fatima to the Qur'anic Maryam. Fatima is referred to by the title "mistress of the women of the worlds," from the Qur'anic phrase used to describe Maryam.[32] The same title is bestowed upon Fatima in the fifth/eleventh-century work of Shi'i miracle tales authored by Ibn 'Abd al-Wahhab. As narrated by 'A'isha in this source, the Prophet himself bestows this epithet upon his daughter in his final conversation with her. The exchange, now embellished with a new honorific for Fatima in a Shi'i source, draws directly upon previous Sunni accounts of the third/ninth century and 'A'isha's role in them for its core. Fatima is now, on 'A'isha's word, referred to as "the mistress of the women of the worlds."[33] Again, implicit in the phrase is the Qur'anic echo of the words applied to Maryam, in sura 3:42, who is chosen by Allah "above [all] the women of the worlds." The elaboration of Fatima's legacy is certainly propelled primarily by Shi'i authors anxious to promote 'Ali, Fatima, and their descendants as preeminent spiritual and political ideals. 'A'isha's role in this task would seem to represent an effective vehicle for the enhancement of Fatima's prestige. Praise from 'A'isha as the opposition in avowedly Shi'i sources, presumably, representing an exceptional demonstration of Fatima's worthiness, is a pattern of praise also found previously in Sunni accounts. The presence of 'A'isha as a foil to Fatima in such a pattern is further echoed in the next century in the hagiographical work of the Shi`i author Ibn Shahrashub (d. 588/1192).[34] It is in this later source that Fatima's preeminence over Maryam is made explicit in a variation of this scene not narrated on `A'isha's authority.

Ibn `Abd al-Wahhab, the Shi`i author who wrote around 448/1056-57, also describes Fatima as al-batul, "the virgin," and "Maryam the greater."[35] The same source further details Fatima's critical maternal role and her similarities with Maryam in this regard. As the mother of sons and particularly of Husayn, the martyr par excellence of Shi`i Muslim memory and ritual, Fatima's link to Maryam becomes more explicit. Indeed, it provides the logical foundation on which to embellish her legacy and the details of her unique sacred biology. Ibn `Abd al-Wahhab recounts, without benefit of a chain of authorities, that Fatima bore Hasan and Husayn from her left thigh while Maryam delivered the messiah from her right.[36] Virginity for Fatima in the Islamic context does not imply a miraculous conception, as it does for Maryam. Indeed, the emphasis on the very human Shi`i genealogy of the imams precludes such a suggestion. Rather, the title "virgin" applied to Fatima signals the absence of menses, a biological factor which was described as "illness" in the Qur'an (2: 222) and necessitated various Islamic purity rituals for all Muslim women. The miraculous forms of childbirth demonstrated by Fatima and Maryam in this Shi`i source also underscore their shared, exceptional freedom from the polluting effects of parturition as defined in Islamic practice. Fatima is also called al-tahira, "the pure," by the same author, a term applied a century earlier as an epithet for `A'isha.[37] The phrase functions rather differently in praise of each woman. In its application to Fatima, the phrase means purity in the sense of freedom from menstruation.[38] The title is a variation of the verbal forms which in the Qur'an refer to both Maryam and the ahl al-bayt, the phrase synonymous with Muhammad's family including Fatima, `Ali, Hasan, and Husayn, all of whom are made pure.[39] In `A'isha's case, the term refers to her chastity as part of her exoneration from adultery, an application stressing the volatile connection between honor and shame, between female chastity and its opposite. The application to Fatima, while a parallel to the earlier usage in `A'isha's case, is a more completely positive feminine usage and links her alone once more in Shi`i works to the Qur'anic Maryam.

In the Qur'an, the mother of Jesus is described as *siddiqa*, the woman who tells the truth. This exact Qur'anic phrase is also applied to Fatima in fourth/tenth-century Shi`i hadith.[40] The epithet *al-siddiqa*, in the previous century had already become synonymous with `A'isha, just as the masculine version of the same phrase had described her father. Following the previous male-female Sunni parallel, in the same Shi`i hadith, Fatima's husband `Ali is also termed *siddiq*. The Shi`i replication of these titles frames an overt religiopolitical definitional struggle, but in Fatima and `Ali's case more clearly linked wife and husband to the Qur'anic Maryam and Jesus, both of whom are mentioned in the Shi`i source as precedents. The pivotal presence of the angel Gabriel is also newly detailed in fourth/tenth-century Shi`i hadith as the divine intercessor in the arrangement of Fatima's marriage to `Ali.[41] Once again, the pattern of `A'isha's early, more developed uniqueness is qualified by Fatima's later evolving medieval historical persona as presented in Shi`i sources.

Both Khadija and Fatima are confirmed as part of the continuum of exemplary female figures within the Islamic community through comparison with Maryam.[42] Yet, in the earliest sources, a challenge to their exclusive connection to the mother of Jesus would also be found in the depiction of `A'isha. The stakes in this contest for merit and demonstrable excellence were high in the medieval Islamic world for what appeared to be a debate about exclusively feminine merit was inextricably bound to larger definitions of communal faith and politics.

`A'isha

`A'isha's portrayal in the earliest written Arabic material developed into an implicit and explicit comparison with her two most notable rivals: Khadija and Fatima. Unlike Khadija and Fatima, `A'isha's long life was extensively documented in the earliest written Arabic materials. `A'isha had been married nine years when the Prophet died. At eighteen she began the remaining fifty years of her life as a childless widow forbidden by the Qur'an to remarry, but still acknowledged as the favorite wife of the late Prophet. As her life was recorded in writing, the authors who preserved and shaped `A'isha's legacy already knew that she had once been accused of adultery, taken part in the first civil war, and contributed as an authority on tradition to the preservation of the communal memory. The determination of `A'isha's legacy, even among her supporters, from the first contended with aspects of an active, controversial historical persona. While the absence of detail about Fatima in early materials might open the way for later positive evolution, `A'isha's known biography came replete with incidents that could not be dismissed or overwritten, only interpreted. The very richness of her life as it first entered into the written record precluded a trajectory of exclusively positive invention. Other strategies would have to be summoned in support of `A'isha's legacy.

Praise of `A'isha also involved reference to the Qur'anic Maryam and the wife of pharaoh. In the earliest traditions, the linkage of `A'isha with these two Qur'anic ideals most often took the form of an implicit, rather than an explicit comparison. Indeed, a series of traditions which may have evolved or coexisted in two versions in the third/ninth-century written record reveals once more the distinctly different pattern taken by the development of `A'isha's legacy. The content of these hadith represents `A'isha's superiority over women in a simile which likens her to al-tharid, a dish of bread and meat said to be the Prophet's favorite meal: "The superiority of `A'isha over [other] women is like the superiority of al-tharid over other food."[43] Tharid consists of bread crumbled into small pieces with broth. Meat is usually part of the concoction.[44] The history of this dish is documented in early sources as part of Muhammad's great-grandfather's legacy. He apparently cooked the dish in Mecca during a time of famine and introduced tharid in Syria where, allegedly, it "attracted the attention of the Byzantine emperor."[45] Given the high visibility of this gastronomic device in the early written Islamic record, Muhammad's preference for it might be seen as a form of respect for a revered ancestor or merely confirmation of his great-grandfather's culinary expertise. However, when the Prophet's preference for special food is transferred to an evocation of `A'isha, praise for his favorite wife takes on a distinctly sensual dimension. A less popular tradition describes the Prophet's predilection for `A'isha in terms of "butter with dates."[46] The Prophet's terms of preference for `A'isha place her in the category of his sexual desire, a description in marked contrast to the more ethereal portraits of Khadija and Fatima.

Eleven third/ninth-century traditions connect tharid with `A'isha's superiority. The majority are related on the authority of Anas ibn Malik

(d. 91-93/709-711), three originate with `A'isha and one with Abu Musa al-Ash`ari (d. 42/662).[47] As a child of ten, Anas ibn Malik was brought to the Prophet as a servant and is attested as the originator of a tremendous amount of hadith.[48] After the Prophet's death, he took part in the wars of conquest and became a resident of Basra. He is described as the last of the Prophet's companions to die in that town. It has been suggested that he supported `Ali against `A'isha in the first civil war. His longevity is attested, but not his date of death. Although he is the originator of eight of the eleven traditions which compare `A'isha's superiority to that of tharid, Anas ibn Malik is also the authority of the three traditions which reckon Khadija, Fatima, Maryam, and Asiya among the women of the worlds.[49] His presence in the promotion of the women closest to the Prophet suggests the importance of his prestige in the process of documenting female idealization. However, the life and trajectory of these reports are not solely dependent on the originator of the tradition, the most probable point of false attribution, but in their later placement and integration into the broader structure of Islamic thought and argument. The fact that `A'isha also reports this utterance of the Prophet suggests that it was received as a positive part of her depiction.

The third source for the transmission of this tradition is Abu Musa al-Ash`ari, who is described as a native of Yemen and companion of the Prophet who traveled to Medina with fifty members of his tribe of al-Ash`ar and accepted Islam in the year 7/628.[50] He served as governor of Basra and Kufa, ruling in Kufa when the first civil war began. He swore allegiance to `Ali on behalf of the Kufans, but called on them to remain neutral, for which stance he was dismissed from the governorship by the fourth caliph. He was chosen, apparently because of his neutrality, as an arbitrator at Siffin, although Shi`i authors argue that Abu Musa was not `Ali's choice to represent him, a suggestion supported by Abu Musa's later declaration that `Ali be deposed as caliph.[51] Abu Musa relates only one of these short hadith about `A'isha and tharid, but he will prove a much cited point of origin for a more elaborate variation of these traditions. He is recorded, in a later biography of `A'isha, concerned with those who related tradition, as one of the Prophet's companions who related from her.[52] In the same source, his single hadith about tharid is included as traceable directly to the Prophet Muhammad.

The short versions of the tradition found in hadith collections, which are divided by subject rather than relater, place this account in sections that record the merits of `A'isha or those dedicated to food.[53] One places two hadith in a section dedicated to explaining why men love some women more than others.[54] The placement of these hadith in the earliest collections indicate that the terms of `A'isha's superiority, as defined by the Prophet's preference for her, merge in the arena of sexual appetite. These references span the third and early fourth Islamic centuries as set down by their earliest and latest compilers from 241/845 to 313/915.[55] Although a chapter is devoted to the excellence of tharid and Muhammad's preference for it, in the fourth/tenth-century Shi`i hadith collection of al-Kulayni, there is no mention of `A'isha in the chapter.[56]

During the same period, a variant of the tradition concerning `A'isha and tharid is recorded that introduces the figures of Maryam, the mother of Jesus, and Asiya, the wife of pharaoh.

There are many perfect men, but there are no perfect women except Maryam bint `Imran and Asiya, the wife of pharaoh. And the superiority of `A'isha over [other] women is like the superiority of tharid over other food.[57]

In these ten traditions the short sentence attested elsewhere during the same period remains, but an additional sentence featuring Maryam and Asiya is also included. All of the long versions of the hadith are related on the authority of Abu Musa al-Ash`ari.[58] The statement that "there are no perfect women except" Maryam and Asiya implicitly rules out Khadija and Fatima as perfect or comparable to these Qur'anic ideals. However, it is also clear that `A'isha, unlike Maryam and Asiya, is described in relation to superiority, not perfection. The separation of these concepts, the chasm between types of praise, is reinforced by the composition of the two-sentence tradition itself. Neither sentence relies upon the other grammatically or semantically. Indeed, in one instance the order of the sentences is completely reversed.[59] The inversion demonstrates that the implications of the tradition are not affected by sentence order. Each can stand alone as, indeed, the short utterance involving `A'isha and tharid does in eleven other instances. In subject-oriented hadith collections, the placement of these longer traditions suggests the variety of categories to which their content was thought to conform. In the category of meritorious praise one is mentioned on the chapter devoted to `A'isha and one, oddly, in the chapter dedicated to Khadija.[60] Two are found in the chapter entitled "prophets," more specifically sections of traditions dedicated to Maryam and Asiya, respectively.[61] Three accounts occur under sections which describe food, two sub-sections being specifically dedicated to tharid.[62] These divisions of presentation suggest at once praise for `A'isha, an attempt at conjoining the Qur'anic images of Maryam and Asiya with the Prophet's wife, and the continued presence of the dish tharid.

Intended as an indictment of the lack of perfect women normative to the abundance of flawless men, the presence of Maryam and Asiya appears to enhance `A'isha's prestige. The implication of the tradition is that `A'isha participates, by association, in an exceptional and perfect female triad. Yet the wife of the Prophet's truest point of comparison is with food, the desirable, superior tharid. Proximity to the two Qur'anic female ideals emphasizes the circumscribed sphere of `A'isha's praise as sexual rather than spiritual. She remains better than other women because of the Prophet's taste. She is Muhammad's wife in the flesh, her sexuality the object of his desire, designated in the tradition's key simile as appetite. Unlike the perfect Maryam and Asiya nowhere does `A'isha transcend her primary fleshly appeal. The categories which emanate from the longer tradition inadvertently reinforce the divide between the Qur'anic ideals Maryam and Asiya and the historical persona of `A'isha. Just as `A'isha's legacy and earthly attributes distinguish between the physical and sacred realities of her role as wife, the tradition in which she is compared to tharid places her solidly in the sexual realm, implicitly separating her from the two ideal women of the Qur'an.

It is critical in the earliest hadith that no tradition combines `A'isha with Khadija and Fatima, although all three Muslim women are praised in regard to the Qur'anic figures of Maryam and Asiya. This division suggests that by the third/ninth century Khadija and Fatima had come to represent a distinct exemplary vision of the Islamic feminine. The proponents of the superiority of all three women utilized parallel, obviously competing precedents to establish their candidates' preeminence as female ideals. Indeed, only Khadija, Fatima, and `A'isha, of all the women closest to the Prophet Muhammad, are compared to female Qur'anic figures. The struggle documented in third/ninth-century hadith collections extends logically into the earliest fourth/tenth-century chronicles and Qur'anic commentary. In his work as historian and exegete, al-Tabari documented the presence of `A'isha in reference to Maryam in chronicle and the critical absence of the Prophet's wife in the explication of key Qur'anic verses.

As the compiler of a voluminous world history which begins with creation, al-Tabari (d. 310/923) includes an explicitly stated comparison between `A'isha and Maryam in his chronicle. In a description of her marriage to the Prophet Muhammad, `A'isha lists the nine special attributes bestowed upon her and no other woman except Maryam.[63] What is curious and significant in al-Tabari's chronicle is the unexplained association of `A'isha with Maryam. It has been observed that the list found in al-Tabari relates `A'isha in no discernible way to Maryam.[64] Certainly it is true that the linkage is not clear from the list given in the chronicle, but there are extant, if implicit, parallels between the two female figures.

Three aspects of the description of `A'isha and Maryam represent strikingly potent and unique points of comparison in their portrayal.[65] It has already been noted that the angel Gabriel plays a significant role in designating both women as the objects of divine intervention. The involvement of the angel in `A'isha's marriage and vindication from adultery form the core of her divine legacy. Maryam is also visited in the Qur'an by the spirit of God in the likeness of a "perfect man" (19: 17). Elsewhere in the Qur'an angels give her tidings (3: 45). In post-Qur'anic literature, the figure of the anonymous man will be positively identified as the angel Gabriel. It is this spirit that announces to Maryam her divinely ordained role as the mother of the prophet Jesus in the Qur'an. Moreover, both women are described as *siddiqa*, "truthful." `A'isha, for whom the title replicates that of her father, has most often been designated as *al-siddiqa*, "the just, believing, or righteous woman." In the context of the accusation of adultery made against her, she is literally "the woman who tells the truth" in maintaining her innocence. The epithet *al-siddiqa* thus separates her from the *ahl al-ifk*, "the people of the lie," who spread and maintain the rumor of her adultery.[66] `A'isha's trial is one brought on by aspersions made against her chastity. In Maryam's Qur'anic portrayal, she too is accused of sexual misconduct when, unmarried, she appears before her people with the baby Jesus. Predictably, they denounce her as unchaste (19:27–28). In both instances the verses that refer implicitly to `A'isha and explicitly to Maryam describe the claims against them as "a tremendous calumny."[67] The baby Jesus defends his mother from the cradle, proving her innocence by the miracle of his speech (19: 29–30). Thus, in the Qur'an, Maryam is termed *siddiqa*, "a truthful woman," the verbal form of the epithet later synonymous with `A'isha (5: 75). Neither woman once accused of adultery is able to vindicate herself by her own testimony. In the depiction of `A'isha and Maryam, it is their unique relationships to male prophets that precipitate their exoneration. Muhammad, husband and prophet, will reveal `A'isha's innocence from Allah as a divine communiqué; Jesus, son and prophet, will miraculously speak in defense of his mother, Maryam.

Finally, both Maryam and `A'isha wish for complete oblivion during moments of personal trial: Maryam in the throes of childbirth (19: 23) and `A'isha at the end of her life.[68] Each woman's use of the exact same powerful phrase is pointed. Maryam wishes to avoid the physical pain of motherhood in the very human birth of Jesus described in the Qur'an. `A'isha, reflecting on her life and forecasting her legacy as she faces death, apparently wished to evade responsibility for her actions in the first civil war. These three shared attributes are specific to each woman in the manifestation of divine significance and Qur'anic epithets and terminology. It is possible that in the development of `A'isha's legacy, these subtle references reflect another form of linkage with the figure of Maryam. Muslim believers, sensitive to the motifs and specificity of Qur'anic language, may have noted these parallels between the descriptions of `A'isha and Maryam. Al-Tabari's account signals that `A'isha's legacy continued to be defined in relation to the Qur'anic Maryam, but it would take nearly five hundred more years before that connection was made explicit.[69] In contrast, Fatima's explicit ties to Maryam emphasized her maternity and purity while `A'isha's relationship to this same Qur'anic ideal promoted the remembrance of the accusation of adultery, an historical episode whose outcome underscored the problematic issue of female sexuality. Through comparison with the same Qur'anic female figure, the legacies of Fatima and `A'isha assumed very different symbolic interpretations.

Al-Tabari's tenuously stated connection between `A'isha and Maryam

in chronicle is confirmed in his Qur'anic exegesis. In this earliest Qur'anic commentary, Fatima and Khadija emerge triumphant in the explication
of Allah's revealed verses about Maryam. These ties are built on the selective employment of traditions written earlier in the third/ninth century.
The critical verses of the Qur'an in which the women closest to the
Prophet Muhammad are featured are not those which define Asiya and
Maryam as examples "for those who believe," as stated in sura 66: 11-12,
but rather those found in sura 3: 42 which define the mother of Jesus
alone as "chosen," "made pure," and "preferred" "above [all] the women of
the worlds."[70]

In explicating these Qur'anic verses, al-Tabari records a microcosm of
preexistent traditions about Khadija and Fatima. Related on `Ali's author-
ity, al-Tabari records two instances which define Maryam and Khadija as
the best of their women or the best of the female inhabitants of heaven.[71]
In one other reference, Maryam is described as preferred by the Prophet
"over [all] the women of the worlds," whereas Khadija is preferred by him
"over [all] the women" of his community. The Qur'anic phrase "women of
the worlds," is also twice applied to the female quartet of Maryam, Asiya,
the wife of pharaoh, Khadija, and Fatima. These references to Maryam are
qualified by asides about the best of women truly belonging to the tribe of
Quraysh because "they ride camels," whereas Maryam rode only an ass.[72]
Muhammad's preference for his own tribe of Quraysh is also an implicit
nod toward the superiority of its most prominent female members,
Khadija and Fatima.

Fatima is compared to Maryam only once in the deathbed scene with
her father which, we are now told, takes place in `A'isha's house. Fatima,
still prompted by `A'isha as interlocutor, recounts details which extol
both her mother and herself. The Prophet refers to the deceased Khadija
as "a wife from among the women of the worlds" of whom he had been
deprived. He then describes his daughter Fatima as "mistress of the
women of heaven, except for Maryam the virgin."[73] As `A'isha had framed
the exaltation of both these women in earlier, separate hadith, the two
objects of her praise are here joined in the same account, thus doubly
diminishing her own prestige.

`A'isha's absence from any positive association with the Qur'anic vers-
es pertaining to Maryam is most obvious in one tradition cited by al-

Tabari, which begins: "There are many perfect men, but there are no perfect women except . . ."The phrase replicates the introductory sentence
of the ten versions which earlier in the third/ninth century link, however indirectly, Maryam, Asiya, and `A'isha:

There are many perfect men, but there are no perfect women except
Maryam bint `Imran and Asiya the wife of pharaoh. And the superiority of
`A'isha over [other] women is like the superiority of tharid over other food.[74]

However, the exceptional women in the version cited by al-Tabari include
Maryam and Asiya, but not `A'isha. Instead, Khadija and Fatima replace her:

There are many perfect men, but there are no perfect women except Maryam
and Asiya the wife of pharaoh and Khadija bint Khuwaylid and Fatima bint
Muhammad.[75]

Al-Tabari's version of this tradition even replicates the exact chain of
transmission, beginning with Abu Musa al-Ash`ari that had once been
applied to earlier, similar accounts dedicated to `A'isha.[76]The presence of
this peculiar, previously unattested tradition in al-Tabari's exegesis raises
questions about attribution, selectivity, and placement of evidence in the
explication of the Qur'an. More importantly, it suggests at least a suspicious borrowing and at worst, a forged tradition, wrought or included
by the author in order to promote Khadija and Fatima in relation to the
Qur'anic Maryam at `A'isha's expense. Indeed, the tradition signals the
possibility that terms of praise for `A'isha could be reworked and circu-
lated, with the same transmitting chain of authorities, to support the rival
exemplary claims of Khadija and Fatima in Sunni sources.[77]
　　The inclusion of this curious tradition about the perfection of Khadija
and Fatima in relation to Maryam and Asiya functions effectively at many
levels. Hadith criticism focused on the reliability of individuals in the
chain of transmission. The chain is impeccable in al-Tabari's commentary
as it was in earlier hadith collections where it appears to support rather
different content concerning `A'isha. Even if it were grafted onto a suspi-
cious core report, the support for that content would stand up to the
usual scrutiny applied to the chain of relaters. The structure of the content

functioned at two levels: structural and semantic. As previously demonstrated, the original phrase recounting the perfection of Maryam and Asiya remained separate grammatically from the additional sentence about `A'isha, superiority, and tharid. Structurally and semantically, it was possible to delete the phrase concerning `A'isha. To praise Khadija and Fatima as perfect exceptions one need only append an "and" to the original sentence featuring Maryam and Asiya.

Moreover, the context in which this tradition appears to emerge promotes consistency with extant traditions which conclude that there are only four women who are the most excellent. Maryam, Asiya, Khadija and Fatima had been previously defined as the best of the women of heaven or among the women of the worlds. Khadija and Fatima could now, without suspicion, be considered among the only four perfect women. The inclusion of Khadija and Fatima in this perfect foursome also worked well to eliminate `A'isha from a kind of praise which had never effectively defined her. Even in the hadith featuring the perfect Maryam and Asiya, `A'isha's presence had not been defined in terms of perfection. `A'isha had never previously been described as among "the women of the worlds," the Qur'anic phrase which gained Khadija and Fatima entry in two early hadith to realms of unqualified excellence. In al-Tabari's exegesis previous inferences about `A'isha and perfection represented in earlier hadith would not simply be lost, they would be expunged and replaced by rival claims. In this context, Sunni exegesis of the Qur'an would seem to confirm the direction of contemporary Shi`i hadith, most particularly concerning Fatima.

Biographical considerations also functioned in smoothing the way of this evolutionary process. Maternity and purity were two powerful factors which promoted Khadija and Fatima as exalted women. Fatima's evocation, in particular, would be propelled by an active religiopolitical constituency who supported her husband and her male children. Despite the earlier, more frequent connections made between Khadija and Maryam, Shi`i Muslim partisanship drove the promotion of Fatima as daughter, wife, and, most importantly, mother par excellence. And it is as mother, that Fatima would finally and most firmly be linked to the Qur'anic Maryam. Sunni Muslims also concurred with their Shi`i coreligionists about Fatima's powerful importance within the family of the Prophet

Muhammad, but for political reasons, they would emphasize her importance as daughter rather than mother thus promoting her tie with Khadija.

In contrast, `A'isha's connections with Maryam although possible to elaborate upon were not so completely positive for the Sunni community. Muslim supporters could describe her in terms of the Qur'anic verses relating to Maryam as "chosen," but the divine arrangement of her marriage by Gabriel would be overshadowed by renewed discussion of her heavenly exoneration from the charge of adultery. They could not easily describe `A'isha as "made pure" in such a context without raising issues which reiterated the aspersions once cast upon `A'isha's chastity.[78] The description of `A'isha as "preferred above the women of the worlds" would never be made in these early centuries. The most consistent linkage between Maryam and `A'isha, divine intervention in defense of their impugned sexual conduct and subsequent vindication, hardly supported a vision of the Prophet's wife as a perfect female. Even Sunni Muslim supporters of `A'isha's specialness could not have been immune from such considerations. Indeed, Shi`i Muslims would capitalize on these very issues to attack the Sunni community through the remembrance of the aspersions cast upon `A'isha in this matter. Purity and maternity would prevail as preeminent ideal categories for the feminine in Qur'anic exegesis, linking Maryam with the women closest to the Prophet. Fatima's limited early biography most easily accommodated such directions for elaboration; `A'isha's did not.

It is impossible to fathom whether or not al-Tabari understood fully the implications of his inclusion of this tradition in his exegesis. He was, apparently, accused of harboring Shi`i sympathies, but a confession of faith made by him late in life suggests that he acknowledged the Sunni Muslim order of caliphs beginning with `A'isha's father Abu Bakr.[79] However, although the acceptance of Abu Bakr as first and `Ali as the fourth caliph became a litmus test for Sunni Muslim affiliation, it has been noted that al-Tabari refers only to `Ali in this declaration as "the commander of the faithful" and "imam."[80] It is possible that his sympathies were more subtle than could be determined by simply stating the Sunni-defined political order of the first four caliphs. The support he summons for the women closest to the Prophet provides additional insight. Although his profession of faith mentions none of these women by name, by stacking the exegeti-

cal deck in favor of Khadija and Fatima, al-Tabari could less conspicuously demonstrate support for `Ali and his family, a position which was not
inconsistent with either Sunni Muslim affiliation or emerging concepts of
Islamic female ideals. Al-Tabari's selectivity reflects a shared Sunni and
Shi`i reverence for Khadija and Fatima in the fourth/tenth century. His
precedent-setting interpretation in the earliest exegesis of the Qur'an
effectively determined the absence of `A'isha and the definitive presence
of Khadija and Fatima in their association with the Qur'anic Maryam. The
effect of al-Tabari's selection of tradition to explain the Qur'anic verses
on Maryam reverberates in later presentations of `A'isha's legacy amidst
the politics of praise, a process in which al-Tabari's selectivity in chronicle and exegesis verifies the shared, unqualified basis of Sunni and Shi`i
Muslim support for Khadija and Fatima over `A'isha.

   Three hundred years later a Sunni jurist in Damascus, in his biographical dictionary dedicated to the wives of the Prophet, would attempt to
reconcile Khadija and Fatima's linkage to Maryam and Asiya with `A'isha.
In this process, Ibn `Asakir (d. 620/1223) at once included and excluded
`A'isha from the predominant, earlier medieval female quartet of ideals.
Thus, he restates al-Tabari's exegetical hadith about perfect women with
an important numerical qualification and, in a novel addition, tacks on the
short separate hadith about `A'isha and al-tharid:

There are many perfect men, but there are no perfect women except four:
Maryam bint `Imran, and Asiya wife of pharaoh, and Khadija bint Khuwaylid
and Fatima bint Muhammad. And the superiority of `A'isha over [other]
women is like the superiority of al-tharid over other food.[81]

Ibn `Asakir makes explicit in his version that there are now only four per-
fect women. Thus, `A'isha's inclusion in the hadith, forged on the prece-
dent of her superiority over other women, also clarifies the terms of her
exclusion from the realm of the two Qur'anic ideals: Maryam and Asiya.
The result of this graft of the tradition concerning `A'isha serves to defin-
itively separate the terms of her praise and solidify the more exalted
medieval precedent of Khadija and Fatima.[82]

   A unique, slightly later treatise by the Egyptian Sunni author al-Zarkashi
(d. 794/1392) suggests that the task of Shi`i Muslims in their attacks on

`A'isha may, inadvertently, have been facilitated by the early failure of her supporters to fully integrate the image of the wife of the Prophet with Qur'anic female ideals. Al-Zarkashi's work is dedicated to `A'isha's corrections of the traditions authored by Muhammad's companions. Al-Zarkashi introduces his work by listing `A'isha's forty special attributes. The number forty, a convention and title in later hadith collections of that number, represents a clear amplification of earlier third/ninth and fourth/tenth-century lists of `A'isha's nine or ten merits. Al-Zarkashi, in seeming defiance of his Shafi`i legal school's doctrinal statements, champions `A'isha's primacy of place as the most exalted female of the Muslim community. In so doing, he acknowledges that there remained much debate concerning the relative ranking of Khadija and `A'isha, but he surprisingly asserts that only Shi`i Muslims believe the best of Muhammad's wives to be Khadija.[83] Sunni Muslims, he states, declare `A'isha to be "the most excellent of the women of the worlds."[84] He supports this claim by stating that `A'isha, Maryam, and Asiya all bear that key Qur'anic designation. Once again, `A'isha's supremacy over other women in the Muslim community depends upon a demonstrated continuity with the exemplary women of the Qur'an.

Al-Zarkashi's approach is unusual in two respects. First, he adopts a Qur'anic phrase that five hundred years earlier had been most consistently associated with `A'isha's rivals, Khadija and Fatima. Then he produces the long version of the hadith that in the third/ninth century had united Maryam and Asiya as perfect women with `A'isha, superiority, and tharid. What is striking about al-Zarkashi is that, for the first time, he attempts to make explicit the import of the tradition. Thus, he contends that "there is no preference which belongs to the first two [Maryam and Asiya] that does not apply to the last [`A'isha]." His statement, in effect, places `A'isha in the realm of Maryam, Asiya, and perfection. Al-Zarkashi's elaboration emphasizes both the problem with the tradition and the potential latent in the comparison of `A'isha with Maryam and Asiya.

Al-Zarkashi's unusual methodology helps explain why his solitary attempt failed as a response to a cultural precedent that would continue to support the preeminence of Fatima and Khadija in association with Qur'anic figures. His unique explication for `A'isha's superiority represents a definite case of too little argumentative assertion on her behalf too late. Al-Zarkashi belatedly demonstrates that `A'isha's implicit association with Maryam and Asiya could not effectively challenge the already predominant image of the four women of the worlds as Khadija, Fatima, Maryam, and Asiya. Early exclusion of `A'isha from this quartet also encouraged al-Tabari's curious adaptation of these same four women as "perfect," despite evidence that Khadija and Fatima were not originally included in such a designation. It is not, therefore, surprising to find this same tradition fully accepted in the city of Basra at the turn of the twentieth century. A missionary who spent many years teaching Muslim girls records in her memoirs that she had so many Fatimas and Khadijas in her class that she had "to number them." When she inquired about the reason for the popularity of these names, one of her students informed her that Fatima and Khadija were considered "two of the four women" designated by the Prophet Muhammad as "perfect." The other two perfect women, stated her source, were Maryam and Asiya.[85] The tradition favored by al-Tabari in the fourth/tenth century would have appealed to the Sunni as well as the numerous Shi`i inhabitants of Basra in the twentieth century.

The Debate About `A'isha and Communal Identity

The debate about the most excellent woman in the Islamic community would continue to draw upon the tissue of associations established in ninth/third-century traditions and tenth/fourth-century chronicle and exegesis. Notions about the premier male and female personages close to the Prophet emerge more explicitly in later declarations and defenses of Sunni Islam. Traditions concerning the women of the worlds, tharid, and Maryam and Asiya represent early points of reference in this debate repeatedly summoned in later doctrinal and theological sources.

In al-Baghdadi's (d. 429/1037) work on Sunni theology, a special section is devoted to his exposition of the ranks of women. He begins with a tradition which collapses previous hadith, but emphasizes Qur'anic precedent in his assertion that the "there are four who are mistresses of the women of the worlds . . . and they are: Asiya the wife of pharaoh and Maryam bint `Imran and Khadija bint Khuwaylid and Fatima the daughter of the Prophet of Allah." He continues with an admission that at once confirms and denies his previous sentence. He admits that disagreements remain "concerning the superiority of `A'isha and Fatima."[86] Al-Baghdadi then states that those who follow the theologian al-Ash`ari (d. 324/935) and the Sunni legal school founded by al-Shafi`i (d. 205/820) "prefer Fatima over `A'isha." However, he notes that *al-Bakriyya*, presumably those who trace their descent from Abu Bakr, "claim that `A'isha is more excellent than Fatima." Despite dissent within his own Sunni community, al-Baghdadi, as a member of the Shafi`i law school, asserts that, based on received tradition, there are four women deemed "the most excellent." Thus, he ranks Fatima and Khadija as the most exalted of all women, followed in order by `A'isha, Umm Salama, and finally the Prophet's wife, Hafsa bint `Umar. After these illustrious women, al-Baghdadi declares that only "Allah knows best who is the most excellent." He concludes with a saying that supports the precedence of Muhammad's direct descendants over his marital ties: "All of the daughters of the Prophet are more excellent than his wives."[87] No chains of transmission are present in this exposition, a demonstration of the popularity and pervasiveness of the previously circulating traditions cited.

A credal statement attributed to the jurist and law-school founder Abu Hanifa (d. 150/767), but compiled by one of his students in the fourth/tenth century, equivocates on the discussion of the best woman of the Muslim community and the disagreement over the respective rankings of Fatima and `A'isha. It states that some Muslims thought `A'isha more excellent than Fatima, while others preferred Fatima, thus confirming the debate signaled among Sunnis of the Shafi`i school.[88] The disagreement on this point is described as a choice made by the supporters of each woman as to their primary male points of distinction. `A'isha's preeminence was founded on her husband Muhammad's place with her in heaven, while Fatima's claims for preeminence were also dependent on her tie to her father. It is noteworthy that neither woman's prestige in this doctrinal equivocation is explicitly linked to the order of male political authority where Abu Bakr's primacy is uncontested and `Ali's place positions him no higher than either third or fourth. The Sunni vision of the past and the religiopolitical order of male successors to the Prophet permitted no opposition to Abu Bakr's first rank in this continuum of male excellence. He is placed immediately after the prophets and messengers of Allah in the order of superior men. `A'isha's legacy, always present in the consideration of the most excellent of women, served to support her father's primacy, but did not effectively promote it. Fatima's own ideal priority was not attached to an argument for `Ali's primacy in the Sunni sphere, but her presence effectively qualified `A'isha's historical persona by contrast for all believers. In another statement attributed to Abu Hanifa about the ranking of the most excellent of women, Khadija is determined to be definitively superior to `A'isha. The latter is described as an object of attack by those Shi`i Muslims who rejected the Sunni order of the first four male political successors to the Prophet Muhammad.

Even later in the eighth/fourteenth century, praise of `A'isha would still be coupled with a discussion of the most exemplary woman in the Islamic community and a defense of her reputation. Ibn Taymiyya (d. 728/1328), a Sunni Muslim theologian and jurist of the Hanbali school, in his own profession of faith stresses that Sunni Muslims revere the wives of the Prophet, the mothers of the believers, as "his wives in the next world." Khadija, he declares, in conformity with his Hanbali legal affiliation, has the highest rank.[89] `A'isha follows next in the discussion, with a citation of the hadith that is now synonymous in discussions of `A'isha's exemplary status: "The superiority of `A'isha over [other] women is like the superiority of tharid over other food."[90]

Ibn Taymiyya is more expansive in his praise and defense of `A'isha in his treatise dedicated to the refutation of Shi`i Muslim theology.[91] Couched in a series of Shi`i statements and Sunni responses, Ibn Taymiyya's section on `A'isha merges praise with a detailed defense of her reputation. In this work he declares that Sunni Muslims do not agree about whether `A'isha is the most excellent of women. He does, however, acknowledge that on the authority of Anas ibn Malik and Abu Musa al-Ash`ari, `A'isha's superiority was once compared in a tradition by the Prophet Muhammad to al-tharid. He does not cite the longer version of the tradition, nor does he develop anywhere a praise or defense of `A'isha in terms of the Qur'anic Maryam and Asiya. Instead, he asserts that while Shi`i Muslims slander the wives of the Prophet and `A'isha in particular, they unduly glorify Fatima and her two sons.[92]

Ibn Taymiyya's defense of `A'isha develops into a refutation of Shi`i Muslim opinion concerning the twin horns of equally explosive controversies: the accusation of adultery and her role in the first civil war. Of

particular interest is his attempt to contradict the Shi`i Muslim linkage of
`A'isha with the wives of the prophets Lot and Noah. In the Qur'an, these
two women are cited as "examples for those who disbelieve." Each woman
is described in relation to the betrayal of their prophet-husbands. Hell is
deemed their certain destination, a punishment their husbands cannot
prevent (66: 10). Reference to them contrasts decisively with the two
verses that follow, dedicated to the positive ideals of Asiya and Maryam.
Clearly by this time, `A'isha exemplified for Shi`i Muslims the opposite of
a female ideal. The notions of unbelief and sexual transgression are central to the Shi`i Muslim association of `A'isha with these two nonideal
Qur'anic females.

Ibn Taymiyya's rebuttal of these assertions reflects a logical Shi`i Mus-
lim reversal of previous Sunni Muslim attempts to rank her with Maryam
and Asiya. If `A'isha's association with Maryam and Asiya proved hard for
Sunni Muslims to consistently substantiate, an effective form of Shi`i Mus-
lim polemic would logically capitalize on the most negative female figures
found in the Qur'an. In comparing `A'isha with the wives of Lot and
Noah, Shi`i Muslims banished all notions of Abu Bakr's daughter as an
exemplary figure. The challenge for Sunni Muslim theologians such as Ibn
Taymiyya remained the articulation of support for `A'isha despite the dual
vulnerabilities of her legacy to condemnation concerning her sexual and
political behavior.

After the third/ninth century, the question of superior men and
women in the Islamic community was much debated. Eventually, these
decisions hardened into doctrine. Sunni and Shi`i Muslims chose different
men and women as reflections of their communal identities. Although for
Sunni Muslims the male order of religiopolitical authority could not be
altered and the order of reverence would reflect exactly the order of rule
of the first four caliphs—Abu Bakr, `Umar, `Uthman, and `Ali—this doc-
trinal rigidity of the fourth/tenth century was not applied as strictly to
notions of the most excellent women in the Muslim community.

On the Sunni side, legal and theological schools split over the rankings
of Khadija, Fatima, and `A'isha. The Hanbali and Hanafi schools regarded
Khadija as the best of women, followed by `A'isha. Those who followed
the Shafi`i school supported the superiority of Fatima along with the the-
ologians of the Ash`ari persuasion. It is clear that both Sunni and Shi`i

Muslims shared an especially high reverence for Khadija, while Sunni Muslims would themselves admit to differences of opinion about the place of `A'isha in relation to both Fatima and Khadija.

The obvious and most bitter communal divide about rank and reputation became pronounced in the contrast between the presentations of Fatima and `A'isha. Whereas Shi`i Muslims unequivocally supported Fatima as their most excellent female figure, they rejected and reviled `A'isha. Sunni Muslims might include `A'isha as a contender in the contest for the most excellent woman of the Muslim community, but they would never present her as the victor in this quest for definitional superiority. Sunni Muslims sought a distinct inclusive path in support of the emerging medieval legacies of both the Prophet's daughter and `A'isha, the two women who would most clearly exemplify religiopolitical differences within the Muslim community.

However, if Sunni Muslims chose to include and praise `A'isha, her preeminence was never effectively established. Even among Sunni Muslim statements of faith, `A'isha was never defined as unequivocally first in rank. She most often came second to Khadija as wife, or was part of a disagreement concerning Fatima as daughter. If the male exemplars after the Prophet remained inflexible in Sunni doctrine in their order of prestige, their female counterparts did not. In the debate over the ranking of the most excellent Muslim women, the basis of their order had as much to do with their affiliation with men as with their own intrinsic symbolic import.

In maintaining `Aisha's historical persona in relation to Khadija and Fatima, Sunni Muslim scholars were forced to defend her flawed historical legacy. `A'isha could not be idealized because even in the Sunni accounts of her life her existence remained problematic, a source of both communal pride and vulnerability.[93] Her impugned sexual and political persona, as stressed by Shi`i Muslims, made the Sunni community more comfortable with female alternatives to `A'isha whose depictions emphasized the more appealing feminine qualities of obedience, chastity, and motherhood, attributes also supported by their Shi`i Muslim brethren. In selecting and promoting Khadija and Fatima over and above `A'isha, Sunni Muslim theologians confirmed a unified Islamic vision of an idealized feminine gender.

Sunni Confirmations of the Female Ideal: The Ottoman Pictorial Dimension

The endpoint in the medieval development of Sunni Muslim reverence for Khadija, Fatima, and `A'isha may be confirmed through the analysis of an illustrated Ottoman Turkish manuscript. In this biography of the Prophet Muhammad, called the *Siyer-i Nebi*, the importance of all three women is rendered both verbally and visually. The text, drawn from a Turkish work completed by the author Mustafa Darir in 790/1388, details the Prophet Muhammad's life story by drawing upon much earlier works, such as that of the third/ninth-century biographer Ibn Hisham, as well as the medieval Shi`i miracle tales of the sixth/twelfth-century and the seventh/thirteenth-century verse passages of Abu al-Hasan al-Bakri. Thus, the work dedicated originally to a Mamluk sultan in Egypt represents an amalgam of extant Islamic notions about the women closest to the Prophet in the late medieval period.

As illustrated over two centuries later at the request of the Ottoman Sultan Murad III and completed around 1004/1595, the cycle of five extant manuscripts details Muhammad's life in word and miniature. The existence of these miniatures in a civilization generally hostile to representational art may be explained within the broader tradition of Islamic miniature painting as a demonstration of royal privilege and artistic patronage.[94] In such a court context, the miniatures would not have been publicly accessible, but would have been viewed only by a small palace elite. Yet even in this constricted environment, these paintings outline the very different historical legacies of Khadija, Fatima, and `A'isha in the late medieval period. Nowhere is the disjunction in the development of these competing female images so strikingly represented. As written and illustrated, the lives of Khadija, Fatima, and `A'isha remain embedded in the story of the Prophet Muhammad, their shared point of historical prestige. Yet each female figure evolves in unique directions in these sources, suggesting at once a profound continuity and change in their symbolic import. The final Turkish text, based as it was on early and late Arabic sources, reveals layers of accretion and embellishment and sometimes a surprising consistency with its earliest third/ninth-century written materials.

In the illustrated Ottoman Turkish biography of the Prophet, there is a tension between the written and visual images of Khadija, Fatima, and `A'isha. Three themes present in the *Siyer-i Nebi*, which may be examined in each woman's life, are the details of her marriage, divine intervention in the form of the angel Gabriel, and the absence or presence of controversy in communal memory. The miniatures provide evidence for the analysis of continuity and disjunction between written description and pictorialization. In these manuscripts, full of syncretic strands of inspiration from Shi`i miracle tales, the contest for superiority is transformed into a hierarchy of female visibility in a Sunni Muslim political context. Although still normative to the life and example of the Prophet Muhammad, the lives of Khadija, Fatima, and `A'isha are each imbued with a distinct visual significance in these eleventh/sixteenth-century miniatures.

Khadija: Consistency of Depiction in Early and Late Sources

In third/ninth-century Arabic sources, Khadija is instrumental in offering Muhammad employment, an aspect of their lives confirmed in both word and image in the Ottoman manuscript. In one illustration, Khadija gazes on Muhammad from the confines of her house.[95] She makes inquiries as to his name and position in the world, eventually offering him a job in the management of her caravan business. In a subsequent miniature, she offers Muhammad a turban as a token of her esteem.[96] Khadija's marriage to the Prophet takes place shortly thereafter in the text of the *Siyer-i Nebi*, but the only illustration of this event, described in a fashion consistent with the earliest Arabic accounts, features servant women readying the bride's house for her wedding to Muhammad.[97] Khadija's initiative in her preliminary dealings with Muhammad as employee and eventual spouse is consistent in both the Arabic and Ottoman Turkish versions.

The role of the angel Gabriel in the life of Khadija in the Ottoman Turkish manuscript is also consistent with earlier Arabic sources. Khadija, pictured with the angel Gabriel, has to be informed of his presence by her husband. In the miniature, Muhammad introduces his wife to the angel even though Gabriel remains invisible to her.[98] In the Ottoman text, prior to this miniature, Khadija had determined that Gabriel was truly an angel and not a demon because when she removed her veil the Prophet informed her that Gabriel had abruptly disappeared. The angel did not transgress the rules of female modesty and thus confirmed his sanctity. This anecdote is found in the earliest Arabic biography of the Prophet and the later Turkish text of Darir.[99] Khadija does not directly encounter the angel Gabriel, nor is she the object of his visit, but her testing of the angel helps confirm the divine inspiration of her husband's mission. Described as the first convert to the faith of Islam, Khadija was also instructed by her husband on the proper ritual ablutions before prayer.[100] She is thus pictured in the Ottoman manuscript learning from Muhammad about what the angel Gabriel had already instructed her husband. The miniature represents the second time Khadija is visually linked to the presence of the angel Gabriel.[101]

Fatima: Late Medieval Constructions

The description of the Prophet's daughter Fatima in the *Siyer-i Nebi* reveals the disjunction between early and late Arabic sources, but also the incorporation of Shi`i materials into the Turkish text authored by Darir in the eighth/fourteenth century. Shi`i influence in this Turkish text is most apparent in miracle tales that enhance the depictions of Fatima and `Ali. The fact that these details were first incorporated for Sunni patrons at the Mamluk court in Egypt and later illustrated at the request of the Sunni Ottoman sultan two centuries later in Istanbul suggests at once a surprising tolerance for the Shi`i materials and, possibly, the dramatic appeal of these stories. Fatima's persona in particular had become, by the author Darir's time, a figure of popular devotion not just for Shi`i Muslims, but also for Sunni Muslims who followed the mystical path of Sufism.[102] The Ottoman rulers were themselves well aware of Bektashi Sufism, a syncretic, indigenously Turkish form of mystical belief that drew its inspiration, in part, from Shi`ism and had many adherents among the military.

Although sparsely documented in the earliest Arabic biography of the Prophet, the arrangement of Fatima's marriage becomes both a textual and visual focal point in the Ottoman Turkish text as a demonstration of divine intervention. Only in the late medieval Turkish version does the angel Gabriel inform the Prophet that Fatima's husband, as directed by heaven, is to be `Ali ibn Abi Talib. The angel's intervention in the arrangement of this marriage draws its earliest written precedent from Shi'i hadith of the fourth/tenth century.[103] The miniature that illustrates the heavenly pronouncement of Fatima's marriage features the angel Gabriel personally conveying this information to the Prophet.[104] On this page of the Ottoman manuscript, Fatima is described by a string of Shi'i honorifics, including "the virgin," "the chaste," and "the radiant."[105] None of these epithets are present in the earliest Arabic sources detailing the Prophet's life. They are the product of distinctly Shi'i works originating in the fourth/tenth century.

Fatima's proposed marriage inspires in the Ottoman miniatures a variety of miracles that emphasizes her special and unique place in Islamic lore. None of these divinely inspired events are present in the earliest biography of the Prophet. In one miniature in the Ottoman manuscript, a feast without end is served while the Prophet looks on.[106] Fatima is absent from this picture, but the heaven-sent feast is provided on her behalf to celebrate her marriage to 'Ali. The event may echo both the Qur'an, in which Maryam is twice miraculously supplied with food, and Shi'i hadith of the fourth/tenth century, in which special food is also presented to Fatima from on high.[107]

Gabriel's role in these miraculous happenings prompts the deliverance of gifts to Fatima, who receives a vial of perfume from a handsome young man—who is none other than the angel Gabriel in disguise. In the miniature, Fatima, in green, holds the perfume bottle while 'A'isha bint Abi Bakr, one of the two wives of the Prophet present in the scene, reacts with awe to the gift.[108] Another heavenly packet arrives for Fatima, who is seated on the upper right in the scene and is flanked on the left by the Prophet's wife Umm Salama and on the lower right by 'A'isha. In the left-hand panel of the same painting, a servant woman reveals to a crowd of Jewish men the parcel of divine cloth delivered by the angel Gabriel. According to the Siyer-i Nebi the cloth, as a demonstration of the divine inspiration of the Islamic faith, prompts the Jews to convert to Islam (figure 3).[109] This miracle tale, as a demonstration of Fatima's unique favor, is drawn directly from a late medieval Shi'i work of the author al-Qummi (d. 573/1177).[110]

The last of these marriage scenes features the central figure of the Prophet Muhammad conferring his blessing upon Fatima and 'Ali.[111] The

Figure 3. Fatima's receipt of the divine cloth and the conversion of the Jews.
—Turkish MS 419, fol. 44a. By permission of the Chester Beatty Library, Dublin.

miniature emphasizes the divine direction and celebration of the union and implies its earthly genealogical significance. The earliest Arabic biography of the Prophet makes no reference to the miracles surrounding the marriage of Fatima and ʿAli. The one reference in Ibn Hisham to the couple so beautifully rendered in the Ottoman miniature is an anecdote of a rather different sort which describes how ʿAli received the honorific *Abu Turab*, "father of dust." According to Ibn Hisham's third/ninth-century account, when ʿAli was angry with Fatima he would not speak to her, but used to sprinkle dust on his head as a sign of annoyance. When the Prophet noticed this, he knew his son-in-law was upset with Fatima and would ask, "What is your trouble, O Abu Turab?"[112] Not surprisingly, this rather different portrait of a marriage is not textually or visually represented in the Ottoman *Siyer-i Nebi.*

`A'isha: Textual Presence and Pictorial Absence

The earliest biography of the Prophet Muhammad does not describe the circumstances of `A'isha's marriage even though equally early third/ninth-century biographical dictionaries do. Darir's Turkish text details the arrangement of `A'isha's marriage to the Prophet and the role of the angel Gabriel in it in a manner reminiscent of third/ninth-century Arabic accounts. According to the narrative of the Turkish text, the Prophet was instructed to marry `A'isha after the angel presented him with a piece of silk cloth bearing her likeness. Two variations on this incident appear in the Turkish text, one of which surpasses the earliest Arabic sources by detailing `A'isha's physical appearance in novel ways. The *Siyer-i Nebi* describes the young `A'isha as having a "fair complexion, black hair, and black eyes," which are described as *surmeli*, or tinged with kohl. `A'isha's beauty is further exalted as matchless. The angel Gabriel instructs the Prophet in the Turkish account to "marry the girl in the picture."[113]

It would seem from the text that `A'isha's marriage to the Prophet, like Fatima's to `Ali, results from a divine directive. Despite the dramatic potential of this scene as written in the Turkish text and its importance for the Sunni Muslim community, there is no visual depiction of `A'isha's marriage. Instead, emphasis is placed upon the more mundane aspects of the situation. A miniature thus features Abu Bakr with his male companions discussing the Prophet's plans to marry.[114] The only other visual reference to the Prophet's marriage to `A'isha features a female matchmaker figure named Umm Hakim. She is depicted in conversation with the Prophet Muhammad discussing `A'isha's age, which at the time was seven.[115]

The visual images in the *Siyer-i Nebi* are in conflict with the angel Gabriel's textual presence and emphasize the earthly arrangement of `A'isha's marriage at the expense of its divine inspiration. Pictorially absented from her primary and most prestigious link to the Prophet Muhammad, `A'isha's marriage is never depicted visually in the Ottoman manuscripts. The presence of the woman known to Sunni Muslims as the

Prophet's favorite wife is thus suspiciously diminished as the object of pictorial representation. Instead, `A'isha's visibility in miniatures is confined to the role of admiring foil in the miracles inspired by Fatima.

In the Turkish text `A'isha is the recipient of divine intervention a second time. The incident that necessitates Gabriel's aid as divine messenger relates to the false accusation of adultery made against `A'isha. Her vindication from the charge of adultery is received in the earliest Arabic sources without explicit reference to the angel Gabriel. However, in the Turkish text it is the angel Gabriel who bears the heavenly message that vindicates `A'isha.[116]

The controversy became the subject of Sunni Muslim celebration with a decided emphasis on `A'isha's miraculous exoneration. Yet even within this Sunni Ottoman manuscript `A'isha's vindication through divine revelation is not transformed into a miniature. The only miniature in the Ottoman Turkish work that features `A'isha during this period of her life depicts an incident not directly linked to the accusation of adultery. The illustration predates the accusation even though it portrays an event that occurred on the same raid during which the scandal about `A'isha began. In the miniature, `A'isha begs her husband to deal charitably with the daughter of the chief of a conquered Arab tribe.[117] This woman, named Juwayriyya, will later become one of the Prophet's wives. `A'isha is never pictured as the divinely vindicated wife of the Prophet, even when she is dramatically saved through the words of Allah as delivered by Gabriel. Although Sunni Muslims accepted `A'isha's exoneration, they also understood that the incident provoked a slanderous response from Shi`i Muslims.

The Ottomans were well aware of their coreligionists' antipathy toward the wife of the Prophet. Five years before the completion of the *Siyer-i Nebi*, in 999/1590, the Ottomans dictated their victorious treaty terms to the Shi`i Safavid dynasty of Iran. Among other things, the Sunni Ottomans instructed their Shi`i military opponents not to slander "`A'isha the chaste."[118] Sunni communal vulnerability regarding this incident may explain why the only visual representation of the accusation made against `A'isha features the Prophet Muhammad forgiving those who spread rumors about his wife.[119]

The last critical role played by `A'isha in the earliest Arabic biography of the Prophet relates to her proximity to her husband during his final illness and death. In the earliest Arabic sources and the Turkish text, the Prophet dies in `A'isha's arms, but there is no extension of the scene as written. Instead, Fatima, who had played no role in the earliest biography of the Prophet, is featured in the visual depiction of Muhammad's last days. In the final series of miniatures in the Ottoman manuscript, `A'isha has not merely been passed over as a part of her husband's life, she has been replaced by his daughter. In one miniature Fatima keeps company with the angel Gabriel at her dying father's bedside. In another, her two sons weep with her in Muhammad's sickroom.[120]

Continuity and Change in the Representation of Islamic Female Ideals

In both early Arabic and late medieval Turkish texts, as in their visual extension, Khadija represents a sanctity defined by stasis. Seven miniatures feature the first wife of the Prophet, two of them with the angel Gabriel. Although Khadija is associated with the angel, their interaction is conducted entirely through the mediation of the Prophet. Khadija's contact with the divine in the pictorial form of the angel Gabriel is indirect and serves primarily to demonstrate her staunch support for the Prophet's religious mission. She is a faithful wife and devout Muslim throughout her textual and pictorial representation, but she is the object of no direct divine blessing or miraculous gift.

In contrast to that of her mother, the depiction of Fatima represents a continuity between text and image based on Arabic, particularly Shi`i, sources of a much later date. If one relied exclusively on the earliest third/ninth-century sources, there would be no written basis for the Ottoman miniatures of Fatima involving the angel Gabriel. Nor would there be any visual evidence for the divine sponsorship of her marriage. The Turkish text definitively demonstrates that Fatima's sparsely detailed early portrayal had been transformed by the time of Darir's work in the eighth/fourteenth century. It is the burgeoning of Shi`i hagiography and miracle tales surrounding Fatima, `Ali, and their children, that establishes the basis for her preeminence in the eleventh/sixteenth-century Ottoman miniatures. Her visual depiction emphasizes the written embellishments which drew upon a particular partisan base for their promotion.

The construction of Fatima's special sanctity is visually unchallenged in the arrangement of her marriage and the role of the angel Gabriel in conveying divine blessings upon her union with `Ali. Ten miniatures feature Fatima in the Ottoman manuscript, three more than her mother and twice as many as `A'isha. Moreover, within these miniatures she, unlike either her mother or `A'isha, is the focus of attention. Although Fatima is exalted in these scenes, she remains the object of others' actions in her marriage as in her miracles. Her passivity makes a clear visual counterpoint to the portrayal of her husband `Ali. He too is featured in the miniatures of the *Siyer-i Nebi*, but it is `Ali's military prowess, his self-engineered, divinely sponsored feats in battle that are celebrated in this same manuscript.

If Fatima's textual and visual image suggests a study in what lends itself to the demonstration of female sanctity for both Sunni and Shi`i believers, the treatment of `A'isha bint Abi Bakr underscores what aspects of an attested historical existence undermine the idealization of a female legacy. Ironically, the role of the angel Gabriel in `A'isha's marriage and divine vindication are more emphasized in the earliest Arabic sources than in either Khadija's or Fatima's treatment. These sources are substantiated in Darir's Turkish text, but none of them are extended to the visual depiction of `A'isha in the Ottoman manuscript illustrated two hundred years later. All of the miniatures involving `A'isha refer to minor incidents that do not emphasize her special place as the Prophet's favorite or the religious prestige attendant upon the role of Gabriel in her marriage and vindication from adultery. Three of the five miniatures depict `A'isha as an admiring spectator when divine blessings are bestowed upon Fatima.

The visual hierarchy for female idealization in these Ottoman miniatures is revealed most clearly by one illustration that exalts Fatima and `A'isha in relation to the Prophet Muhammad (figure 4).[121] The scene is part of a series of miracles bestowed upon Fatima by the angel Gabriel. The mysterious package in the center foreground is the superficial focus of the viewer's gaze. Yet the placement of Fatima and `A'isha in relation to the Prophet Muhammad is also noteworthy. It is Fatima who is seated next to the Prophet. `A'isha follows Fatima moving right to left, the visual order implicit in a civilization where literacy dictated this same direc-

Figure 4. The Prophet Muhammad, Fatima, and ʿAʾisha.
—Turkish MS 419, fol. 40b. By permission of the Chester
Beatty Library, Dublin.

tion of eye movement. In the miniature, Muhammad touches ʿAʾisha's
hand while Fatima places her own hand upon ʿAʾisha. Although Fatima is
the object of the gift from Gabriel, ʿAʾisha's special relationship to the
Prophet is tacitly demonstrated by the placement of Muhammad's hands.

This scene thus brilliantly balances the Sunni Ottoman position, which
emphasizes ʿAʾisha's primacy as the Prophet's favorite wife with the pronounced demonstration of Fatima's unique idealization for both Sunni and
Shiʿi Muslims. In the Ottoman manuscript, as in Sunni medieval doctrinal
statements, the determination of the most excellent Muslim woman never

effectively placed `A'isha above Khadija or Fatima. Both Sunni and Shi`i Muslims agreed that Khadija and Fatima were superior to `A'isha. However, while all Muslims might find communality in their preference for female ideals, they could not agree about the order of male merit. Thus, the Ottoman manuscript ends with a miniature in which `A'isha's father, Abu Bakr, receives the oath of allegiance as caliph after the Prophet's death.[122] No Shi`i text or illustrator would have permitted such a Sunni affirmation of the religiopolitical order.

There appear to be three visual modes of development represented by the miniatures featuring Khadija, Fatima, and `A'isha in the Ottoman manuscript. A separate type of pictorialization may be assigned each female figure, one that conforms with overarching notions of gender and the sacred. Khadija's textual stasis in early and late Arabic sources is affirmed by her visual depiction. She is revered, but her image in the miniatures does not represent a change in her position in Islamic communal perception. The greatest contrast in the depiction of these three female personages may be seen in the nature of the images generated by Fatima and `A'isha.[123] They represent an inversion. Fatima's later but dynamic Shi`i textual development promotes her primacy of place in the miniatures as a reflection of her sanctity. As daughter, wife, and mother, Fatima remains a woman who, unlike other women, neither menstruates nor experiences the ritually polluting effects of childbirth. The epithets in the Ottoman manuscript emphasizing her chastity and transcendence of the usual rules of female biology define an Islamic female ideal who escapes the normal dictates of her sexuality. `A'isha's reputation, in contrast, emphasized her sexuality as the result of a controversy that cast aspersions on her chastity and prompted continued Shi`i slander in the medieval period. `A'isha's prestigious connection to the Prophet is only visually realized once.

What these miniatures do, collectively, is mark the visual endpoint in a medieval process of selection in which the image of the most exalted female figure in Islamic society had already been determined. The lives of Khadija and Fatima possessed the least content and controversy. They thus became the easiest to idealize. Only in one brief series of third/ninth-century traditions did the portrayal of `A'isha threaten their more elevated status, but by definition superiority cannot be qualified and `A'isha's past made the development of an unflawed legacy impossible. Khadija and Fatima alone, therefore, would be developed as ideals and defined, unconditionally, as models for new generations of Sunni and Shi'i Muslim believers. `A'isha's legacy alone defied idealization as completely as it denied comfortable categorization, a point on which medieval Muslims reached consensus about her controversial historical persona.

six *the last word:*

a note in conclusion

> `A'isha's services to Islam entitle her to an eminent
> position in the pages of history . . . . The Muslims
> respect her as the wife of the Prophet and the Moth-
> er of the Believers but no student of history can min-
> imize the supreme qualities of her character or the
> magnitude of her achievement.   —Mumtaz Moin

isha bint Abi Bakr's legacy as a woman allows the historian access to the minds of medieval Muslim men. Their depiction of `A'isha reveals the historiographical process through which her remembrance assumed new, contested meanings in their representations of the past. In defining this controversial woman, these men revealed much about themselves and the importance of interpretation. As configured in communal preservation, `A'isha's life and legacy fused inextricably so that memory and meaning became one. Her life, subsumed into the sphere of multifaceted symbol, became the focus of a struggle to define the past, to assert the truth about critical events long over, but ever-present in the elaboration of communal identity. In studying `A'isha, one studies male intellectual history, not a woman's history, but reflections about the place of a woman, and by extension all women, in exclusively male assertions about Muslim society.

`A'isha's legacy forced debate and disagreement, but also a shared synthesis within the medieval Muslim community. Shi`i Muslims were most consistent in subjecting `A'isha to a detailed critique, a form of communal censure that was redolent with religiopolitical significance. Yet `A'isha's negative valence for this minority of Muslims was also effectively applied to support their distinct vision of a shared past, a direction that selected critical details about `A'isha from earlier, non-Shi`i sources. In the Shi`i view, `A'isha was flawed first by association with her father, but also in her actions as wife and widow. Her sexuality and her direct interference in the politics of succession served to enhance her high profile as a negative female figure. Accused of adultery and not exonerated of this charge in Shi`i interpretations of the relevant Qur'anic verses, `A'isha symbolized in one historical persona both the sexual and political dangers of female power. Cast as an assertive figure in the first civil war, her opposition to `Ali incarnated all that was wrong with the Sunni assertion of religiopolitical authority. She could not be a model for women, but she served as a warning directed to them by men about the evils of uncontrolled female intervention in Muslim society. Her words were worthless in transmitting the past, except when they affirmed the excellence of Shi`i paragons such as Fatima and `Ali ibn Abi Talib. `A'isha might serve to enhance their untarnished profiles in the historical record. She might even act out the bases for her own censure, but she would never be allowed more than a monochromatic representation in the Shi`i sphere.

Sunni Muslims best understood `A'isha's complexities and made striking attempts to maintain her difficult presence in the record of their communal experience. While both Shi`i and Sunni Muslims deplored `A'isha's political actions, Sunni Muslims alone found aspects of her historical persona to celebrate. The Sunni Muslim community retained a more nuanced vision of `A'isha, one that allowed both negative and positive components of her depiction to exist simultaneously. They praised her miraculous marriage, her divine exoneration from the charge of adultery, and her ability to transmit hadith. Yet praise for `A'isha was always qualified in the Sunni sphere by the need for a defense of her place in the past, a posture provoked, in part, by Shi`i polemic.

The didactic potential of `A'isha's legacy in the medieval period had potent appeal in Sunni and Shi`i Muslim societies. Through her example, Muslim authors honed their vision of the female and valorized selective aspects of the feminine. Disagreement about `A'isha's inclusion among the most excellent women of the Islamic community ostensibly supports a major communal conflict, but such a divide masks a critical and conciliatory realm of consensus. Both Sunni and Shiʿi Muslims agreed to exclude ʿAʾisha from their most ideal designations of the feminine because they found alternative female figures about whose completely positive qualities all Muslims could concur. In this process of defining communal values, ʿAʾisha's presence appears to challenge cultural constructs, but in the end serves only to confirm them.

In the medieval period Muslim scholars based the elaboration of real women upon female archetypes found in the Qurʾan. They conflated the lives of the women closest to the Prophet Muhammad with those female figures described by Allah in their sacred book. Qurʾanic precedent both directed and constricted the potential meaning of the feminine in Islamic society. Thus, the most positive women of the Qurʾan, by association, determined the most excellent women of Islam. Such a synthesis demanded the development of an artificial consistency between the real and the ideal, between the individual and the communal. ʿAʾisha's historical persona would not easily conform to such narrow definitions of the feminine. Unlike the women supported by all Muslims as unequivocally ideal, ʿAʾisha would be associated not just with the best of Qurʾanic images— Maryam, the mother of Jesus, and Asiya, the wife of pharaoh, but also with the more problematic female figures of Zulaykhaʾ and the wives of the prophets Lot and Noah. The range of ʿAʾisha's associations with Qurʾanic female figures was far greater than any other historical Muslim woman because her persona was impossible to reconcile with the simple prescriptives of perceived positive feminine attributes.

The choices made about ʿAʾisha's presentation in the written historical record involve three separate stages of development. Her elaboration in the medieval period resulted from the confluence of time, place, and the varied tactics of those dedicated to the control of communal memory. In the first phase of ʿAʾisha's development, the singularity of her marital attributes were promoted as a series of divine and human distinctions. The intervention of the angel Gabriel, stressed in the arrangement of her marriage, is further attested by her miraculous exoneration from the charge of adultery. In each of these areas, ʿAʾisha conspicuously narrates the details of her own uniqueness with the pivotal promotion of her relatives and those associated with the Medinan school of history in the second/ eighth century.

These earliest recollections of 'A'isha's positive place in the past were effectively challenged when, in the fourth/tenth century, the majority of Muslims began to define themselves as Sunni in the urban environments of Iraq and Iran. In this same critical century, Shi'i Muslims asserted most fully their own rejection of 'A'isha's historical persona. Her words and those of her partisans would be denied legitimacy, just as 'A'isha's marital legacy, and with it her sexual reputation, would be condemned. Without partisans other than the few descendants of Abu Bakr who alone attested to her primacy of place among the women of the past, Sunni Muslims reworked 'A'isha's precarious presence in light of Shi'i polemic. They did not abandon 'A'isha, but they ceased to make a case for her as the best model for women, for Shi'i Muslims had fully defined her volatile sexual and political liabilities for them. In Sunni exegesis and theology scholars defended 'A'isha, but accepted shared lessons about her contested meaning within the Muslim community. It is during this pivotal century that Sunni and Shi'i Muslims found implicit common ground in their definition of Islamic female ideals.

'A'isha's late medieval resurgence was the result of a new group of Sunni Muslim partisans who promoted her importance in eighth/fourteenth-century Syria and Egypt. She symbolized the transmission of the past for these male Sunni scholars. They championed her legacy, briefly even her primacy, as an extension of their own communal identity. In poems and works of hadith criticism, these men asserted the importance of 'A'isha as a revered conduit of the founding truths of their society. Her prestige and theirs had become intertwined. Their communal honor rested upon the words of a woman scorned, as they knew well, by their Shi'i coreligionists. Support for her truthfulness represented their own exclusive right to prestige as guardians of the past and pillars of the present.

The construction of 'A'isha's legacy represents a case study in the formation of historical reality. The struggle over her meaning definitively reveals that the exclusivity of historical truth in the Muslim community would be belied by its very assertion. The arguments documenting 'A'isha's historical persona reveal that Muslims developed effective strategies for making the past work in their medieval present. Whether they did this in consonance or dissonance, whether they agreed or disagreed, they participated in this process together and, in reaction, arrived at their varied positions. They made choices of consequence in the interpretation of `A'isha and, in so doing, they fashioned future directions and possibilities for all Muslims. In ascertaining what had been, they sought to assert what should be. The power of the past to mimic stasis when presented as historical reality actually masked the hard fought need to conceal conflict, for to allege a single reality meant the certain proof that some truths were irreconcilable, that beneath the mask of effective rationales, there was slippage and other possible directions for the representation of the past.

The Pakistani author Mumtaz Moin, in attacking the single Western biography of `A'isha, defines the author as "like most of the western orientalists" who use "every possible opportunity to make insinuating remarks on Islam and prominent figures in its history."[1] Muslims may not always agree about the modern implications of `A'isha's life, but her legacy is too important to allow Western scholarship to dictate the last word to those for whom her meaning is more than an academic pursuit. Their vehemence on her behalf provides proof not only of the esteem in which Sunni Muslims continue to hold `A'isha, but of their ability to rely upon their own history for sources of present-day direction. Muslims will, ultimately, have the final say in determining `A'isha's modern legacy, but this work suggests that, in so doing, they are the true inheritors of a medieval process of Islamic interpretation. In the modern, as in the medieval period, `A'isha's presence continues to be summoned to support varied ideological strategies.

notes

1. Approaches to the Study of a Legacy: An Introduction

1. David Lowenthal, *The Past Is a Foreign Country*, p. xvii.

2. Muhammad Ibn Saʿd, *al-Tabaqat al-kubra*, 8:78. The earliest, but briefest, written biography may be found in ʿAbd al-Razzaq Ibn Hammam al-Sanʿani, *al-Musannaf*, 11:429–33. Al-Sanʿani (d. 211/827) often cites in his chain of authorities transmitters who can be dated to the late second/eighth century. For the argument that many of these oral sources were originally copied in writing much earlier in the first/seventh century, but survived only in later compilations, see Nabia Abbott, "Hadith Literature," pp. 289–98; and Nabia Abbott, *Studies in Arabic Literary Papyri I: Historical Texts*.

3. Ibn Saʿd derived much of his biographical material on the wives of the Prophet Muhammad from al-Waqidi (d. 207/822), his contemporary and the man he served as secretary in Baghdad. Al-Waqidi's written account on the wives of the Prophet is not extant except as preserved in Ibn Saʿd. If adjusted for an earlier written source, Ibn Saʿd's materials date from twenty-three years earlier, or just under one hundred and fifty years after ʿAʾisha's death. It is also of interest that the written version of Ibn Saʿd, the biographical dictionary which bears his name, appears to have been completed and preserved after his death. Gertrude Stern, *Marriage in Early Islam*, p. 3.

4. ʿAʾisha was born four or five years after Muhammad's prophetic mission began, according to Ibn Saʿd, *Tabaqat*, 8:79. However, a slightly later chronicle suggests that ʿAʾisha was born in the *jahiliyya*, the period before the revelation of Islam to Muhammad. If the latter is true, then ʿAʾisha's age at the time of her marriage might have been twelve

or thirteen, rather than the usually stated nine given in most early sources. Such a suggestion would also throw off her age at the date of her death. For the contradiction, see al-Tabari, *Ta'rikh al-rusul wa al-muluk*, 4:2135.

5. The root in Arabic is `*ysh*. For the potential benefit of such names in a period of high infant mortality, see Annemarie Schimmel, *Islamic Names*, p. 20.

6. For the term as one not generally used until the fourth/tenth century by Muslims, see W. Montgomery Watt, *The Formative Period of Islamic Thought*, pp. 269–70; and Roy Mottahedeh, *Loyalty and Leadership in an Early Islamic Society*, pp. 1–24.

7. Those Shi`i Muslims who supported the fifth Imam Zayd ibn `Ali would not dismiss Abu Bakr as the first caliph, but would designate him as inferior to `Ali.

8. For a more recent reflection of this antithetical pairing, `Umar Abu al-Nasr, `*Ali wa `A'isha*.

9. Joan Scott, *Gender and the Politics of History*, p. 43. Her complex definition of gender does not suggest potential conflations between symbolic and real historical figures and their ability to define social constructions of the female as well as feminine.

10. See, for example, Susan A. Spectorsky, *Chapters on Marriage and Divorce: Responses of Ibn Hanbal and Ibn Rahwayh*, pp. 12, 18, 52, 161, 165, 216, 304.

11. What is true of medieval Christian historical sources is instructive for medieval Islamic ones. See Caroline Bynum, "Jesus as Mother and Abbott as Mother," pp. 167–68.

12. Abbott, *Studies in Arabic Literary Papyri*, 1:6–7; and for specific importance in third/ninth- and fourth/tenth-century chronicles, see R. Stephen Humphreys, *Islamic History: A Framework for Inquiry*, pp. 73–74.

13. G. H. A. Juynboll, *Muslim Tradition: Studies in Chronology, Provenance, and Authorship of Early Hadith*, p. 200; and E. Kohlberg, "Shi`i Hadith," p. 300. In fact, the emphasis is most often on imams as the sources of precedent for the Twelver Shi`i community.

14. For the early critical bases of hadith as they fed more complex Sunni legal articulation, see Spectorsky, *Chapters in Marriage and Divorce*; and for the later maintenance of hadith in these processes, Jonathan Berkey, *The Transmission of Knowledge in Medieval Cairo: A Social History of Islamic Education*, pp. 12–14.

15. Berkey, *Transmission of Knowledge*, pp. 175–81.

16. Nabia Abbott, *Two Queens of Baghdad: The Mother and Wife of Harun al-Rashid*; and Gertrude Stern, *Marriage in Early Islam*, pp. 19 and 22, where she states that after the first generation of Muslim women, it was increasingly unusual for women to be prominent in transmitting Islamic tradition, which explains, for example, why critical early third/ninth-century compilers such as Ibn Hanbal and Ibn Sa`d had few, if any, women teachers. This was not the case in much later medieval environments, see E. M. Sartain, *Jalal al-Din al-Suyuti: Biography and Background*, 1:125–26; and Huda Lutfi, "Al-Sakhawi's Kitab al-Nisa' As A Source for the Social and Economic History of Muslim Women During the Fifteenth Century A.D.," pp. 104–24.

17. For an early example of this position, see Ignaz Goldziher, *Muslim Studies*, 2: 38–189; Joseph Schacht, *The Origins of Muhammadan Jurisprudence*; and more recently,

Michael Cook, *Early Muslim Dogma*, p. 107; and N. J. Coulson, "European Criticism of Hadith Literature," pp. 317–21.

18. Nabia Abbott, *Studies in Arabic Literary Papyri*, II: *Qur'anic Commentary and Tradition*; G. Juynboll, *Muslim Traditions*; M. M. Azmi, *Studies in Early Hadith Literature*; and Muhammad Abdul Rauf, "Hadith Literature I: The Development of the Science of Hadith," in *Arabic Literature*, pp. 271–279.

19. For the discussion of this methodological problem as an essentially historiographical one, see Humphreys, *Islamic History*, pp. 69–103.

20. Michael Cook and Patricia Crone, *Hagarism: The Making of the Islamic World*.

21. John Wansbrough, *The Sectarian Milieu: Content and Composition of Islamic Salvation History*; and Albrecht Noth, *Quellenkritische Studien zu Themen, Formen, und Tendenzen fruhislamischen Geschichtsuberlieferung. I: Themen und Formen*.

22. For an important approach to the dilemma, see R. Stephen Humphreys, "Qur'anic Myth and Narrative Structure in Early Islamic Historiography," pp. 271–90.

23. For examples of this approach, see Erling L. Petersen, `Ali and Mu`awiya in Early Arabic Tradition*; Fred M. Donner, "The Death of Abu Talib"; Marilyn Waldman, "The Otherwise Unnoteworthy Year 711," pp. 240–48; and Marilyn Waldman, *Toward a Theory of Historical Narrative*.

24. As an oral process devalued in contemporary Western society, see Jan Vansina, *Oral Tradition as History*; Nabia Abbott, *Studies in Arabic Literary Papyri*, 2:5–9; Michael Cook, *Muhammad*, pp. 61–67; Patricia Crone, *Meccan Trade and the Rise of Islam*, pp. 215–16, 222; and *Encyclopaedia of Islam*, 2d ed., s.v. "Kissa" and "Kass."

25. Humphreys, *Islamic History: A Framework*, pp. 72–74.

26. For example, Crone, *Meccan Trade*, p. 230, where she argues forcefully: "Without correctives from outside Islamic tradition, such as papyri, archeological evidence, and non-Muslim sources, we have little hope of reconstituting the original shapes of the early period. Spurious information can be rejected, but lost information cannot be regained." This approach is also echoed in Cook, *Muhammad*, p. 67, where he concurs: "The usual practice is to accept whatever in the sources we lack specific reason to reject. This may be the right approach; doubtless there is a historical core to the tradition of Muhammad's life, and perhaps a little judicious selectivity is enough to uncover it. Yet it may equally be the case that we are nearer the mark in rejecting whatever we do not have specific reason to accept, and that what is usually taken for bedrock is no more than shifting sand."

27. Donner, "Death of Abu Talib"; Cook, *Dogma*; Joseph B. Roberts, "Early Islamic Historiography: Ideology and Methodology"; Yahya Khalid Blankenship, "Translator's Foreword," *The History of al-Tabari*, 11: xiii-xxx; Petersen, `Ali and Mu`awiya.

28. Roberts, "Early Islamic Historiography."

29. Donner, "Death of Abu Talib"; Petersen, `Ali and Mu`awiya; and Robertson, "Early Islamic Historiography."

30. Blankenship, "Introduction," pp. xxvii-xxviii.

31. Barbara Herrnstein Smith, "Narrative Versions, Narrative Theories," pp. 209–32, who notes among other things, multiple motivations and sets of interests in any "story."

32. Although most historians of the early Islamic period have ceased to speculate about the nature of history in deference to their own methodologically isolating issues, medievalists of the European past have plunged into the debate: see Gabrielle M. Spiegel, "History, Historicism and the Social Logic of the Text in the Middle Ages," pp. 59–86; Susan Mosher Stuard, "The Chase After Theory: Considering Medieval Women," pp. 135–45; and Judith M. Bennett, "Medievalism and Feminism," pp. 309–32.

33. Michael M. J. Fischer, *Iran: From Religious Dispute to Revolution*, p. 173.

34. For example, Muhammad Khamis, *Al-sayyida `A'isha umm al-mu'minin*; `Abd al-Ghani Hamada, *Al-Mar'a al-khalida fi ta'rikh al-Islam*; `Abd al-Hamid Tahmaz, *Al-sayyida `A'isha*; Zahiyya Mustafa Qaddura, *`A'isha umm al-mu'minin*; `Ali Ahmad Abu al-`Izz, *Umm al-mu'minin `A'isha al-mubarra'a*.

35. Muhammad Baraniq, *`A'isha al-`alima*; Yakub Kenan Necefzade, *Ayse Anamiz*; and Ahmed Cemil Akinci, *Hazretli Aise*.

36. Nawal al-Sa`dawi, *The Hidden Face of Eve*, p. 131. For the negative point of view with less medieval documentation, see Mahmud al-`Aqqad, *Al-Siddiqa bint al-siddiq*, pp. 132–33.

37. Fatima Mernissi, *Le harem politique*; and Magali Morsy, *Les Femmes du Prophete*.

38. For a discussion of modern Muslim ideology on such matters and women's self-definition within Islamist ideology, see Yvonne Y. Haddad, "Islam, Women and Revolution in Twentieth-Century Arab Thought," pp. 275–307.

39. `Umar R. Kahhala, *A`lam al-nisa: fi a`lam al-`Arab wa al-Islam*, 3:9–131; `A'isha bint `Abd al-Rahman, *Nisa' al-nabi*, pp. 69–117.

40. Sa`id al-Afghani, *`A'isha wa al-siyasa*. For a more popular treatment for youthful audiences, see Muhammad Baraniq, *`A'isha al-siyasa*.

41. Al-Afghani, *`A'isha*, pp. 9–14.

42. Fatima Mernissi, *Women and Islam*, pp. 5–8; also the refutation of this stance by Ghassan Ascha, *Du Statut Inferieur de la Femme en Islam*, p. 224.

43. In the commanding methodological handbook by Humphreys, *Islamic History*, there is no chapter on research methods concerning women in medieval or modern times. For a similar omission, see also Claude Cahen and Jean Sauvaget, *Introduction to the Study of the Muslim East*; and most recently, with a section on modern, but not medieval women, the otherwise encyclopedic work by Ira Lapidus, *A History of Islamic Societies*. In such a vacuum, anthologies take the place of in-depth studies, see Nikki R. Keddie and Beth Baron, *Women in Middle Eastern History*. Six articles are featured on medieval Muslim women; one by the author treats `A'isha, "Political Action and Public Example: `A'isha and the Battle of the Camel," pp. 58–74.

44. For example, Jane I. Smith, "Women, Religion and Social Change in Early Islam," pp. 19–37; Barbara Freyer Stowasser, "The Status of Women in Early Islam," pp. 11–43; Leila Ahmed, "Women and the Advent of Islam," pp. 665–91, and Leila Ahmed, *Women and Gender in Islam*, pp. 49–52.

45. Ahmed and Stowasser most particularly exemplify these oppositional tendencies and the ability to draw opposing arguments from the same body of limited early materials.

46. Elizabeth W. Fernea and Basima W. Bezirgan, "`A'ishah bint Abi Bakr, Wife of the Prophet Muhammad," p. 27.

47. M. E. Combs-Schilling, *Sacred Performances*, pp. 69–90; and Fedwa Malti-Douglas, *Woman's Body, Woman's Word*, pp. 51–53. For a brief treatment of popular literature concerning women of the Prophet's family, see Esko Naskali, "Women in the Prophet's Family as They Feature in Popular Bazaar Literature," pp. 245–50. Although his categories of analysis do not include gender, one cannot ignore the important contribution of Joseph B. Roberts to the analysis of `A'isha's political career in "Early Islamic Historiography" or the popular but peculiar mention of `A'isha in Antonia Frazier, *The Warrior Queens*, p. 110.

48. Nabia Abbott, *Aishah: The Beloved of Mohammed*, p. xvii; Nabia Abbott, "Women and the State in Early Islam," pp. 106–27. Other pioneering Western works on women include Henri Lammens, *Fatima et les filles de Mahomet*; Ilse Lichtenstadter, *Women in the Aiyam al-Arab*; and Stern, *Marriage in Early Islam*.

49. Abbott, *Aishah*, p. xvii.

50. Yvonne Haddad, "Women," p. 295.

51. Abbott, *Aishah*, p. 218.

52. *Encyclopaedia of Islam*, 2d ed. s.v. "`A'isha" by W. Montgomery Watt. Additional brief biographies of `A'isha include Fred M. Donner, "`A'isha," 1:112–13; and Jane D. McAuliffe, "`A'isha," 1:162–63.

53. Or, as Roland Barthes once described biography, "a counterfeit integration of the subject."

54. Morton Smith, *Jesus the Magician*, p. 8.

55. Jane Austen, *Northanger Abbey*, p. 87.

56. W. Montgomery Watt, *Muhammad at Mecca*, pp. xiii-xiv.

57. Abbott, *Aishah*, p. xviii.

58. Watt, *Muhammad at Mecca*, p. xiv.

59. Ibid., p. xiv.

60. Adrian Wilson and T. G. Ashplant, "Whig History and Present-Centred History," pp. 1–16.

61. See for outlines of available medieval sources, Leone Caetani, *Chronographia Islamica*, 3:631–32; and Kahhala, *A`lam al-nisa'*, 3:130–31. For `A'isha as relater or subject in Sunni hadith collections, see A. J. Wensinck et al. eds., *Concordance et Indices de la Tradition Musulmane*, 8:135–40. Indeed, the work on `A'isha's exclusive contributions as the originator of hadith as a source of legal precedent and ritual life has yet to be effectively studied despite an amazing range of early Sunni sources.

2. Privileges and Problems: The Shaping of `A'isha's Historical Persona

1. `Abd al-Malik Ibn Hisham, *Kitab sirat rasul Allah*: vol. 1, pt. 2: 1001; and al-Tabari, *Ta'rikh*, 4: 1766. Al-Tabari says the Prophet married fifteen women, but only consummated the bond with thirteen women.

2. Qur'an, S. 33: 6, 53.

3. In this respect, `A'isha's life is more fully developed in early written sources than either Khadija's or Fatima's.

4. Parts of `A'isha's remembered life, as subsumed into the communal record, diverge significantly in their placement by genre. Her presence as one of the Prophet's wives is briefly, if consistently, noted in early works on the Prophet's life and exploits. In the works of major biographers of the Prophet from the early third/ninth century, including Ibn Hisham (d. 218/833), who emended and preserved sections of an earlier work by Ibn Ishaq (d. 150/767), al-Waqidi (d. 207/823), and `Abd al-Razzaq ibn Hammam al-San`ani (d. 211/827), `A'isha's life is noted only where it intersects with the major events of the Prophet's life. `A'isha makes brief appearances as narrator or witness to early battles in these accounts, but of the two great controversies in her life, it is the accusation of adultery, known as the hadith al-ifk, which receives the most attention as an occasion for both communal tension at Medina and Qur'anic revelation. See Ibn Hisham, Kitab sirat rasul Allah, vol. 1, pt. 1:163; pt. 2:731–40 (hadith al-ifk); pt. 2: 1001–5 (wives of Prophet); Muhammad ibn `Umar al-Waqidi, Kitab al-maghazi, 2: 427–40 (hadith al-ifk); `Abd al-Razzaq al-San`ani, Musannaf, 5: 410–20 (hadith al-ifk); 11: 429–33 (azwaj al-nabi). `A'isha's political action as a widow at the Battle of the Camel belongs to chronicle and selective hadith, but for obvious reasons of chronology is not part of her remembered life with the Prophet. As in the case of the accusation of adultery, the Battle of the Camel is hardly mentioned in her biography, but is a controversy detailed elsewhere in the communal record.

5. Ibn Sa`d, Tabaqat, 8: 58–81; Stern, Marriage in Early Islam, pp. 3–20; Fedwa Malti-Douglas, "Biography, Islamic," 2: 237–38.

6. Khalifa ibn Khayyat al-`Usfuri, Kitab al-tabaqat, pp. 333–34; Ahmad ibn Yahya al-Baladhuri, Ansab al-ashraf, 1: 409–22.

7. They include the six collections of hadith considered canonical by Sunni Muslims by the fourth/tenth century, including the works of Muhammad ibn `Abd Allah al-Bukhari (d. 256/870), Muslim ibn al-Hajjaj al-Qushayri (d. 261/875), Sulayman ibn al-Ash`ath Abu Da`ud (d. 275/888), Muhammad ibn `Isa al-Tirmidhi (d. 279/892), Ahmad ibn Shu`ayb al-Nasa'i (d. 303/915), and Muhammad ibn Yazid Ibn Maja (273/886). I also included the works of `Abd Allah ibn `Abd al-Rahman al-Darimi (d. 225/869) and Ibn Hanbal (241/855).

8. Watt, Formative Period, pp. 269–70. For earlier ninth-century formulations, see Wilferd Madelung, "Early Sunni Faith," pp. 233–54.

9. Ibid., p. 266. Although the notion of the past as central to later medieval definition has been raised before with regard to the affirmation of the order of the first four caliphs, the extension of this assumption to include `A'isha has not been made.

10. Ibn Sa`d, Tabaqat, 8: 64. The Arabic is more evocative of both Allah's intervention in Muhammad's death and the Prophet's proximity to his wife. He was literally between `A'isha's lungs and throat.

11. Ibn Sa`d, Tabaqat, 8: 63–64; Shihab al-Din Ibn Hajar al-`Asqalani, Al-Isaba fi tamy-iz al-sahaba, 4: 250. This list is related from `A'isha by her paternal nephew Qasim ibn

Muhammad. As a partisan of `Ali ibn Abi Talib in the first civil war, he would not always be cited as a source of praise for his aunt. See chapter 4.

12. Ibn Sa`d, *Tabaqat*, 8: 65.

13. What she stresses here is her Islamic genealogy, not her tribal ties. For the latter, see al-`Usfuri, *Tabaqat*, pp. 333–34.

14. Ibn Sa`d, *Tabaqat*, 8: 59.

15. Ibid., 3: 170.

16. Al-San`ani, *Musannaf*, 5: 328.

17. Toshihiko Izutsu, *Ethico-Religious Concepts in the Qur'an*, pp. 91–92.

18. *Suras* 12: 46 and 19: 41; Izutsu, *Ethico-Religious Concepts*, pp. 92–95.

19. Ibn Sa`d, *Tabaqat*, 8: 64, 66.

20. Ibn Sa`d, *Tabaqat*, 8: 65, 67; al-Tirmidhi, *Sahih al-Tirmidhi*, 5: 364, 365, 366.

21. Ibn Sa`d, *Tabaqat*, 8: 65, 67; Muhammad ibn `Abd Allah al-Bukhari, *Sahih al-Bukhari*, 5: 6. In the first instance, the Prophet's reference to Abu Bakr as the most beloved of men is listed among `A'isha's ten special privileges. For `Ali and Fatima, see al-Tirmidhi, *Sahih al-Tirmidhi*, 5: 360, 362, 299.

22. Husayn Ibn `Abd al-Wahhab, `*Uyun al-Mu`jizat*, p. 61.

23. Muhammad ibn Abi Bakr Ibn Khallikan, *Wafayat al-a`yan*, 3: 141.

24. Ibn Sa`d, *Tabaqat*, 3: 171–72; al-Tirmidhi, *Sahih al-Tirmidhi*, 5: 306. In the first account, Abu Bakr is described as converting first, then `Ali when he was only a boy of eight. This tradition also says that the first woman to convert was Khadija. The second tradition on the page asserts that `Ali was first to convert, but then this is denied and Abu Bakr declared the first. For both, see al-San`ani, *Musannaf*, 5: 325. Ibn Hisham, *Kitab sirat rasul Allah*, vol. 1 pt. 1: 158–59, where `Ali alone is described as the first. See also L. Veccia Vaglieri, "`Ali," *Encyclopaedia of Islam*, 1: 381–86, where the dispute is also admitted.

25. Al-Bukhari, *Sahih al-Bukhari*, 5: 10–11 (Abu Bakr); al-Tirmidhi, *Sahih al-Tirmidhi*, 5: 300 (`Ali).

26. Muhammad Ibn Hanbal, *Musnad*, 3: 64, 80.

27. Ibn Sa`d, *Tabaqat*, 8: 65, 79.

28. George Ostrogorsky, *History of the Byzantine State*, pp. 67–68.

29. Al-Tabari, *Ta'rikh*, 2: 1424; Isma`il ibn `Umar Ibn Kathir, *Al-Bidaya wa al-nihaya*, 10: 323–24; and Reuben Levy, *A Baghdad Chronicle*, p. 106.

30. Moojan Momen, *An Introduction to Shi`i Islam*, p. 73.

31. Ibn Kathir, *Al-Bidaya*, 10: 324.

32. As quoted in Richard W. Bulliet, *The Patricians of Nishapur*, p. 234.

33. Muslim ibn al-Hajjaj al-Qushayri, *Sahih Muslim*, 7: 135–36; al-San`ani, *Musannaf*, 11: 431–32.

34. Ibid. `A'isha's words of praise for Zaynab may reflect the latter's support for her during the accusation of adultery. In this matter, `A'isha would also find kind words for Zaynab. See chapter 3.

35. Ibn Sa`d, *Tabaqat*, 8: 64.

36. Al-Baladhuri, *Ansab*, 1: 415–16; al-Bukhari, *Sahih al-Bukhari*, 6: 13.

37. Al-Tabari, *Ta'rikh*, 4: 1766.

38. Ibid., 4: 1814; Ibn Hisham, *Kitab sirat rasul Allah*, vol. 1, pt. 2: 1011.

39. It is, therefore, not surprising that `A'isha in particular and the wives of the Prophet in general should figure prominently in relating traditions concerning menstruation and marital conduct. See, for example, any hadith collection's chapter on *al-tahara*, "ritual purity." For one example of `A'isha as a source on female ritual purity, marital cohabitation, and the Prophet's ablutions for prayer, see Ibn Hanbal, *Musnad*, 6: 143.

40. Al-Tirmidhi, *Sahih al-Tirmidhi*, 5: 362–63.

41. Ibn Sa`d, *Tabaqat*, 8: 64; Muslim, *Sahih Muslim*, 7:137; al-Bukhari, *Sahih al-Bukhari*, 6: 14, 15, 16.

42. Ibn Sa`d, *Tabaqat*, 8: 64; al-Bukhari, *Sahih al-Bukhari*, 6: 16; Ibn Hanbal, *Musnad*, 6: 117.

43. Al-Bukhari, *Sahih al-Bukhari*, 5: 37; Muslim, *Sahih Muslim*, 7: 135. In an unrelated demonstration of deference to the Prophet's preference, Sawda, the eldest of Muhammad's wives, had previously given her day and night with the Prophet to `A'isha. See Ibn Hanbal, *Musnad*, 6: 117.

44. Ibn Sa`d, *Tabaqat*, 8: 64.

45. Ibid., 8: 65; al-San`ani, *Musannaf*, 5: 428–30; Ibn Hisham, *Kitab sirat rasul Allah*, vol. 1, pt. 2: 1005–6.

46. See for example the account of the fifth/eleventh-century Twelver Shi`i author on the matter of Ghadir Khumm and `Ali's thwarted access to the Prophet Muhammad during his final hours, due in part to `A'isha. Muhammad ibn Muhammad al-Mufid, *Kitab al-irshad*, pp. 91–96.

47. Ibid., pp. 96–103, but especially p. 99.

48. Ibn Sa`d, *Tabaqat*, 8: 60, 62.

49. Qur'an, 33: 53.

50. Ibn Sa`d, *Tabaqat*, 8: 58, 63; Ibn Hisham, *Kitab sirat rasul Allah*, vol. 1, pt. 2: 1001.

51. Ibn Sa`d, *Tabaqat*, 8: 80.

52. Ibid., 8: 58–62, where hadith concerning her age are repeated more than ten times. Al-Bukhari, *Sahih al-Bukhari*, 4: 71; Ibn Hanbal, *Musnad*, 6: 118. Both al-Bukhari and Ibn Hanbal maintain the ages as six and nine.

53. Ibn Hisham, *Kitab sirat rasul Allah*, vol. 1, pt. 2: 1001.

54. For disputed date of birth, see al-Tabari, *Ta'rikh*, 4: 2135 and its contradiction within the same chronicle, *Ta'rikh*, 4: 1262. For her death date at sixty-seven, not sixty-six, see Ibn Khallikan, *Wafayat al-a`yan*, 3: 16.

55. Ibn Sa`d, *Tabaqat*, 8: 65.

56. Ibid., 8: 58, 60; Ibn Hisham, *Kitab sirat rasul Allah*, vol. 1, pt. 2: 1001.

57. Ibn Sa`d, *Tabaqat*, 8: 60; Al-Baladhuri, *Ansab*, 1: 410.

58. Al-Baladhuri, *Ansab*, 1: 410.

59. Ibn Sa`d, *Tabaqat*, 8: 60–61.

60. Stern, *Marriage in Early Islam*, pp. 84–85.

61. Ibn Sa`d, *Tabaqat*, 8: 63, 66. The two references on p. 66 make specific reference to Ibn al-Zubayr by name or as `A'isha's nephew. The lone reference on p. 63 is related from `A'isha by `Abd Allah ibn al-Zubayr himself. See Schimmel, *Islamic Names*, p. 6, who suggests that the kunya might refer to `A'isha's nephew or, oddly, "to a miscarriage."

62. G. R. Hawting, *The First Dynasty of Islam: The Umayyad Caliphate A.D. 661–750*, pp. 46–57.

63. Ibn Sa`d, *Tabaqat*, 8: 63. From `A'isha to her paternal nephew Qasim b. Muhammad. The marriage of the Prophet to Zaynab bint Jahsh, confirmed by Qur'anic revelation, that she should divorce the Prophet's adopted son Zayd ibn al-Harith. See Qur'an, 33: 37–38; Stern, *Marriage in Early Islam*, p. 106. Zaynab's marriage was sanctioned by a verse in the Qur'an in which she is not named, but in which she takes great pride in her biography. For Zaynab as the Prophet's wife in heaven, see Ibn Sa`d, *Tabaqat*, 8: 103; 108.

64. Ibn Sa`d, *Tabaqat*, 8: 65.

65. Ibid., 8: 64. From `A'isha to `Urwa ibn al-Zubayr to Hisham ibn `Urwa, his son.

66. For the `A'isha–`Urwa ibn al-Zubayr–Hisham ibn `Urwa traditions, see Ibn Sa`d, *Tabaqat*, 8:59, 64, 67. `Urwa, the son of `A'isha's sister Asma' and al-Zubayr, `A'isha's ally in the first civil war, was the rebel `Abd Allah's brother and a famous relater of hadith in Medina; see A. A. Duri, *The Rise of Historical Writing Among the Arabs*, pp. 76–78. One of the references is narrated on the authority of `Urwa's *mawla*, or "client," Habib; see Ibn Sa`d, *Tabaqat*, 8: 78; Stern, *Marriage in Early Islam*, p. 106, where she incorrectly states that all of these traditions originate with `A'isha. In one of the lists in which Gabriel figures, the report is transmitted from `A'isha to her paternal nephew Qasim ibn Muhammad. Ibn Sa`d, *Tabaqat*, 8: 63.

67. Al-Baladhuri, *Ansab*, 1: 411; Muslim, *Sahih Muslim*, 7: 134; al-Bukhari, *Sahih al-Bukhari*, 4: 71, all with a family isnad. Only al-Tirmidhi does not have the same chain of transmission, *Sahih al-Tirmidhi*, 5: 363.

68. Al-Bukhari, *Sahih al-Bukhari*, 4: 171.

69. Muslim, *Sahih Muslim*, 7: 134.

70. Al-Tirmidhi, *Sahih al-Tirmidhi*, 5: 363.

71. Ibid. Al-Tirmidhi himself admits to problems with the chain of transmitters.

72. Ibn Sa`d, *Tabaqat*, 8: 64–65; al-Baladhuri, *Ansab*, 1: 412.

73. Ibn Sa`d, *Tabaqat*, 8: 63.

74. Al-Baladhuri, *Ansab*, 1: 419–20. See also chapter 3.

75. For example, Al-Waqidi, *Kitab al-maghazi*, 2:427–40; Ibn Hisham, *Kitab sirat rasul Allah*, vol. 1, pt. 2: 731–40; al-San`ani, *Musannaf*, 5: 410–19; and al-Bukhari, *Sahih al-Bukhari*, 5: 149–55. The separation out of the accusation in Ibn Sa`d, in particular, may also reflect his acknowledgement that al-Waqidi, the man from whom he borrowed heavily in his biographies of the wives of the Prophet, had already dealt with the scandal in his work. The placement of the account in the early Islamic corpus raises question of categorization of events by genre and their position as part of the communal record rather than exclusively as part of `A'isha's life.

76. Ibn Sa`d, *Tabaqat*, 8: 65; Shihab al-Din Ibn Hajar al-`Asqalani, *Kitab al-isaba fi tamyiz al-sahaba*, 8: 694.

77. Ibn Sa`d, *Tabaqat*, 8: 67–68

78. Muslim, *Sahih Muslim*, 7: 144. Narrated on the authority of the Iranian convert Salman al-Farisi, a popular and important figure for Shi`i Muslims who, like Umm Salama, figures prominently in the narration of their past.

79. For reference to scholarly debate about this incident and reference to Ibn Ishaq's account, which also features Gabriel inciting the Prophet, without `A'isha as witness, to attack the Banu Qurayza, see Gordon D. Newby, *A History of the Jews of Arabia: From Ancient Times Until Their Eclipse Under Islam*, pp. 90–96.

80. Ahmad ibn Yayha al-Baladhuri, *Futuh al-Buldan*, pp. 21–22. From `A'isha to `Urwa ibn al-Zubayr to Hisham ibn `Urwa.

81. Ibn Sa`d, *Tabaqat*, 8:79; al-Bukhari, *Sahih al-Bukhari*, 5:36; al-Tirmidhi, *Sahih al-Tirmidhi*, 5: 363–64; Ibn Hanbal, *Musnad*, 6: 117.

82. Muslim, *Sahih Muslim*, 7: 139 (3 times); al-Tirmidhi, *Sahih al-Tirmidhi*, 5: 34; al-San`ani, *Musannaf*, 11: 429 (twice, once from `A'isha to `Urwa to Zuhri; once on Qutada's authority).

83. Ibn Hisham, *Kitab sirat rasul Allah*, vol. 1, pt. 1: 154.

84. Ibid. A second briefer account is narrated on the authority of the granddaughter of Khadija, Fatima bint Husayn via her son `Abd Allah b. Hasan, who reports Khadija's words in their essence: "He [Gabriel] is an angel, not a devil."

85. *Sura* 33: 53. Stern, *Marriage in Early Islam*, pp. 123–24, asserts that two traditions about the khimar as a face veil may have been fabricated at a later date in order to legitimate later Islamic practice. `A'isha does indeed narrate many hadith concerning khimar in the early third/ninth century, but these give little clue as to how they were worn, despite much detail on color and fabric. For example, Ibn Sa`d, *Tabaqat*, 8: 70–73; particularly p. 72, where `A'isha scolds her co-wife Hafsa about the flimsiness of her khimar and reminds her about the Qur'anic injunctions of 24: 31, which indicates that women should use their khimars to cover their bosoms. In a Christian tradition based on Jewish religious precedent, women were admonished generally to cover their heads "because of the angels" (1 Corinthians 11:10). I am indebted to Dr. Bernadette Brooten of Harvard Divinity School for this reference, which suggests an alternative possibility of a previous monotheist precedent in the Middle East for Muslims regarding head covering. See further, Constance F. Parvey, "The Theology and Leadership of Women in the New Testament," pp. 123–28.

86. Ibn Sa`d, *Tabaqat*, 8: 64, 66.

87. It has been remarked that the laudatory emphasis in Ibn Sa`d's biography may disqualify it as a helpful historical source for the study of the Prophet's wife. Yet such praise, even if extreme, had a purpose at the time of its inception and qualification. See, for example, Harris Birkeland, *The Lord Guideth: Studies on Primitive Islam*.

88. Al-Tabari, *Ta'rikh*, 3: 1262.

89. Al-Tirmidhi, *Sahih al-Tirmidhi*, 5: 362–63.

90. See for example, al-Tabari's Shi`i contemporary `Ali ibn Ibrahim al-Qummi (d. 307/919), *Tafsir al-Qummi*, 2: 99.

91. From the seventh/thirteenth through the tenth/sixteenth centuries, authors of biographical dictionaries dedicated to the wives of the Prophet as well as `A'isha and her hadith criticism reiterate both the lists of Ibn Sa`d and al-Tabari in their works. See Fakhr al-Din Ibn `Asakir (d. 620/1223), *Kitab al-arba`in fi manaqib ummahat al-mu'minin*, p. 78, who cites the first list of Ibn Sa`d; Muhammad ibn Bahadur al-Zarkashi (d. 794/1392), *Al-Ijaba li-irad ma istadrakathu `A'isha `ala al-sahaba*, p. 20, who cites the list found originally in al-Tabari; Ibn Hajar al-`Asqalani (d. 852/1448), *Al-Isaba fi tamyiz al-sahaba*, 4: 350, who cites both lists of Ibn Sa`d; Jalal al-Din al-Suyuti (d. 911/1505), `Ayn al-isaba, fol. 14a, where al-Tabari's list is included; Qadir ibn Muhammad al-Shadhili (d. 920/1514), Radd al-`uqul al-ta'isha ila ma`rifa ma ikhtassat bihi Khadija wa `A'isha, fols. 120b-121b, where both Ibn Sa`d's list of ten qualities and al-Tabari's list of nine may be found. It should be noted that al-Shadhili's version of al-Tabari is qualified so that `A'isha remains the most beloved of people to the Prophet.

92. Juynboll, *Muslim Tradition*, p. 200.

93. Ibn Sa`d, *Tabaqat*, 8: 73; al-Baladhuri, *Ansab*, 1: 416.

94. Al-Baladhuri, *Ansab*, 1: 418.

95. Ibn Hanbal, *Musnad*, 6: 67; al-Baladhuri, *Ansab*, 1: 416.

96. Al-Baladhuri, *Ansab*, 1: 416.

97. Jamila Shaukat, "A Critical Edition . . . of Tradition Recounted by `A'isha," fols. 178a, 176b, 185b, 186b, 187b; Ibn Hanbal, *Musnad*, 6: 45, 47, 66, 93 on marriage; 6: 96, 150, 238 on clothing; and 6: 91, 113, 123, 182 on menstruation.

98. Ibn Sa`d, *Tabaqat*, 8: 66; al-Baladhuri, *Ansab*, 1: 415.

99. Al-Baladhuri, *Ansab*, 1: 418.

100. `Abd Allah ibn Muslim Ibn Qutayba, *Kitab ta'wil mukhtalif al-hadith*, pp. 10–11, 27.

101. Muhammad Ibn Idris al-Shafi`i, *Al-Imam Muhammad ibn Idris al-Shafi`i's al-risala fi usul al-fiqh*, pp. 213–14.

102. Muhibb al-Din Ahmad Ibn `Abd Allah al-Tabari, *Al-Simt al-thamin fi manaqib ummahat al-mu'minin*, pp. 60–61; Ibn Rahawayh, a source for both al-Bukhari and Muslim preserves over one thousand hadith on `A'isha's authority; see Shaukat, "Ibn Rahawayh."

103. Ibn Hanbal, *Musnad*, 6: 29–282.

104. Al-Tabari, *Al-Simt al-thamin fi manaqib ummahat al-mu'minin*, p. 60.

105. Shams al-Din ibn Ahmad `Uthman al-Dhahabi, *Siyar `alam al-nubala'*, 2: 98.

106. Al-Zarkashi, *Al-Ijaba*, pp. 32–40; for modern negative reactions to this treatise as among other things, a Zionist plot, see Mernissi, *Women and Islam*, pp. 77–79.

107. Al-Zarkashi, *Ijaba*, pp. 17, 24.

108. Jalal al-Din al-Suyuti, `Ayn al-isaba fi istidrak `A'isha `ala al-sahaba, fol. 14a.

109. Sartain, *Al-Suyuti*, 1: 125–26.

110. Abu al-Hasan al-Mawardi, *Ahkam al-sultaniyya*, p. 28.

111. Sartain, *Al-Suyuti*, 2: 126.

112. Farid al-Din `Attar, *Tadkhirat al-awliya'*, 1: 59.

113. Annemarie Schimmel, *Mystical Dimensions of Islam*, pp. 40–41; Margaret Smith, *Rabi`a the Mystic and Her Fellow Saints in Islam*, pp. 3–4.

114. `Attar, *Tadkhirat al-awliya'*, 1:59.

115. Najm al-Din `Umara al-Hakimi, *Ta'rikh al-Yaman*, p. 171.

116. Smith, *Rabi`a the Mystic*, p. 19; Schimmel, "Women in Mystical Islam," pp. 145–51; Jamal Elias, "Female and Feminine in Islamic Mysticism," pp. 209–24; Ahmed, *Women and Gender*, pp. 96–98.

117. Smith, *Rabi`a the Mystic*, p. 19; Schimmel, "Women in Mystical Islam," pp. 146–47; Elias, "Female and Feminine," pp. 209, 224, Ahmed, *Women and Gender*, p. 96.

118. Carolyn G. Heilbrun, *Writing A Woman's Life*, p. 81.

119. `Attar, *Tadhkirat al-awliya'*, 1: 59.

3. The Accusation of Adultery and Communal Debate

1. The date of the event varies between the year A.H. 5/A.D. 627 and 6/628. In Ibn Hisham, *Kitab sirat rasul Allah*, vol. 1, pt. 2: 731, the year given is A.H. 6; but in al-Dhahabi, *Siyar `alam al-nubala'*,2: 153, the year given is A.H. 5. The year 5/627 is also found in the *Encyclopedia of Islam*, s.v. "`A'isha."

2. See J. G. Peristiany, ed., *Honour and Shame: The Values of Mediterranean Society*; David D. Gilmore, ed., *Honor and Shame and the Unity of the Mediterranean*; Jane Schneider, "Of Vigilance and Virgins," pp. 1–24.

3. Schneider, "Vigilance and Virgins"; and Maureen J. Giovanni, "Female Chastity Codes in the Circum-Mediterranean," pp. 61–74.

4. Bishr Fares, *Honneur chez les Arabes avant l'Islam*, p. 53; Leila Abu Lughod, *Veiled Sentiments: Honor and Poetry in Bedouin Society*, p. 166.

5. John K. Campbell, *Honour, Family, and Patronage*; Gilmore, *Honor and Shame*, p. 4.

6. Abu Lughod, *Veiled Sentiments*, p. 130.

7. Peristiany, *Honour and Shame*, p. 10.

8. Gilmore, *Honor and Shame*, p. 4.

9. Ibn Sa`d, *Tabaqat*, 8: 63–64.

10. Al-Baladhuri, *Ansab*, 1: 420.

11. Ibn Hisham, *Kitab sirat rasul Allah*, vol. 1, pt. 2: 731–40; al-Waqidi, *Kitab al-maghazi*, 2: 427–40; al-San`ani, *Musannaf*, 5: 410–20; Wensinck, *Concordance et Indices*, 1: 67–68.

12. Al-Bukhari, *Sahih al-Bukhari*, 3:173–76; 5: 116–21; Muslim, *Sahih Muslim*, 8: 112–19; and Ibn Hanbal, *Musnad*, 6: 194–97.

13. Al-Bukhari, *Sahih al-Bukhari*, 5: 115. See also the succinct reference of Khalifa ibn Khayyat al-`Usfuri (d. 240/854), *Ta'rikh Khalifa ibn Khayyat*, 1: 42.

14. For other references, see al-Bukhari, *Sahih al-Bukhari*, 3: 167–68; 6: 76–77, 100–109; 8: 172; 8: 168; 9: 139.

15. Duri, *Historical Writing*, p. 106; Watt, *Formative Period*, pp. 69–70.

16. Ibn Hisham, *Kitab sirat rasul Allah*, vol. 1, pt. 2: 731. The other narrative chain featured is also transmitted via the family of Abu Bakr in the person of 'Amra bint Abi al-Rahman, Abu Bakr's aunt. Al-San'ani, *Musannaf*, 5: 410, features a similar chain of transmission as does al-Bukhari, *Sahih al-Bukhari*, 3: 173; 5: 116; Muslim, *Sahih Muslim*, 8: 113; and Ibn Hanbal, *Musnad*, 6: 194.

17. Sahair El Calamawy, "Narrative Elements in the Hadith Literature," p. 313.

18. Ibn Hisham, *Kitab sirat rasul Allah*, vol. 1, pt. 2: 731–32; al-Bukhari, *Sahih al-Bukhari*, 3: 173–74; 5: 116; Muslim, *Sahih Muslim*, 8: 113; Ibn Hanbal, *Musnad*, 6: 195.

19. Ibn Hisham, *Kitab sirat rasul Allah*, vol. 1, pt. 2: 732.

20. Ibid., 731; al-Bukhari, *Sahih al-Bukhari*, 3: 174; 5: 117; Muslim, *Sahih Muslim*, 8: 113; Ibn Hanbal, *Musnad*, 6: 195 .

21. Ibid.; Muslim, *Sahih Muslim*, 8: 114.

22. Ibn Hisham, *Kitab sirat rasul Allah*, vol. 1, pt. 2: 733; al-Bukhari, *Sahih al-Bukhari*, 3: 174; Muslim, *Sahih Muslim*, 8: 115; Ibn Hanbal, *Musnad*, 6: 195.

23. Ibn Hisham, *Kitab sirat rasul Allah*, vol. 1, pt. 2: 733–34.

24. Ibid., 734; al-Bukhari, *Sahih al-Bukhari*, 3: 175; 5: 118; 9: 139; Ibn Hanbal, *Musnad*, 6: 196.

25. Muhammad ibn Muhammad al-Mufid, *Kitab al-jamal*, p. 220.

26. Ibn Hisham, *Kitab sirat rasul Allah*, vol. 1, pt. 2: 734.

27. Ibid., 737. On the poem, see W. Arafat, "A Controversial Incident and the Related Poem in the life of Hassan B. Thabit," pp. 197–206.

28. Ibn Hisham, *Kitab sirat rasul Allah*, vol. 1, pt. 2: 739.

29. Ibid., 735; al-Bukhari, *Sahih al-Bukhari*, 5: 119; Muslim, *Sahih Muslim*, 8: 116.

30. Ibn Hisham, *Kitab sirat rasul Allah*, vol. 1, pt. 2: 735; see also El Calamawy, "Narrative Elements," p. 313, where he oddly and incorrectly asserts that "Her father believes her . . . "

31. Ibn Hisham, *Kitab sirat rasul Allah*, vol. 1, pt. 2: 735; al-Bukhari, *Sahih al-Bukhari*, 3: 176; 6: 76–77; al-San'ani, *Musannaf*, 5: 417. She cites Qur'an 12: 18, where Jacob is shown the false evidence of his son Joseph's bloody shirt.

32. Ibn Hisham, *Kitab sirat rasul Allah*, 735–36.

33. Ibid., 739; al-Bukhari, *Sahih al-Bukhari*, 5: 121; Muslim, *Sahih Muslim*, 8: 118.

34. Ibn Hisham, *Kitab sirat rasul Allah*, vol. 1, pt. 2: 740.

35. John Wansbrough, *Qur'anic Studies*, p. 2, who argues that Muhammad's biography "provided the framework for the extended narratio" or the "narratio was itself the framework for frequent if not continuous allusion to scripture."

36. Qur'anic verses are cited in Ibn Hisham, *Kitab sirat rasul Allah*, vol. 1, pt. 2: 736; al-Bukhari, *Sahih al-Bukhari*, 3: 176; Muslim, *Sahih Muslim*, 8: 117.

37. Fares, *Honneur chez les Arabes*, p. 77; see also Robert Roberts, *The Social Laws of the Qoran*, p. 38.

38. *The Oxford Annotated Apocrypha*, p. 213.

39. Mary D. Garrard, "Artemesia and Susanna," pp. 147–72.

40. Christine de Pizan, *The Book of the City of Ladies*, p. 155; Margaret Miles, *Carnal*

Knowing: Female Nakedness and Religious Meaning in the Christian West, pp. 121–25.

41. *Annotated Apocrypha*, p. 214.

42. Ibid., pp. 214–15.

43. Norman Daniel, *Islam and the West*, p. 215.

44. Al-Zarkashi, *Ijaba*, p. 14.

45. In the Hindu epic the *Ramayana*, doubt is cast upon the chastity of the faithful wife Sita. When she is not believed she beseeches Mother Earth to prove her purity. Whereupon, the Earth opens up and, at Sita's request, takes her back as divine proof of her innocence. See William Buck, *Ramayana: King Rama's Way*, pp. 340–41.

46. Al-Qummi, *Tafsir al-Qummi*, 2: 99.

47. Qur'an 66:10; al-Qummi, *Tafsir al-Qummi*, 2: 375–77.

48. Al-Qummi, *Tafsir al Qummi*, 2: 98.

49. Al-Tabari, *Jami` al-bayan `an ta'wil ay al-Qur'an*, 18: 86–101.

50. Al-Fadl Ibn al-Hasan al-Tabarsi, *Majma` al-bayan fi tafsir al-Qur'an*, 4: 129–32.

51. M. E. Combs-Schilling, *Sacred Performances*, pp. 91–92, where she draws a comparison with the Christian Mary Magdalene in the matter of sexuality. Sunni Muslims, the majority of the faithful, would also find blasphemous the idea that `A'isha could be called a prostitute. Her chastity and her truthfulness are instead miraculously confirmed by divine revelation.

52. Ibn Kathir, *Al-Bidaya*, 11: 243.

53. Henri Laoust, *La Profession de Foi d'Ibn Batta*, p. xxiv.

54. Ibid., p. 75, where the Arabic text is given.

55. Jane Smith and Yvonne Haddad, "The Virgin Mary in Islamic Tradition and Commentary," p. 187; Louis Massignon, "La notion de voeu et la devotion Musulmane a Fatima," p. 580.

56. Laoust, *La Profession de Foi d'Ibn Batta*, p. 65.

57. Abu Mansur al-Samarqandi, *Sharh al-fiqh al-akbar*, p. 91.

58. Al-Hasan ibn `Ali Nizam al-Mulk, *Siyar al-muluk*, p. 87.

59. Ibn Taymiyya, *Minhaj al-sunna al-nabawiyya*, 2: 192; Henri Laoust, "La critique du sunnisme dans la doctrine d'al-Hilli," pp. 35–60.

60. Ibn Taymiyya, *Minhaj*, 2: 192–93.

61. Al-Qummi, *Tafsir al-Qummi*, 2: 377.

62. Ibn Taymiyya, *Minhaj*, 2: 192.

63. Lois Giffen, *The Theory of Profane Love Among the Arabs*, p. 33.

64. J. De Von Hammer, *Histoire de l'Empire Ottoman*, 3: 258.

65. `Ali Ibn al-Athir, *Usd al-ghaba fi ma`rifa al-sahaba*, 5: 504.

66. Al-Dhahabi, *Siyar*, 2: 153.

67. `Abd al-Karim ibn al-Haytham, "Hadith al-ifk," Cairo, Ma`had al-Makhtutat, Hadith no. 244.

68. Ibn Hisham, *Kitab sirat rasul Allah*, vol. 1, pt. 2: 734.

69. Ibn al-Haytham, "Hadith al-ifk," fol. 44b.

70. Abu `Imran Musa ibn Muhammad ibn `Abd Allah al-Wa`iz al-Andalusi, "Qasida

fi madh ʾAʾisha," no. 4066, fol. 13a, where the term *wazir*, "prime minister," is used. Al-Afghani, ʾAʾisha, p. 262, where he cites two manuscripts from Damascus, Dar al-Kutub al-Zahiriyya, Taʾrikh, no. 828 and 441, which use the term for military commander. All three manuscripts specify the one hundred dinar fee for the poet.

71. Al-Andalusi, Qasida, MS 4066, fol. 13a.

72. Al-Andalusi, Qasida, OR 5509 (776/1374); Qasida, MS 4066 (745/1344); "Madh umm al-muʾminin ʾAʾisha," al-Kutub al-Zahiriyya, Taʾrikh, no. 828 and 441 (800/1397). The poem has not been published in the West and is not mentioned by Carl Brockelmann, but Saʾid al-Afghani did publish a complete version of the poem in his work ʾAʾisha, pp. 262–65. However, he was aware only of the two Syrian copies. See also Michael W. Dols, *The Black Death in the Middle East*, pp. 43, 57, 113.

73. Al-Andalusi, Qasida, Adab no. 657 (1028/1618). A partial copy of the poem is also cited in Qadir ibn Muhammad al-Shadhili, Radd al-ʾuqul al-taʾisha . . . wa ʾAʾisha," MS 3678, fols. 178b-181a (c. 920/1514), but the work is not attributed to al-Andalusi.

74. Al-Andalusi, Qasida, MS 4066, fol. 13a. In this copy, the names of many scholars are mentioned. The biographer al-Shadhili mentions that he took the poem from his contemporary, Jalal al-Din al-Suyuti (d. 911/1505), MS. 3678, fol. 178b.

75. Al-Andalusi, Qasida, OR 5509, fol. 19b.

76. For example, the variations in line six between OR 5509, fols., 23a-26b and al-Afghani's version in ʾAʾisha, pp. 263.

77. Al-Andalusi, Qasida, OR 5509, fol.23b; Qasida, MS 4066, fol. 11b; al-Afghani, ʾAʾisha, p. 263; al-Shadhili, Radd, MS 3678, fol. 178b.

78. Al-Dhahabi, Siyar, 2: 153. The usage is also found in third/ninth-century sources; see Ibn Hanbal, *Musnad*, 6: 196 and al-Sanʾani, *Musannaf*, 5: 411, 413.

79. Al-Andalusi, Qasida, OR 5509, fol. 23b; Qasida, MS 4066, fol. 11b; al-Afghani, ʾAʾisha, p. 263; al-Shadhili, Radd, MS. 3678, fol. 178b.

80. Al-Andalusi, Qasida, OR 5509, fol. 24a.; Qasida, MS 4066, fol. 11b; Al-Afghani, ʾAʾisha, p. 263; al-Shadhili, Radd, MS. 3678, fol. 179a.

81. Al-Andalusi, Qasida, OR 5509, fol. 24b-25a; Qasida, MS. 4066, fol. 12a; al-Afghani, ʾAʾisha, p. 264.

82. Al-Andalusi, Qasida, OR 5509, fol. 25b; Qasida, MS 4066, fol. 12b; al-Afghani, ʾAʾisha, p. 264.

83. Al-Andalusi, Qasida, OR. 5509, fol. 26a; Qasida, MS 4066, fol. 13a; al-Afghani, ʾAʾisha, p. 265.

84. Ibn Hisham, *Kitab sirat rasul Allah*, vol. 1, pt. 2: 744.

85. Daniels, *Islam and the West*, p. 101.

86. Salman Rushdie, *Satanic Verses*, p. 387.

87. Qurʾan 33: 37–38.

88. Lisa Appignanesi and Sara Maitland, eds., *The Rushdie File*, p. 39.

89. Erika Friedl, *Women of Deh Koh*, p. 221.

90. Yasar Nuri Ozturk, "Son Peygamberʾin Hanimlari: Hz. Aise," p. 4.

4. Gender and the Politics of Succession

1. Qur'an 4:3.

2. Lichtenstadter, *Women in Aiyam al-Arab*, p. 65.

3. Combs-Schilling, *Sacred Performances*, p. 72.

4. Abbott, "Women and the State in Early Islam," pp. 120–21.

5. For the matrilineal argument, see W. Robertson Smith, *Kinship and Marriage in Early Islam*. For opposition, see Stern, *Marriage in Early Islam*; and Watt, *Muhammad at Medina*, pp. 272–89.

6. Barbara F. Stowasser, "The Status of Women in Early Islam," p. 15.

7. Abbott, "Women and the State in Early Islam," p. 107.

8. Fatima Mernissi, *The Veil and the Male Elite*, pp. 120–24, who argues that the egalitarian components of the Qur'an were misinterpreted later, a position also espoused by Abbott, "Women and the State," and challenged by Ahmed, "Women and the Advent of Islam," p. 690.

9. Ahmed, "Women and the Advent of Islam," pp. 690–91.

10. Lichtenstadter, *Women in Aiyam al-Arab*, p. 81; Ahmed, "Women and the Advent of Islam," p. 691.

11. Ibn Sa'd, *Tabaqat*, 8: 301–4; al-Baladhuri, *Futuh al-buldan*, p. 343; Abbott, "Women and the State," p. 118.

12. Al-Baladhuri, *Ansab*, 5: 341–63; al-Tabari, *Ta'rikh*, 6: 3000–3130. For the most recent synthesis of the motivations of participants and historians alike, see Roberts, "Early Islamic Historiography."

13. Al-Baladhuri, *Ansab*, 5: 34; 102.

14. Al-Tabari, *Ta'rikh* 6: 3040; al-Baladhuri, *Ansab*, 5: 91. For an examination of the socioeconomic rivalries animating this event, see Martin Hinds, "The Murder of the Caliph 'Uthman," pp. 450–69.

15. Al-Tabari, *Ta'rikh*, 6: 3112.

16. Al-Baladhuri, *Ansab*, 5: 70.

17. 'Ali al-Mas'udi, *Muruj al-dhahab wa ma'adin al-jawhar*, 2: 366.

18. Lichtenstadter, *Women in Aiyam al-Arab*, p. 43.

19. Al-Tabari, *Ta'rikh*, 6: 3120–21.

20. For an earlier outline of this argument, see Spellberg, "Political Action," pp. 58–73.

21. Ibn Sa'd, *Tabaqat* 8: 65.

22. Ibn Sa'd, *Tabaqat*, 8: 66; for the suggestion that the isnad is suspicious, see Stern, *Marriage in Early Islam*, p. 85.

23. Ibn Sa'd, *Tabaqat*, 8: 64.

24. Al-Baladhuri, *Ansab*, 1: 412.

25. Al-Bukhari, *Sahih al-Bukhari*, 5: 37.

26. Al-Kulayni, *Al-Usul min al-kafi*, 8: 331.

27. Khalifa ibn Khayyat al-'Usfuri, *Ta'rikh Khalifa ibn Khayyat*, 1: 49.

28. Al-Baladhuri, *Ansab*, 1: 417.

29. Al-Tabari, *Ta'rikh* 6: 3128–29.

30. Al-Baladhuri, *Ansab*, 1: 421.

31. Suliman Bashear, "Riding Beasts on Divine Missions: An Examination of the Ass and Camel Traditions," pp. 71–72, who raises the possiblity that in nomenclature and apocalyptic precedent there may be more than humor or censure at work in the camel and mule issue.

32. Ibid. See also Schimmel, *Islamic Names*, p. 64, who notes that Abu Bakr had been given the *laqab*, or nickname, 'Atiq Allah, as one who had been freed by God from hell-fire. 'Abd Allah reiterated the familial connection by taking a variation of his great grand-father's nickname for his own.

33. 'Amr al-Jahiz, *Al-Qawl fi al-bighal*, pp. 22–25.

34. Charles Pellat, *The Life and Works of Jahiz*, p. 186.

35. Al-Jahiz, *Qawl*, p. 24.

36. Al-Tabari, *Ta'rikh*, 6: 3231.

37. Al-Jahiz, *Qawl*, p. 25.

38. Ibn Khallikan, *Wafayat al-a'yan*, 3: 17.

39. Abbott, *'A'ishah*, pp. 198–99, without citing any sources for her supposition, supports the idea that 'A'isha had initially given permission for Hasan to be buried beneath her house. Assuming such an event actually occurred, even Abbott admits that such an admission from 'A'isha would have been unlikely.

40. Al-Ya'qubi, *Ta'rikh*, 2: 267.

41. Al-Mufid, *Kitab al-irshad*, 193.

42. Ibn 'Abd al-Wahhab, *'Uyun*, p. 69.

43. Lewis Pelly, ed., "The Martyrdom of Hasan," 2: 168–69.

44. Ibn Kathir, *Al-Bidaya*, 11: 275.

45. Mayel Baktash, "Ta'ziyeh and Its Philosophy," p. 97.

46. 'Abd Allah Ibn Muslim Ibn Qutayba, *'Uyun al-akhbar*, 1: 108.

47. Ibn Sa'd, *Tabaqat*, 8: 74.

48. Al-Tabari, *Ta'rikh*, 6: 3201, 3222.

49. Wensinck, *Concordance et Indices*, 8: 315; Ibn Hanbal, *Musnad*, 6: 52, 92.

50. Ibn Hanbal, *Musnad*, 6: 52, 92.

51. Al-Ya'qubi, *Ta'rikh*, 2: 210.

52. Al-Jahiz, *Kitab al-hayawan*, 2: 208.

53. Goldziher, *Muslim Studies*, 2: 1212.

54. Al-Tabari, *Ta'rikh*, 6: 3108.

55. Ibid., 6: 3109; al-Mas'udi, *Muruj*, 2: 357, who states in contrast that the camel was purchased in Yemen for two hundred dinars, that is, gold not silver.

56. Al-Tabari, *Ta'rikh*, 6: 3109.

57. Al-Mas'udi, *Muruj*, 2: 358. For al-Mas'udi's Shi'i affiliation, see Ahmad M. Shboul, *Al-Mas'udi and His World*, pp. 39–41.

58. Al-Mas'udi, *Muruj*, 2: 358.

59. Ahmad Ibn 'Abd Rabbih, *Al-'Iqd al-farid*, 3: 332.

60. Ibn Taymiyya, *Minhaj*, 2: 185.

61. Al-Mufid, *Kitab al-irshad*, pp. 131–32.

62. Ibid., p. 132.

63. Al-Mufid, *Jamal*, p. 125 .

64. Muhammad ibn `Ali Ibn Shahrashub, *Manaqib Al Abi Talib*, 3: 149.

65. On the Sunni side, for example, the positions of the Murji`a and the Mu`tazila represent cases in point. A determination was made about each of the key players involved in the first civil war as a matter of communal debate which combined both theology and politics in the Sunni sphere.

66. Ibn al-Nadim, *Kitab al-fihrist*, pp. 93–94, where this fourth/tenth-century author cites the work of the Shi`i author Abu Mikhnaf (d. 158/774) on the Battle of the Camel and that of the much-cited oral Sunni source Sayf ibn `Umar (d. 200/815) on the same subject.

67. Al-Tabari, *Ta'rikh*, 6: 3120–21.

68. Muhammad ibn Yazid al-Mubarrad, *Al-Kamil*, 1: 267.

69. `Abd al-Qahir al-Baghdadi, *Al-Farq bayn al-firaq*, p. 99.

70. Muhammad ibn `Abd al-Karim al-Shahrastani, *Kitab al-mihal wa'l-nihal*, p. 21.

71. Al-Shahrastani, *Milal*, p. 21; Ibn Taymiyya, *Minhaj*, 2: 184.

72. Ibid., pp. 103, 136; al-Tirmidhi, *Sahih al-Tirmidhi*, 5: 308.

73. Al-Mas`udi, *Muruj*, 2: 370.

74. Ibn Taymiyya, *Minhaj*, 2: 182–202.

75. Ibn Shahrashub, *Manaqib*, 3: 148.

76. Al-Mufid, *Jamal*, pp. 218–20; for an apparent inconsistency, see Martin J. McDermott, *The Theology of al-Shaikh al-Mufid*, p. 249.

77. Al-Mufid, *Jamal*, pp. 220.

78. Ibn Shahrashub, *Manaqib*, 3: 152.

79. Al-Ya`qubi, *Ta'rikh*, p. 209.

80. Al-Tabari, *Ta'rikh*, 6: 3101.

81. Ibn `Abd Rabbih, *Al-`Iqd al-farid*, 3: 316.

82. Ibid., p. 317; Abbott, *`A'ishah: The Beloved*, pp. 140–41, uses the exchange to flesh out her narrative, but never questions the polemical nature of the source material.

83. Al-Mufid, *Jamal*, p. 126.

84. Ibn `Abd Rabbih, *Al-`Iqd al-farid*, 3: 314.

85. Ibn Sa`d, *Tabaqat*, 8: 81.

86. Al-Mas`udi, *Muruj*, 2: 369–70.

87. Al-Tabari, *Ta'wil*, 22: 2–3.

88. Al-Baghdadi, *Farq*, p. 342; Ibn Taymiyya, *Minhaj*, 2: 185.

89. Ibn Taymiyya, *Minhaj*, 2: 185–86.

90. Al-Mufid, *Jamal*, p. 81.

91. Ibn Shahrashub, *Manaqib*, 3: 148.

92. Al-Mas`udi, *Muruj al-dhahab wa ma`adin al-jawhar*, 6: 485–86.

93. Edward W. Lane, *An Arabic-English Lexicon*, 6: 2335–36; s.v. "Fitna," *Encyclopae-*

dia of Islam, 2d ed. The Persian poet Nizami (d. 606/1209) named one of his female characters Fitna in his work the *Khamsa*.

94. For example, al-Bukhari, *Sahih al Bukhari*, 7: 8; Ibn Hanbal, *Musnad*, 3:22; 5: 200; Ibn Maja, *Sunan*, 2: 1325.

95. Al-Bukhari, *Sahih al Bukhari*, 1: 14, 83; Ibn Hanbal, *Musnad*, 5:210; 6: 363; Ibn Maja, *Sunan*, 2: 1326.

96. Ibn Hanbal, *Musnad*, 5: 38, 45.

97. Al-Bukhari, *Sahih al-Bukhari*, 6:10.

98. Ibn Hanbal, *Musnad*, 5: 45.

99. Al-Mawardi (d. 450/1058), *Ahkam al-Sultaniyya*, p. 28.

100. "Perspectives," *Newsweek*, May 11, 1992, p. 23; Mernissi, *Women and Islam*, p. 1, who cites a variation of this as addressed to her by a male schoolteacher in conversation.

101. Nizam al-Mulk, *Siyar al-muluk*, pp. 242–50; and for an early analysis of this chapter, see Spellberg, "Nizam al-Mulk's Manipulation of Tradition," pp. 111–17.

102. Nizam al-Mulk, *Siyar al-muluk*, p. 242.

103. Fatima Mernissi, *Beyond the Veil*, p. 12; Wilhelm Barthold, *Turkestan Down to the Mongol Invasion*, p. 310, where the author suggests that toward the end of Nizam al-Mulk's life he saw "a special danger in the growing strength of the heretical Ismailites [and] in the influence of women."

104. 'Ali ibn Anjab Ibn al-Sa'i (d. 674/1275), *Nisa' al-khulafa'*, pp. 131–32.

105. M. T. Houtsma, "The Death of Nizam al-Mulk and Its Consequences," pp. 147–60.

106. Nizam al-Mulk, *Siyar al-muluk*, p. 242.

107. Aristotle, *The Politics*, pp. 49–52; Jean B. Elshtain, *Public Man, Private Woman*, pp. 12–35; and R. W. Southern, *The Making of the Middle Ages*, p. 109.

108. Nizam al-Mulk, *Siyar al-muluk*, p. 246.

109. Ibid., p. 247.

110. Ibn Hisham, *Kitab sirat rasul Allah*, vol. 1, pt. 2: 1008–9 (especially 1008); Ibn Sa'd, *Tabaqat*, 3: 178–81. For other early hadith sources on this incident as narrated by 'A'isha, Ibn Hanbal, *Musnad*, 6: 34, 96, 159, 210, 224, 228, 231, 249, 251, 270.

111. Ibn Sa'd, *Tabaqat*, 3: 178–79.

112. Ibn Hanbal, *Musnad*, 6: 34, 96, 159, 210, 224, 228–29, 231, 249, 251, 270.

113. Ibn Hisham, *Kitab sirat rasul Allah*, vol. 1, pt. 2: 1008; Ibn Sa'd, *Tabaqat*, 3: 178–80; Ibn Hanbal, *Musnad*, 6: 34, 96, 159, 210, 224, 270.

114. Al-Mufid, *Kitab al-irshad*, pp. 97–98.

115. Ibid., p. 99. For another indirect reference to 'A'isha and Hafsa as the female personifications of "friendly advice," possibly in cynical reference to this incident, see Ibn Shahrashub, *Manaqib*, 3: 321. Henri Lammens, "Le Triumvirat Abou Bakr," pp. 113–44, where 'A'isha's role in the succession of her father portrays her as an early player in the politics of succession.

116. Abdelwahab Bouhdiba, *Sexuality in Islam*, pp. 19–20.

117. Nizam al-Mulk, *Siyar al-muluk*, p. 247.

118. Al-Saʿi, *Nisa'*, p. 132.
119. Al-Mufid, *Jamal*, pp. 79–81.
120. Ascha, *Du Statut Inferieur de la Femme en Islam*, p. 224.

5. The Politics of Praise: ʿAʾisha and the Development of Islamic Female Ideals

1. For the early hadith material on Asiya, see Wensinck, *Concordance et Indices*, 8:14; for the early hadith material on Maryam, see Wensinck, 8: 252.

2. The Qur'anic phrase *ʿala nisa' al-ʿalamin*, "above [all] the women of the worlds" will prove pivotal in the depiction of Khadija and Fatima.

3. These associations need not be exclusively positive for ʿAʾisha will also be compared to the more negative Qur'anic figures of the wife of al-ʿAziz, who figures in the story of the prophet Joseph in sura 12: 23, and the wives of Lot and Noah, who are cited as examples for the faithless in sura 66:10. For the male half of this continuum see Gordon Newby, *The Making of the Last Prophet*, pp. 1–32.

4. Ibn Saʿd, *Tabaqat*, 8: 17; al-Baladhuri, *Ansab*, 1: 471; and for a partial version of this argument, Spellberg, "The Politics of Praise," pp. 130–49.

5. Ibn Saʿd, *Tabaqat*, 1: 131–33; 8:15–17; Ibn Hisham, *Kitab sirat rasul Allah*, vol. 1, pt. 1: 119–22. The assumption particularly of Muhammad's age at the time of his marriage is effectively questioned by Lawrence I. Conrad, "Abraha and Muhammad," pp. 225–40. His argument also suggests that Khadija's age at the time of her marriage to Muhammad is also a topoi that calls into question the numerous children produced by Khadija, supposedly at the age of forty. Ibn Saʿd, *Tabaqat*, 8:17. The fifteen-year difference in ages between Muhammad and Khadija is supported in Ibn Saʿd, 8: 15, but questioned in Muhammad Ibn Habib (d. 245/860), *Kitab al-muhabbar*, p. 79, where the ages of twenty-eight and forty are both given for Khadija. Although forty is the age at which Muhammad received his prophetic calling, the religious resonance of the number also transforms the Prophet's sexual prowess in early Islamic sources. Thus, the Prophet is described as having "the power of forty men" in *jimaʿ*, sexual intercourse, after the angel Gabriel brought him some special food. Ibn Saʿd, *Tabaqat*, 1: 374. Clearly forty was a very potent designation.

6. Ibn Saʿd, *Tabaqat*, 8: 16; Ibn Hisham, *Kitab sirat rasul Allah*, vol. 1, pt. 1: 119, 155.

7. Ibn Saʿd, *Tabaqat*, 1: 133–34; 8: 19; Ibn Hisham, *Kitab sirat rasul Allah*, vol. 1, pt. 1: 120–21; al-Bukhari, *Sahih al-Bukhari*, 5: 47–51; al-Baladhuri, *Ansab*, 1: 396–402 and al-Sanʿani, *Musannaf*, 5: 320–22. The children produced by Muhammad and Khadija include his four daughters Zaynab, Ruqayya, Umm Kulthum, and Fatima. Both Ruqayya and Umm Kulthum would, in succession, marry and predecease the Prophet's companion and the third caliph, ʿUthman. Fatima became the wife of ʿAli b. Abi Talib, the Prophet's first cousin, companion, and fourth caliph. Muhammad's son al-Qasim died at an early age before Muhammad became a prophet in the period known retrospectively as the *jahiliyya*, the time of ignorance. His other son, ʿAbd Allah, called by the epithets al-

Tayyib and al-Tahir, died after the advent of Islam, Ibn Hisham, *Kitab sirat rasul Allah*, vol. 1, pt. 1: 121; Ibn Sa`d, *Tabaqat*, 1: 133. The only child born to a woman other than Khadija was Ibrahim, the son of the concubine Maryam the Copt, who also died in infancy. Ibn Hisham, *Kitab sirat rasul Allah*, vol. 1, pt. 1: 121.

8. Sura 33: 6; Ibn Hisham, *Kitab sirat rasul Allah*, vol. 1, pt. 2: 1001, where Khadija is described under category *ummahat al-mu'minin*.

9. The title *umm al-mu'minin*, sometimes applied in medieval sources as synonymous with `A'isha, apparently remains an esteemed epithet even in modern, somewhat different circumstances as an honorary title for P.L.O. Chairman Yasir Arafat's eldest sister, a woman also known for her involvement in Palestinian affairs. I am indebted to Dr. Laurie A. Brand of the University of Southern California's School of International Relations for this information.

10. "Mu'minin," is the Arabic word in question. Ibn Sa`d, *Tabaqat*, 8: 64; 67.

11. Ibn Sa`d, *Tabaqat*, 8: 78; Ibn Hisham, *Kitab sirat rasul Allah*, vol. 1, pt. 1: 217.

12. Al-Baladhuri, *Ansab*, 1:412; al-Bukhari, *Sahih al-Bukhari*, 5:47–48; al-Tirmidhi, *Sahih al-Tirmidhi*, 5:366; Muslim, *Sahih Muslim*, 7:134.

13. Ibn Hanbal, *Musnad*, 6: 154.

14. Al-Mufid, *Jamal*, p. 219.

15. Al-Bukhari, *Sahih al-Bukhari*, 4: 200; 5: 38; Muslim, *Sahih Muslim*, 7: 132; Ibn Hanbal, *Musnad*, 1: 84,116, 132, 143; al-Tirmidhi, *Sunan*, 5: 366–67; al-Baladhuri, *Ansab*, 1: 406. The epithet is *khayr nisa'iha*. All hadith originate with `Ali ibn Abi Talib.

16. Ibn Hanbal, *Musnad*, 3: 135; al-Tirmidhi, *Sahih al-Tirmidhi*, 5:367; al-San`ani, *Musannaf*, 11: 430. Same isnads, all originate with Anas ibn Malik.

17. Al-Tabari, *Tafsir*, 6: 393–401.

18. Ibn Hanbal, *Musnad*, 1: 293, 316, 322. All on the authority of Ibn `Abbas.

19. Ibn Hisham, *Kitab sirat rasul Allah*, vol. 1, pt. 1: 156; Bukhari, *Sahih al-Bukhari*, 5: 39; al-Tirmidhi, *Sahih al-Tirmidhi*, 5: 366; Muslim, *Sahih Muslim*, 7:133; al-San`ani, *Musannaf*, 11: 430; 5: 324, where the house described is of pearl.

20. The best overview of the post third/ninth-century explosion of detail and elaboration surrounding Fatima's life remains L. Veccia Vaglieri's article "Fatima" in the *Encyclopedia of Islam*, which directly addresses the plethora of post-ninth-century Shi`i-authored accounts. However, some Western works have mentioned Fatima's legacy in conjunction with both `A'isha and Maryam—most notably, Lammens, *Fatima et les filles de Mahomet* and Neal Robinson, *Christ in Islam and Christianity*, pp. 158–60. On Fatima, see Louis Massignon, "Fatima et La Mubahala de Medine et l'hyperdulie de Fatima," and "La Notion du Voeu et la Devotion Musulmane a Fatima," pp. 550–618; and, more recently, Jane Dammen McAuliffe, "Chosen of All Women," pp. 19–28; and Mahmoud Ayoub, *Redemptive Suffering in Islam*, pp. 27–52. On the symbolic import of Mary's role as mother in medieval Western Christian society, see Clarissa W. Atkinson, *The Oldest Vocation*, pp. 101–43.

21. Ibn Sa`d, *Tabaqat*, 8:19–30; al-Baladhuri, *Ansab*, 1:402–6; al-San`ani, *Musannaf*, 5:485–92; al-Bukhari, *Sahih al-Bukhari*, 5: 36–37; Muslim, *Sahih Muslim*, 7: 140–44; and al-Tirmidhi, *Sahih al-Tirmidhi*, 5: 359–62.

22. Marshall Hodgson, "How Did the Early Shi`a Become Sectarian?" p. 1: "For the early Shi`ites, as for other Arabs, it was descent in the male line which counted—that is from `Ali, not primarily from Muhammad's daughter. Indeed, the whole family of `Ali was given precedence." Although this may have been true for early Shi`i Muslims, by the fourth/tenth century, the ending of the line of imams with the twelfth, all of whom were descended through both Fatima and `Ali led, retrospectively, to the promotion of her hitherto understated historical persona in Twelver Shi`i sources during this period. See also Massignon, "La Notion du voeu," p. 573.

23. Al-Tirmidhi, *Sahih al-Tirmidhi*, 5: 305; al-Tabari, *Ta'wil*, 13: 6–8. The explication of these verses describes Umm Salama as one of the wives of the Prophet, but also among the "people of the house," as well as among "the best." Umm Salama's proximity to the verses concerning Muhammad's family is explained by the fact that she says they were revealed in her house. Despite the association of the *ahl al-bayt* with `Ali, Fatima, Hasan, Husayn, and Muhammad, some traditions suggest, for grammatical reasons concerning the preceding sentence of the same verse explictly addressed to the wives of the Prophet, that this part of the revelation also refers to them.

24. Al-Tirmidhi, *Sahih al-Tirmidhi*, 5: 361; Ibn Hanbal, *Musnad*, 6: 296, 304, 323.

25. Ibn Sa`d, *Tabaqat*, 8: 24.

26. Al-Bukhari, *Sahih al-Bukhari*, 5:36; Muslim, *Sahih Muslim*, 7:141; al-Tirmidhi, *Sahih al-Tirmidhi*, 5: 359, 360.

27. Only al-Bukhari does not feature Muhammad's exchange with `Ali.

28. Al-Bukhari, *Sahih al-Bukhari*, 6: 12; Muslim, *Sahih Muslim*, 7: 142; al-Tirmidhi, *Sahih al-Tirmidhi*, 5: 361–62. See also the Shi`i author al-Mufid, *Kitab al-irshad*, p. 100, who notes this incident without `A'isha's presence.

29. Al-Tirmidhi, *Sahih al-Tirmidhi*, 5: 142–43, 144.

30. Ibn Hanbal, *Musnad*, 3: 64, 80.

31. McAuliffe, "Chosen of All Women," p. 28.

32. Al-Kulayni, *Al-Usul min al-kafi*, 1: 459.

33. Ibn `Abd al-Wahhab, `*Uyun al-mu`jizat*, p. 61.

34. Ibn Shahrashub, *Manaqib Al Abi Talib*, 3: 322.

35. Ibn `Abd al-Wahhab, `*Uyun al-mu`jizat*, pp. 56–57. Perhaps the earliest recorded instance of the epithet *al-batul*, "the virgin," is used explicitly for Maryam, not Fatima, in traditions that refer to the Muslim mission to Christian Ethiopia before the hijra. See Ibn Hanbal, *Musnad*, 1: 203, 461; 5: 292.

36. Ibn `Abd al-Wahhab, `*Uyun al-mu`jizat*, pp. 61–62.

37. Ibid., p. 58; Laoust, *La profession de foi d'Ibn Batta*, p. 65, for `A'isha.

38. Smith and Haddad, "The Virgin Mary in Islamic Tradition," p. 187; Massignon, "La Notion du Voeu," p. 580.

39. Qur'an, 3:42, for Maryam; 33:33 for the ahl al-bayt.

40. Al-Kulayni, *Al-Usul min al-kafi*, 1: 459; Ibn `Abd al-Wahhab, `*Uyun al-mu`jizat*, p. 57.

41. Al-Kulyani, *Al-Usul min al-kafi*, 1: 460–61.

42. Baha'i female ideals also appear to build on the precedent of Islamic historical women and Qur'anic ideals as a basis for their own. Thus they cite Sarah, Asiya, Maryam, and Fatima in addition to their own exemplary females Bahiyyih Khanum and Tarihih. See Shoghi Effendi, *God Passes By*, p. 347.

43. Ibn Sa`d, *Tabaqat*, 1: 393, where *al-tharid* as the Prophet's favorite food is mentioned. Ibn Sa`d, 8: 79 (twice); al-Bukhari, *Sahih al-Bukhari*, 5: 29; Muslim, *Sahih Muslim*, 6: 138; Ibn Hanbal, *Musnad*, 3: 156, 264; 6: 159; al-Tirmidhi, *Sahih al-Tirmidhi*, 5: 365; `Abd Allah al-Darimi, *Sunan al-Darimi*, 2: 106; Abu `Abd al-Rahman al-Nasa'i, *Sunan al-Nasa'i*, 7: 63.

44. The male association of women with food, particularly meat, is not limited to medieval Islamic history. See Carol J. Adams, *The Sexual Politics of Meat*.

45. Crone, *Meccan Trade and the Rise of Islam*, p. 109.

46. Ibn Sa`d, *Tabaqat*, 8: 79.

47. Al-Bukhari, *Sahih al-Bukhari*, 5: 29; al-Darimi, *Sunan al-Darimi*, 2: 106; Muslim, *Sahih Muslim*, 6: 138; Ibn Hanbal, *Musnad*, 3: 156, 264; 6: 159; al-Nasa'i, *Sunan al-Nasa'i*, 7: 63–64; al-Tirmidhi, *Sahih al-Tirmidhi*, 5: 365; Ibn Sa`d, *Tabaqat*, 8: 79 (twice).

48. Al-`Asqalani, *Al-Isaba*, 1: 84–85.

49. Ibn Hanbal, *Musnad*, 3: 135; al-Tirmidhi, *Sahih al-Tirmidhi*, 5: 367; and al-San`ani, *Musannaf*, 11: 430.

50. Ibn Sa`d, *Tabaqat*, 1: 348–49.

51. Al-`Asqalani, *Al-Isaba*, 8: 694; S. Husain Jafri, *The Origins and Early Development of Shi`a Islam*, pp. 122, 130.

52. Al-`Asqalani, *Al-Isaba*, 4: 350.

53. As part of `A'isha's merits, al-Bukhari, *Sahih al-Bukhari*, 5: 29; Muslim, *Sahih Muslim*, 6: 138; al-Tirmidhi, *Sahih al-Tirmidhi*, 5: 365 and Ibn Sa`d, *Tabaqat*, 8: 79 (twice). In conjunction with tharid, al-Darimi, *Sunan al-Darimi*, 2: 106.

54. Al-Nasa'i, *Sunan al-Nasa'i*, 7: 63–64.

55. Ibn Sa`d would appear to be the earliest author and al-Nasa'i the latest.

56. Al-Kulayni, *Al-Usul min al-kafi*, 6: 317–18.

57. Al-Bukhari, *Sahih al-Bukhari*, 6:97.

58. Ibid., 4: 193, 200; 5: 29; 6: 97; Muslim, *Sahih Muslim*, 7: 132–33; Ibn Hanbal, *Musnad*, 4: 394, 409; Ibn Maja, *Sunan Ibn Maja*, 2: 29; al-Tirmidhi, *Sahih al-Tirmidhi*, 8:30; al-Baladhuri, *Ansab*, 1: 413.

59. Al-Bukhari, *Sahih al-Bukhari*, 4: 200. He offers three other versions with the predominant sentence order.

60. Ibid., 5: 29; and Muslim, *Sahih Muslim*, 7: 132–33.

61. Al-Bukhari, *Sahih al-Bukhari*, 4: 193, 200.

62. Ibid., 6: 97; Ibn Maja, *Sunan Ibn Maja*, 2: 29; al-Tirmidhi, *Sahih al-Tirmidhi*, 8: 30.

63. Al-Tabari, *Ta'rikh al-rusul wa al-muluk*, 3: 1362.

64. Al-Tabari, *The History of al-Tabari*, 7: 7, note 13.

65. Robinson, *Christ in Islam*, pp. 158–60. Robinson justifiably notes the problem of accusations against both women of "sexual immorality," but does not document either

heavenly intervention through angels or the notion of each as a truthtelling woman in the face of slander. He also offers other links which, I believe, are more tenuous. For a brief mention of the tie between Maryam and `A'isha, see Smith and Haddad, "Virgin Mary in Islamic Tradition," p. 186.

66. Izutsu, *Ethico-Religious Concepts*, pp. 89–95. Of particular interest is Izutsu's argument that the root is recognized by medieval lexicographers as the exact opposite of *kadhib*, a "lie" or "falsehood." In relation to the epithet *siddiq*, the meaning shifts from the "highly veracious," or "one who never lies" to someone, Izutsu states, who "testifies to the truth of something" (p. 92). He asserts this in the case of Abu Bakr as well as the Qur'anic figures of Maryam, Abraham, and Joseph, to whom the epithet is applied. Such an interpretation of the epithet thus also applies to `A'isha, who testifies to the truth of her own innocence from the charge of adultery, but whom Izutsu does not mention.

67. Qur'an, 24:16, 4:156; also Robinson, *Christ in Islam*, p. 160, who points this parallel out.

68. Ibn Sa'd, *Tabaqat*, 8: 73–74 and 75, where `A'isha utilizes the exact phrase uttered by Maryam in the Qur'an.

69. See chapter 3 and al-Zarkashi, *Al-Ijaba*, p. 14.

70. For Qur'an, 66: 11–12, see al-Tabari, *Ta'wil*, 28: 170–72. For Qur'an, 3: 42, al-Tabari, *Tafsir*, 6: 393–401.

71. Al-Tabari, *Tafsir*, 6: 394.

72. Ibid., 6: 395–96. As also recounted by Abu Hurayra, see Muslim, *Sahih Muslim*, 6: 182; and Ibn Hanbal, *Musnad*, 2: 269.

73. Al-Tabari, *Tafsir*, 6: 399.

74. Al-Bukhari, *Sahih al-Bukhari*, 4: 193, 200; 5: 29; 6: 97; Ibn Hanbal, *Musnad*, 4: 394, 409; Ibn Maja, *Sunan Ibn Maja*, 2: 29; Muslim, *Sahih Muslim*, 7: 132–33; al-Tirmidhi, *Sahih al-Tirmidhi*, 8: 30; al-Baladhuri, *Ansab*, 1: 413.

75. Al-Tabari, *Tafsir*, 6: 397–98.

76. Abu Musa al-Ash'ari (d. 42/662), Murra al-Hamdani (d. 76/695), `Amr ibn Murra (d. 116/734), and Shu'ba (d. 160–161/776–777) comprise the core of first four relaters in every extant version of this hadith in which the content mentions `A'isha.

77. Lammens, *Fatima et les filles de Mahomet*, p. 136, believes that just as `Ali's development is a response to the "legend" of Abu Bakr, so too Fatima's development is "the Shi'i reply" to `A'isha. In fact, the argument may be made that Sunni material, including al-Tabari's exegesis drawing upon early hadith, helped solidify the bases of both Khadija and Fatima's later Sunni and Shi'i superiority in the creation of Islamic female ideals.

78. Robinson, *Christ in Islam*, p. 159, where he cites discussion of verse 33:33, whose third sentence, if applied to the wives of the Prophet, might include `A'isha among the "purified." However, al-Tabari's exegesis of these verses suggests debate over whether they apply to the *ahl al-bayt* (Muhammad, Fatima, `Ali, Hasan, and Husayn) or the wives of the Prophet. `A'isha is not specifically mentioned, nor do wives prevail in further explications of this part of the verse; see al-Tabari, *Ta'wil*, 22: 2–8.

79. Dominique Sourdel, "Une profession de foi de l'historien al-Tabari," pp. 190,

197. For reference to al-Tabari's collected hadith on Ghadir Khumm, the place at which in Shi`i history Muhammad is supposed to have designated `Ali as his choice to succeed him, see Henri Laoust, *La profession de foi d'Ibn Batta*, p. xxxvi, note 82; and al-Mufid, *Kitab al-irshad*, pp. 93–95.

80. Sourdel, "Une profession de foi," pp. 190, 197.

81. Ibn `Asakir, *Kitab al-arba`in*, p. 57.

82. See also McAuliffe, "Chosen of All Women," pp. 20, 28, who asserts, as a result of her analysis of exegesis beginning with al-Tabari, that "Fatima's status as the first female of Islam is unchallenged" for both Shi`i and most Sunni Muslims. Such an assertion omits any hint of a an earlier debate by ignoring pre-fourth/tenth-century hadith sources.

83. Al-Zarkashi, *Al-Ijaba*, pp. 13–31.

84. Ibid. In this reference he cites the Shafi`i theologian `Ali al-Amidi's (d. 631/ 1233) work, *Abkar al-afkar*.

85. Dorothy Van Ess, *Fatima and Her Sisters*, p. 53.

86. Al-Baghdadi, *Kitab usul al-din*, p. 306.

87. Ibid., p. 306; Henri Laoust, *Les schismes dans l'Islam*, p. 428.

88. Abu Hanifa, *Sharh al-fiqh al-akbar*, p. 42. This compilation was authored by Abu Mansur al-Samarqandi (d. 333/944)

89. Ibn Taymiyya, *Sharh al-`aqida al-wasitiyya*, p. 147.

90. Ibid., p. 148.

91. Ibn Taymiyya, *Minhaj*, 2: 182–202. Written in response to the Shi`i Muslim theologian al-`Allama al-Hilli (d. 726/1325), see Laoust, "La critique du sunnisme," pp. 35–60.

92. Ibn Taymiyya, *Minhaj*, 2: 193.

93. Combs-Schilling, *Sacred Performances*, p. 92, argues that "Muslims on the whole find blasphemous the notion that it might have been good for `A'isha to have won at the Battle of the Camel, to have become an important political actor in Islam and a public model for other women." In fact, this work argues that while Sunni and Shi`i Muslims deplored `A'isha's political actions, Sunni Muslims found aspects of her historical persona to promote and celebrate as a model for other women. Contrary to Combs-Schilling's blanket assertion, the Sunni Muslim community held a more nuanced vision of `A'isha, one that allowed both negative and positive components of her depiction to exist simultaneously.

94. Thomas W. Arnold, *Painting in Islam*; Walter B. Denny, "Women and Islamic Art," pp. 148–49.

95. Mustafa Darir, Siyer-i Nebi, Hazine 1221, fol. 8a; and for the modern Turkish translation, Mustafa Darir, *Kitab-i Siyer-i Nebi*, 1: 463. For the significance of these manuscripts in Islamic art history, see Zeren Tanindi, *Siyer-i Nebi: Islam Tasvir Sanatinda Hazreti Muhammed'in Hayati*; and Carol Garret Fisher, "The Pictorial Cycle of `Siyer-i Nebi.'"

96. Darir, Siyer-i Nebi, Hazine 1221, fol. 30a; Darir, *Kitab-i Siyer*, 1: 552.

97. Darir, Siyer-i Nebi, Hazine 1221, fol. 88b; Darir, *Kitab-i Siyer*, 1: 552.

98. Darir, Siyer-i Nebi, Hazine 1221, fol. 168a.

99. Darir, *Kitab-i Siyer*, 1: 623; Ibn Hisham, *Kitab sirat rasul Allah*, vol. 1, pt. 1: 154.

100. Ibn Hisham, *Kitab sirat rasul Allah*, vol. 1, pt. 1: 155.

101. Darir, Siyer-i Nebi, Hazine 1221, fol. 170b; Darir, *Kitab-i Siyer*, 1: 625–26; Ibn Hisham, *Kitab sirat rasul Allah*, vol. 1, pt. 1: 158 where Khadija is not mentioned.

102. Massignon, "La notion du voeu"; Goldziher, *Muslim Studies*, 2: 274; and Margaret Smith, *Rabi`a the Mystic*, pp. 179–80, where she details the Muslim veneration of Fatima's tomb in Medina.

103. Al-Kulayni, *Al-Usul min al-kafi*, 1: 460–61.

104. Darir, Siyer-i Nebi, T. 1974, fol. 12b.

105. Ibid.; Darir, *Kitab-i Siyer*, 2: 578, which in modern Turkish reads "Betul-i Azra Fatimetuzzehra'yi Ali evlendir."

106. Darir, Siyer-i Nebi, T. 1974, fol. 21b.

107. Qur'an, 3: 37; 19: 25–26; al-Kulayni, *Al-Usul min al-kafi*, 1: 460.

108. Darir, Siyer-i Nebi, Turkish MS. 419, fol. 22a; Darir, *Kitab-i Siyer*, 2: 588–89.

109. Ibid., Turkish MS. 419, fol. 44a; *Kitab-i Siyer*, 2: 603–4.

110. Massignon, "La notion du voeu," p. 579, who cites the text and the tale.

111. Darir, Siyer-i Nebi, Turkish MS. 419, fol. 24b; Darir, *Kitab-i Siyer*, 2: 594.

112. Ibn Hisham, *Kitab sirat rasul Allah*, vol. 1, pt. 1: 422. For other, more positive, explanations of this title, see al-Tabari, *Ta'rikh*, 3: 1272–73; for Shi`i Muslims, see Schimmel, *Islamic Names*, p. 34.

113. Darir, *Kitab-i Siyer*, 2: 277.

114. Darir, Siyer-i Nebi, Turkish MS. 3, fol. 106b; *Kitab al-Siyer*, 2:274–75.

115. Darir, Siyer-i Nebi, Turkish Ms. 3, fol. 115a; Darir, *Kitab-i Siyer*, 2: 278. `A'isha's age at the time of the proposal is also seven in early Arabic accounts; see Ibn Sa`d, *Tabaqat*, 8: 64–65.

116. Darir, *Kitab-i Siyer*, 3: 320.

117. Darir, Siyer-i Nebi, Hazine 1223, fol. 136b.

118. De Von Hammer, *Histoire de l'empire Ottoman*, 2: 258.

119. Darir, Siyer-i Nebi, Hazine 1223, fol. 144b.

120. Ibid., fol. 410b.; Darir, *Kitab-i Siyer*, 3: 761.

121. Darir, Siyer-i Nebi, Turkish MS. 419, fol. 40b; Darir, *Kitab-i Siyer*, 2: 601–2.

122. Darir, Siyer-i Nebi, Hazine 1223, fol. 417a.

123. For a brief outline of this argument, see Spellberg, "Marriages Made in Heaven and Illustrated on Earth," pp. 47–54.

6. The Last Word: A Note in Conclusion

1. Mumtaz Moin, *Umm al-Mu'minin `A'ishah Siddiqah*, p. 40.

glossary

Abu Bakr. Companion of the Prophet, first caliph, and father of `A'isha bint Abi Bakr. Died in 13 A.H./A.D. 634.

`Ali ibn Abi Talib.* First cousin of the Prophet, fourth caliph, and husband of the Prophet's daughter Fatima. He became the first of the Shi`i imams and fought `A'isha bint Abi Bakr during the first civil war, which began in 36/656. He died in 41/661.

Battle of the Camel. First conflict in the first civil war in the Islamic community. The battle was fought near Basra in 36/656 between the forces of `A'isha, Talha, and al-Zubayr and the fourth caliph, `Ali ibn Abi Talib. `A'isha's party was defeated, her two male supporters killed, and she retired from the politics of succession. The conflict determined the first doctrinal split within the Islamic community between the supporters of `Ali, the Shi`i, and the rest of the community who, over the next two to three centuries, would identify themselves as the Sunni majority.

Fatima bint Muhammad. Longest-lived daughter of the Prophet Muhammad (d. 11/633), wife of Ali ibn Abi Talib, and mother of the Shi`i imams Hasan and Husayn, the Prophet's grandsons. Shi`is revere her as the most excellent of women.

fitna. Civil war, but a term also applied to women as sources of beauty, sexual power, and loss of male control.

hadith. Written reports or traditions that preserve the Prophet's precedent. Hadith consist of two parts: the **isnad**, or chain of named, originally oral, transmitters, and the **matn**, the core content of the report.

hadith al-ifk. The "affair of the lie," the accusation of adultery made against `A'isha in 5/627. Sunni Muslims believe `A'isha vindicated by the revelation of Qur'anic verses proving her innocence, while Shi`i Muslims dispute her exoneration.

kayd. A term for "guile" or "wile" found in the Qur'an and applied, among others, to the wife of the vizier in the story of the Prophet Joseph, later known as Zulaykha'.

Khadija bint Khuwaylid. First wife of the Prophet (d. 619), first convert to Islam, and the mother of Fatima. A business woman before her marriage, she supported Muhammad economically and spiritually, and is esteemed by Sunni and Shi`i Muslims.

Muhammad. The last Prophet of Allah, the founder of the first religiopolitical community of Muslims. He died in 11/632.

Qur'an. The holy scripture of Islam, revealed by the one god Allah to the prophet Muhammad in Arabic via the angel Gabriel. The Qur'an consists of 114 chapters, or **suras**.

al-Rawafid. Negative Sunni term for Twelver Shi`i Muslims who are "the rejectors" of the first three Islamic caliphs, including Abu Bakr, `Umar, and `Uthman. Shi`is argue that `Ali, the fourth caliph in this continuum for Sunnis, was unfairly denied primacy of place, making his predecessors usurpers.

*Shi`i.* Originally, the "party" (**shi`a**) of `Ali ibn Abi Talib, the fourth caliph, the Prophet Muhammad's cousin and his son-in-law. A minority in the Islamic world, Shi`is believe that the only true political and spiritual authority is vested in patrilineal descendants of `Ali. These men are called the **imams**.

sunna. The Prophet Muhammad's example in word and deed, preserved orally after his death.

Sunni. Designation for the majority of Muslims who accept the original order of the first four caliphs and supported `A'isha.

tabaqat. Biographical dictionaries.

tafsir. Qur'anic exegesis.

ta'rikh. Chronicle.

al-tharid. The Prophet Muhammad's favorite dish, a combination of bread and broth, usually with meat included.

`*ulama'.* Islamic male religious authorities, learned in Qur'an, hadith, law, and theology. This exclusively male group articulated the medieval debate about `A'isha.

ummahat al-mu'minin. "Mothers of the believers," the term applied as an honorific to all of Prophet Muhammad's wives as the new Muslim female elite. The Qur'an directed special injunctions explicitly to them about behavior and dress.

bibliography

Manuscripts

al-Andalusi, Abu ʿImran Musa ibn Muhammad ibn ʾAbd Allah al-Waʿiz. Qasida fi madh ʾAʾisha. MS. no. 4066, Yahuda Arabic Collection, Princeton University Library, Princeton, N.J.

—— Qasida. OR no. 5509, British Museum Library, London.

—— Qasida fi madh umm al-muʾminin ʾAʾisha. Adab no. 657, Maʿhad al-Makhtutat, Cairo.

Darir, Mustafa. Siyer-i Nebi. Hazine MS. 1221, Topkapi Palace Museum, Istanbul.

—— Siyer-i Nebi. Hazine MS. 1223, Topkapi Palace Museum, Istanbul.

—— Siyer-i Nebi. MS. T. 1974, Museum of Turkish and Islamic Arts, Ibrahim Pasha Palace, Istanbul.

—— Siyer-i Nebi. Turkish MS. 419, Chester Beatty Library, Dublin.

—— Siyer-i Nebi. Turkish MS. 3, Spencer Collection, New York Public Library. New York City.

Ibn al-Haytham, ʿAbd al-Karim. Hadith al-ifk. Hadith no. 244, Maʿhad al-Makhtutat, Cairo.

al-Shadhili, Qadir ibn Muhammad. Radd al-ʿuqul al-taʾisha ila maʿrifa ma ikhtassat bihi Khadija wa ʾAʾisha. MS. 3678, Chester Beatty Library, Dublin.

al-Suyuti, Jalal al-Din. ʾAyn al-isaba. MS. Majamiʿ no. 123, Dar al-kutub, Cairo.

Published Works

Abu al-Nasr, ʿUmar. ʾAli wa ʾAʾisha. Cairo: ʾIsa al-Babi al-Halabi, 1947.

Abbott, Nabia. `A'ishah: The Beloved of Mohammed*. Chicago: University of Chicago Press, 1942.

—— "Hadith Literature II: Collection and Transmission of Hadith." In A. Beeston, T. Johnstone, R. Serjeant, and G. Smith, eds., *Arabic Literature to the End of the Umayyad Period*, pp. 289–98. Cambridge: Cambridge University Press, 1983.

—— *Studies in Arabic Literary Papyri I: Historical Texts*. Chicago: University of Chicago Press, 1957.

—— *Studies in Arabic Literary Papyri II: Qur'anic Commentary and Tradition*. Chicago: University of Chicago Press, 1967

—— *Two Queens of Baghdad: The Mother and Wife of Harun al-Rashid*. Chicago: University of Chicago Press, 1946.

—— "Women and the State in Early Islam." *Journal of Near Eastern Studies* 1 (1942): 106–27.

Abdul Rauf, Muhammad. "Hadith Literature I: The Development of the Science of Hadith." In A. Beeston, T. Johnstone, R. Serjeant, and G. Smith, eds., *Arabic Literature to the End of the Umayyad Period*, pp. 271–79. Cambridge: Cambridge University Press, 1983.

Abu al-`Izz, `Ali Ahmad. *Umm al-mu'minin `A'isha al-mubarra'a*. Cairo, n.d.

Abu Hanifa, Al-Nu`man Ibn Thabit. *Sharh al-fiqh al-akbar*. Beirut: Al-Maktabat al-`Asriyya, 1983.

Abu Lughod, Leila. *Veiled Sentiments: Honor and Poetry in Bedouin Society*. Berkeley: University of California Press, 1986.

Adams, Carol. *The Sexual Politics of Meat: A Feminist-Vegetarian Critical Theory*. New York: Continuum, 1991.

al-Afghani, Sa`id. `A'isha wa al-siyasa*. Cairo: Lajnat al-Ta'lif wa al-Tarjuma, 1957.

Ahmed, Leila. "Women and the Advent of Islam." *Signs* 11, no. 4 (1986): 665–91.

—— *Women and Gender in Islam: Historical Roots of A Modern Debate*. New Haven: Yale University Press, 1992.

Akinci, Ahmed C. *Hazretli Aise*. Istanbul: Sinan Yayinevi, 1980.

Appignanesi, Lisa and Sara Maitland, eds. *The Rushdie File*. Syracuse, N.Y.: Syracuse University Press, 1990.

al-`Aqqad, Mahmud. *Al-Siddiqa bint al-siddiq*. Cairo: Dar al-Ma`ani, 1953.

Arafat, W. "A Controversial Incident and the Related Poem in the Life of Hassan B. Thabit." *Bulletin of the School of Oriental and African Studies* 17 (1955): 197–206.

Aristotle. *The Politics*. T. Sinclair, tr. Harmondsworth, Eng.: Penguin, 1962.

Arnold, Thomas. *Painting in Islam: A Study in the Place of Pictorial Art in Muslim Culture*. New York: Dover, 1965.

Ascha, Ghassan. *Du Statut Inferieur de la Femme en Islam*. Paris: L`Harmattan, 1981.

al-`Asqalani, Shihab al-Din Ibn Hajar. *Kitab al-Isaba fi tamyiz al-sahaba*. 8 vols. Cairo: Matba`at Mustafa Muhammad, 1939.

—— *Kitab al-Isaba fi tamyiz al-sahaba*. 4 vols. Osnabruck: Biblio Verlag, 1980.

—— *Tahdhib al-Tahdhib*. 12 vols. Beirut, 1964.

Atkinson, Clarissa. *The Oldest Vocation: Christian Motherhood in the Middle Ages.* Ithaca, N.Y., Cornell University Press, 1991.

'Attar, Farid al-Din. *Tadhkirat al-awliya'.* 2 vols. R. Nicholson, ed. London: Luzac, 1905.

Austen, Jane. *Northanger Abbey.* New York: Dutton, 1980.

Ayoub, Mahmoud. *Redemptive Suffering in Islam: A Study of the Devotional Aspects of 'Ashura' in Twelver Shi'ism.* The Hague: Mouton, 1978.

Azmi, M. M. *Studies in Early Hadith Literature.* Beirut: al-Maktab al-Islam, 1968.

al-Baghdadi, 'Abd al-Qahir. *Al-Farq bayn al-firaq.* Beirut: Dar al-'Afaq al-Jadida, 1973.

—— *Kitab usul al-din.* Istanbul: Matba'at al-Dawla, 1928.

Baktash, Mayel. "Ta'ziyeh and Its Philosophy." In P. Chelkowski, ed., *Ta'ziyeh: Ritual Drama in Iran,* pp. 95–120. New York: New York University Press, 1979.

al-Baladhuri, Ahmad ibn Yahya. *Ansab al-ashraf,* vol. 1. M. Hamidullah, ed. Cairo: Dar al-Ma'arif, 1959.

—— *Ansab al-ashraf.* vol. 5. S. Goitein, ed. Jerusalem: Jerusalem University Press, 1936.

—— *Futuh al-buldan.* M. J. De Goeje, ed. Leiden: E. J. Brill, 1866.

Baraniq, Muhammad. *'A'isha al-'alima.* Cairo: Dar al-Ma'arif, 1983.

—— *'A'isha al-siyasa.* Cairo: Dar al-Ma'arif, 1983.

Barthold, Wilhelm. *Turkestan Down to the Mongol Invasion.* London: Luzac, 1958.

Bashear, Suliman. "Riding Beasts on Divine Missions: An Examination of the Ass and Camel Traditions." *Journal of Semitic Studies* 37, no. 1 (Spring 1991): 37–76.

Bennett, Judith. "Medievalism and Feminism." *Speculum* 68, no. 2 (April 1993): 309–32.

Berkey, Jonathan. *The Transmission of Knowledge in Medieval Cairo: A Social History of Islamic Education.* Princeton: Princeton University Press, 1992.

Bint 'Abd al-Rahman, 'A'isha. *Nisa' al-nabi.* Beirut: Dar al-Kitab al-'Arabiyya, 1983.

Birkeland, Harris. *The Lord Guideth: Studies on Primitive Islam.* Oslo: H. Aschehoug, 1956.

Blankenship, Khalid Y., tr. *The History of al-Tabari: Challenge to Empires.* Albany: SUNY Press, 1993.

Bouhdiba, Abdelwahab. *Sexuality in Islam.* A. Sheridan, tr. London: Routledge and Keegan Paul, 1985.

Buck, William. *Ramayana: King Rama's Way.* Berkeley: University of California Press, 1976.

al-Bukhari, Muhammad ibn 'Abd Allah. *Sahih al-Bukhari.* 9 vols. Cairo: Mustafa al-Babi al-Halabi, 1958.

Bulliet, Richard. *The Patricians of Nishapur: A Study in Medieval Social History.* Cambridge: Harvard University Press, 1972.

Bynum, Caroline. "Jesus as Mother and Abbott as Mother: Some Thoughts in Twelfth-Century Cistercian Writing." *Jesus as Mother: Studies in the Spirituality of the High Middle Ages.* Berkeley: University of California Press, 1982.

Caetani, Leone. *Chronographia Islamica.* 5 vols. Paris: Librairie Paul Geuthner, 1912.

Cahen, Claude and Jean Sauvaget, *Introduction to the Study of the Muslim East.* Berkeley: University of California Press, 1965.

El Calamawy, Sahair. "Narrative Elements in the Hadith Literature." In A. Beeston, T. Johnstone, R. Serjeant, and G. Smith, eds., *Arabic Literature to the End of the Umayyad Period*, pp. 308–16. Cambridge: Cambridge University Press, 1983.

Campbell, John. *Honour, Family, and Patronage*. Oxford: Oxford University Press, 1964.

Combs-Schilling, M. E. *Sacred Performances: Islam, Sexuality, and Sacrifice*. New York: Columbia University Press, 1989.

Conrad, Lawrence. "Abraha and Muhammad: Some Observations Apropos of Chronology and Literary Topoi in the Early Arabic Historical Tradition." *Bulletin of the School of Oriental and African Studies* 50, no. 2 (1987): 225–40.

Cook, Michael. *Early Muslim Dogma: A Source Critical Study*. New York: Cambridge University Press, 1981.

—— *Muhammad*. Oxford: Oxford University Press, 1983.

Cook, Michael and Patricia Crone. *Hagarism: The Making of the Islamic World*. Cambridge: Cambridge University Press, 1977.

Coulson, N. J. "European Criticism of Hadith Literature." In A. Beeston, T. Johnstone, R. Serjeant, and G. Smith, eds., *Arabic Literature to the End of the Umayyad Period*, pp. 317–21. Cambridge: Cambridge University Press, 1983.

Crone, Patricia. *Meccan Trade and the Rise of Islam*. Princeton: Princeton University Press, 1987.

Daniel, Norman. *Islam and the West: The Making of an Image*. Edinburgh: University of Edinburgh Press, 1960.

al-Darimi, `Abd Allah ibn `Abd al-Rahman. *Sunan al-Darimi*. 2 vols. Beirut: Dar al-Ihya' al-Sunna al-Nabawiyya, n.d.

Darir, Mustafa. *Kitab-i Siyer-i Nebi: Peygamber Efendemizin Hayati*. 3 vols. Mehmet Faruk Gurtunca, ed. Istanbul: Saglam Yayinevei, 1985.

Denny, Walter. "Women in Islamic Art." In Y. Haddad and E. Findly , eds., *Women, Religion, and Social Change*, pp. 147–80. Albany: SUNY Press, 1985.

De Von Hammer, J. *Histoire de l'Empire Ottoman*. 3 vols. M. Dochez, tr. Paris: Bethune et Plon, 1844.

al-Dhahabi, Shams al-Din ibn Ahmad `Uthman. *Kitab tadhkirat al-huffaz*. 4 vols. Hyderabad, 1968.

—— *Siyar `alam al-nubala'*. 2 vols. Cairo: Dar al-Ma`arif, 1957.

Dols, Michael. *The Black Death in the Middle East*. Princeton: Princeton University Press, 1977.

Donner, Fred M. "`A'isha." *Dictionary of the Middle Ages*. 13 vols. John Strayer, ed. New York: Scribners, 1989.

—— "The Death of Abu Talib." In J. Marks and R. Good, eds., *Love and Death in the Ancient Near East: Essays in Honor of Marvin H. Pope*, pp. 237–45. Guildford, Conn.: Four Quarters, 1987.

Duri, A. A. *The Rise of Historical Writing Among the Arabs*. L. Conrad, ed. and tr. Princeton: Princeton University Press, 1983.

Effendi, Shoghi. *God Passes By*. Wilmette, Ill.: Baha'i, 1944.

Elias, Jamal. "Female and Feminine in Islamic Mysticism." *The Muslim World* 58, nos. 3/4 (July–October 1988): 209–24.

Elshtain, Jean. *Public Man, Private Woman.* Princeton: Princeton University Press, 1953.

Fares, Bishr. *Honneur chez les Arabes avant l'Islam.* Paris: Adrian Maisonneuve, 1932.

Fernea, Elizabeth W. and Basima W. Bezirgan, "`A'ishah bint Abi Bakr, Wife of the Prophet Muhammad." In E. Fernea and B. Bezirgan, eds., *Middle Eastern Muslim Women Speak*, pp. 27–36. Austin: University of Texas, 1977.

Fischer, Michael M. *Iran: From Religious Dispute to Revolution.* Cambridge: Harvard University Press, 1980.

Fisher, Carol Garret. "The Pictorial Cycle of Siyer-i Nebi: A Late Sixteenth-Century Manuscript of the Life of Muhammad." Ph.D. dissertation, Michigan State University, 1981.

Frazier, Antonia. *The Warrior Queens.* New York: Knopf, 1989.

Friedl, Erika. *Women of Deh Koh: Lives in An Iranian Village.* Washington, D.C.: Smithsonian Institution Press, 1989.

Gardet, L. "Fitna." *Encyclopaedia of Islam.* 2d ed., 2:930–31.

Garrard, Mary. "Artemesia and Susanna." In N. Broude and M. Garrard, eds., *Feminism and Art History: Questioning the Litany*, pp. 147–72. New York: Harper and Row, 1982.

Giffen, Lois. *The Theory of Profane Love Among the Arabs: The Development of the Genre.* New York: New York University Press, 1971.

Gilmore, David, ed., *Honor and Shame and the Unity of the Mediterranean.* Washington, D.C.: American Anthropological Association, 1987.

—— "Introduction: The Shame of Dishonor." In D. Gilmore, ed., *Honor and Shame and the Unity of the Mediterranean*, pp. 2–21. Washington, D.C.: American Anthroplogical Association, 1987.

Giovanni, Maureen. "Female Chastity Codes in the Circum-Mediterranean: Comparative Perspectives." In D. Gilmore, ed., *Honor and Shame and the Unity of the Mediterranean*, pp. 61–74. Washington, D.C.: American Anthropological Association, 1987.

Goldziher, Ignaz. *Muslim Studies.* 2 vols. S. M. Stern and C. R. Barber, trs. London; Allen and Unwin, 1971.

Haddad, Yvonne Y. "Islam, Women and Revolution in Twentieth-Century Arab Thought." In Y. Haddad and E. Findly, eds., *Women, Religion, and Social Change*, pp. 275–307. Albany: SUNY Press, 1975.

al-Hakimi, Najm al-Din `Umara. *Ta'rikh al-Yaman.* Cairo: Matba`at al-Sa`ada, 1976.

Hamada, `Abd al-Ghani. *Al-Mar'a al-khalida fi ta'rikh al-Islam.* Aleppo: Matba`at al-Thabit, 1974.

Hawting. G. *The First Dynasty of Islam: The Umayyad Caliphate A.D. 661–750.* Carbondale: Southern Illinois University Press, 1987.

Heilbrun, Carolyn. *Writing a Woman's Life.* New York: Ballantine Books, 1988.

Hinds, Martin. "The Murder of the Caliph `Uthman." *International Journal of Middle Eastern Studies* 3 (1972): 450–69.

Hodgson, Marshall. "How Did the Early Shi`a Become Sectarian?" *Journal of the American Oriental Society* 75 (1955): 1–13.

Houtsma, M. T. "The Death of Nizam al-Mulk and Its Consequences." *Journal of Indian History* 3 (1924): 147–60.

Humphreys, R. Stephen. *Islamic History: A Framework for Inquiry.* Princeton: Princeton University Press, 1991.

——"Qur'anic Myth and Narrative Structure in Early Islamic Historiography." In R. Clover and R. S. Humphreys, eds., *Tradition and Innovation in Late Antiquity* , pp. 271–90. Madison: University of Wisconsin Press, 1989.

Ibn 'Abd Rabbih, Ahmad Ibn Muhammad. *Al-'Iqd al-farid.* 3 vols. Cairo: al-Matba'at al-Amira, 1876.

Ibn 'Abd al-Wahhab, Husayn. *'Uyun al-mu'jizat.* Beirut: n.p., 1983.

Ibn 'Asakir, Fakhr al-Din. *Kitab al-arba'in fi manaqib ummahat al-mu'minin.* Damascus: Matba'at al-'Ilmiyya, 1986.

Ibn al-Athir, 'Izz al-Din Abu al-Hasan. *Usd al-ghaba fi ma'rifat al-sahaba.* 5 vols. Cairo: al-Matba'at al-Wahbiyya, 1863.

Ibn Habib, Muhammad. *Kitab al-muhabbar.* Beirut: Matba'at al-Da'ira, 1942.

Ibn Hanbal, Muhammad. *Musnad.* 6 vols. Cairo: n.p., 1895.

Ibn Hisham, 'Abd al-Malik. *Kitab sirat rasul Allah.* 2 vols. F. Wustenfeld, ed. Gottingen, 1858–60; rptd. Frankfurt: Minerva, 1961.

Ibn Kathir, Isma'il ibn 'Umar. *Al-Bidaya wa al-nihaya.* 14 vols. Cairo, 1939.

Ibn Khallikan, Muhammad ibn Abi Bakr. *Wafayat al-a'yan.* 7 vols. Ihsan 'Abbas, ed. Beirut: Dar al-Thiqafa, 1968.

Ibn Maja, Muhammad ibn Yazid. *Sunan Ibn Maja.* 2 vols. Beirut, 1980.

Ibn al-Nadim. *Kitab al-fihrist.* G. Flugel, ed. Beirut: Khayyat, 1964.

Ibn Qutayba, 'Abd Allah ibn Muslim. *Kitab ta'wil mukhtalif al-hadith.* Cairo, 1909.

—— *'Uyun al-akhbar.* 4 vols. Cairo: Dar al-Kutub al-Misriyya, 1930.

Ibn Sa'd, Muhammad. *Al-Tabaqat al-kubra.* 8 vols. Beirut: Dar Sadir, 1957–58.

Ibn al-Sa'i, 'Ali ibn Anjab. *Nisa' al-khulafa'.* M. Jawad, ed. Cairo: Dar al-Ma'rif, 1968.

Ibn Shahrashub, Rashid al-Din. *Manaqib Al Abi Talib.* 4 vols. Qumm: Mataba'at al-'Ilmiyya, 1959.

Ibn Taymiyya, Taqi al-Din Ahmad. *Minhaj al-sunna al-nabawiyya.* 4 vols. Cairo: Matba'at al-Kubra al-Aminiyya, 1904.

—— *Sharh al-'aqida al-wasitiyya.* Cairo: Matba'at al-Jadida, 1966.

Izutsu, Toshihiko. *Ethico-Religious Concepts in the Qur'an.* Montreal: McGill-Queens University Press, 1966.

Jafri, S. Husain. *The Origins and Early Development of Shi'a Islam.* London: Longman, 1979.

al-Jahiz, 'Amr. *Al-Qawl fi al-bighal.* Charles Pellat, ed. Cairo, 1955.

—— *Kitab al-hayawan.* 7 vols. Cairo: al-Bab al-Halabi, 1938.

Juynboll, G.H.A. *Muslim Tradition: Studies in Chronology, Provenance, and Authorship of Early Hadith.* Cambridge: Cambridge University Press, 1983.

Kahhala, 'Umar R. *'Alam al-nisa' fi 'alam al-'Arab wa al-Islam.* 5 vols. Damascus: al-Hashimiyya, 1958–1959.

Keddie, Nikki and Beth Baron, eds. *Women in Middle Eastern History: Shifting Boundaries in*

Sex and Gender. New Haven: Yale University Press, 1991.

Khalifa ibn Khayyat al-`Usfuri. *Kitab al-tabaqat*. Riyadh: Dar Tiba, 1982.

―― *Ta'rikh Khalifa ibn Khayyat*. 2 vols. `Akram al-`Umari, ed. Najaf: Matba`at al-Adab, 1967.

Khamis, Muhammad. *Al-sayyida `A'isha umm al-mu'minin*. Aleppo: Dar al-Da`wa, 1976.

Kohlberg, E. "Shi`i Hadith." In A. Beeston, T. Johnstone, R. Sergeant, and G. Smith, ed., *Arabic Literature to the End of the Umayyad Period*, pp. 299–303. Cambridge: Cambridge University Press, 1983.

al-Kulayni, Muhammad ibn Ya`qub. *Al-Usul min al-kafi*. 8 vols. A. al-Ghifari, ed. Tehran, 1969–71.

Lammens, Henri. *Fatima et les filles de Mahomet*. Rome: Scripta Pontificii Instituti Biblici, 1912.

―― "Le Triumvirat Abou Bakr, `Omar et Abou `Obaida." *Melanges de la Faculte Orientale* 4 (1910): 113–44.

Lane, Edward. *An Arabic-English Lexicon*. 8 vols. London: Williams and Norgate, 1877.

Laoust, Henri. "La critique du sunnisme dans la doctrine d'al-Hilli." *Revue des Etudes Islamiques* 34 (1966): 35–60.

―― *La profession de foi d'Ibn Batta*. Damascus: Institut Francais de Damas, 1958.

―― *Les schismes dans l'Islam*. Paris: Payot, 1977.

Lapidus, Ira M. *A History of Islamic Societies*. Cambridge: Cambridge University Press, 1988.

Levy, Reuben. *A Baghdad Chronicle*. Cambridge: Cambridge University Press, 1929.

Lichtenstadter, Ilse. *Women in Aiyam al-Arab*. London: Royal Asiatic Society, 1935.

Lowenthal, David. *The Past Is a Foreign Country*. Cambridge: Cambridge University Press, 1985.

Lutfi, Huda. "Al-Sakhawi's Kitab al-Nisa' As a Source for the Social and Economic History of Muslim Women During the Fifteenth Century A.D." *The Muslim World* 71 (1981): 104–24.

Madelung, Wilferd. "Early Sunni Doctrine Concerning Faith as Reflected in the Kitab al-Iman of Abu `Ubayd al-Qasim ibn Sallam (d. 224/834)," *Studia Islamica* 32 (1970): 233–54.

Malti-Douglas, Fedwa. "Biography, Islamic." *Dictionary of the Middle Ages*. 13 vols. New York: Scribners, 1983.

―― *Woman's Body, Woman's Word: Gender and Discourse in Arabo-Islamic Writing*. Princeton: Princeton University Press, 1991.

Massignon, Louis. *Opera Minora*. 2 vols. Y. Moubarac, ed. Paris: Presses Universitaires de France, 1969.

――"La Mubahala de Medine et l'hyperdulie de Fatima," 1:550–72.

―― "La Notion du Voeu et la Devotion Musulmane à Fatima," 1: 573–91.

al-Mas`udi, `Ali ibn al-Husayn. *Muruj al-dhahab wa ma`adin al-jawhar*. 9 vols. C. Barbier de Meynard and P. de Courteille, eds. Paris: 1861–77.

―― *Muruj al-dhahab wa ma`adin al-jawhar*. 4 vols. Y. Daghir, ed. Beirut: Dar al-Andalus, 1965.

al-Mawardi, Abu al-Hasan. *Ahkam al-sultaniyya.* Cairo: Dar al-Tawfiqiyya, 1983.

McAuliffe, Jane. "'A'isha." *Encyclopedia of Religion.* 16 vols. Mircea Eliade, ed. New York: Macmillan, 1987.

—— "Chosen of All Women: Mary and Fatima in Qur'anic Exegesis." *Islamochristiana* 7 (1981): 19–28.

McDermott, Marin J. *The Theology of al-Shaikh al-Mufid.* Beirut: Dar al-Mashriq, 1978.

Mernissi, Fatima. *Beyond the Veil.* Cambridge: Schenkman, 1975.

—— *Le harem politique.* Paris: Albin Michel, 1987.

—— *The Veil and the Male Elite: A Feminist Interpretation of Women's Rights in Islam.* Reading, Mass.: Addison Wesley, 1992.

—— *Women and Islam: A Historical and Theological Enquiry.* M. Lakeland, tr. London, 1991.

Miles, Margaret. *Carnal Knowing: Female Nakedness and Religious Meaning in the Christian West.* Boston: Beacon Press, 1982.

Moin, Mumtaz. *Umm al-Mu'minin 'A'ishah Siddiqah.* Karachi: Royal Book Co., 1979.

Momen, Moojan. *An Introduction to Shi'i Islam: The History and Doctrines of Twelver Shi'ism.* New Haven: Yale University Press, 1985.

Morsy, Magali. *Les Femmes du Prophete.* Paris: Mercure de France, 1989.

Mottahedeh, Roy. *Loyalty and Leadership in an Early Islamic Society.* Princeton: Princeton University Press, 1980.

al-Mubarrad, Muhammad ibn Yazid. *Al-Kamil.* 4 vols. M. Ibrahim and S. Shahata, eds. Cairo: Maktabat Nahdat Misr, 1956.

al-Mufid, Muhammad ibn Muhammad. *Kitab al-irshad.* Najaf: Matba'at al-Haydariyya, 1962.

—— *Kitab al-jamal.* Qumm, 1963.

Muslim, Ibn Hajjaj al-Qushayri. *Sahih Muslim.* 8 vols. Cairo: Matba'at Muhammad 'Ali wa awladihi, 1963.

al-Nasa'i, Abu 'Abd al-Rahman. *Sunan al-Nasa'i.* 8 vols. Cairo: Mustafa al-Babi al-Halabi, 1964.

Naskali, Esko. "Women in the Prophet's Family as They Feature in Popular Bazaar Literature." In Bo Utas, ed., *Women in Islamic Societies: Social and Historical Perspectives,* pp. 245–50. London: Curzon Press, 1983.

Necefzade, Yakub K. *Ayse Anamiz.* Istanbul, 1967.

Newby, Gordon. *A History of the Jews of Arabia: From Ancient Times Until Their Eclipse Under Islam.* Columbia: University of South Carolina Press, 1988.

—— *The Making of the Last Prophet: A Reconstruction of the Earliest Biography of Muhammad.* Columbia: University of South Carolina Press, 1989.

Nizam al-Mulk, al-Hasan ibn 'Ali. *Siyar al-muluk.* Hubert Darke, ed. Tehran: Bunjah-i va Nashr-i Kitab, 1962.

Noth, Albrecht. *Quellenkritische Studien zu Themen, Formen, und Tendenzen fruhislamischen Geschichtsuberlieferung.* 1: *Themen und Formen.* Bonn: Selbstverlag des Orientalischen Seminars der Universitat Bonn, 1973.

Ostrogorsky, George. *History of the Byzantine State*. J. Hussey, tr. New Brunswick, N.J.: Rutgers University Press, 1969.

The Oxford Annotated Apocrypha. B. Metzger, ed. New York: Oxford University Press, 1977.

Ozturk, Yasar. "Son Peygamber'in Hanimlari: Hz. Aise." *Hurriyet*, June 19, 1985, p. 4.

Parvey, Constance. "The Theology and Leadership of Women in the New Testament." In Rosemary Ruether, ed., *Religion and Sexism: Images of Women in the Jewish and Christian Traditions*, pp. 117–49. New York: Simon and Schuster, 1974.

Pellat, Charles. "Kass." *Encyclopaedia of Islam*. 2d ed., 4: 733–35.

—— "Kissa." *Encyclopaedia of Islam*. 2d ed., 5: 185–87.

—— *The Life and Works of Jahiz*. D. Hawke, tr. London: Routledge Kegan Paul, 1969.

Pelly, Lewis, ed. and tr. *The Miracle Play of Hasan and Husain*. 2 vols. London: Allen, 1879.

Peristiany, J., ed. *Honour and Shame: The Values of Mediterranean Society*. Chicago: University of Chicago Press, 1966.

"Perspectives." *Newsweek*, May 11, 1992, p. 23.

Petersen, Erling L. *`Ali and Mu`awiya in Early Arabic Tradition: Studies on the Genesis and Growth of Islamic Historical Writing Until the End of the Ninth Century*. Copenhagen: Munksgaard, 1964.

de Pizan, Christine. *The Book of the City of Ladies*. E. Richard, tr. New York: Persea Books, 1982.

Qaddura, Zahiyya M. `A'isha *umm al-mu'minin*. Cairo: Matba`at Misr, 1947.

al-Qummi, `Ali ibn Ibrahim. *Tafsir al-Qummi*. 2 vols. Najaf: Matba`at al-Najaf, 1966.

Roberts, Joseph B. "Early Islamic Historiography: Ideology and Methodology." Ph.D. dissertation, Ohio State University, 1986.

Roberts, Robert. *The Social Laws of the Qoran*. London: Curzon Press, 1925.

Robinson, Neal. *Christ in Islam and Christianity*. Albany: SUNY Press, 1991.

Rushdie, Salman. *Satanic Verses*. New York: Harper and Row, 1988.

al-Sa`dawi, Nawal. *The Hidden Face of Eve: Women in the Arab World*. S. Hetata, tr. London: Zed Press, 1980.

al-Samarqandi, Abu Mansur. *Sharh al-fiqh al-akbar*. Beirut: al-Maktabat al-`Asriyya, 1983.

al-San`ani, `Abd al-Razzaq. *Al-Musannaf*. 11 vols. Habib al-Rahman al-A`zami, ed. Beirut: Dar al-Qalam, 1983.

Sartain, E. M. *Jalal al-Din al-Suyuti: Biography and Background*. 2 vols. Cambridge: Cambridge University Press, 1975.

Schacht, Joseph. *The Origins of Muhammadan Jurisprudence*. Oxford: Clarendon Press, 1950.

Schimmel, Annemarie. *Islamic Names*. Edinburgh: University of Edinburgh Press, 1989.

—— *Mystical Dimensions of Islam*. Chapel Hill: North Carolina University Press, 1975.

—— "Women in Mystical Islam." *Women's Studies International Forum* 5, no. 2 (1982): 145–51.

Schneider, Jane. "Of Vigilance and Virgins: Honor, Shame and Access to Resources in Mediterranean Societies." *Ethnology* 10 (1971): 1–24.

Scott, Joan. *Gender and the Politics of History.* New York: Columbia University Press, 1988.

al-Shafi`i, Muhammad Ibn Idris. *Al-Imam Muhammad ibn Idris al-Shafi`i's al-Risala fi usul al-fiqh.* M. Khadduri, tr. Baltimore: Johns Hopkins University Press, 1961.

al-Shahrastani, Muhammad ibn `Abd al-Karim. *Kitab al-Mihal wa'l-Nihal.* M. Kazi and J. Flynn, trs. London: Kegan Paul International, 1984.

Shaukat, Jamila. "A Critical Edition, with Introduction, of Tradition Recounted by `A'isha, Extracted from the Musnad of Ishaq b. Rahawayh." Ph.D. dissertation, Cambridge University, 1984.

Shboul, Ahmad. *Al-Mas`udi and His World.* London: Ithaca Press, 1979.

Smith, Barbara H. "Narrative Versions, Narrative Theories." In W. J. T. Mitchell, ed., *On Narrative,* pp. 209–32. Chicago: University of Chicago Press, 1981.

Smith, Jane I. "Women, Religion, and Social Change in Early Islam." In Y. Haddad and E. Findly, eds., *Women, Religion, and Social Change,* pp. 19–37. Albany: SUNY Press, 1985.

Smith, Jane and Yvonne Haddad. "The Virgin Mary in Islamic Tradition and Commentary." *The Muslim World* 79, nos. 3/4 (July–October 1989): 161–87.

Smith, Margaret. *Rabi`a the Mystic and Her Fellow Saints in Islam.* Cambridge: Cambridge University Press, 1928.

Smith, Morton. *Jesus the Magician.* New York: Harper and Row, 1978.

Smith, W. Robertson. *Kinship and Marriage in Early Islam.* Cambridge: Cambridge University Press, 1885.

Sourdel, Dominique. "Une profession de foi de l'historien al-Tabari." *Revue des Etudes Islamiques* 36, no. 2 (1968): 177–99.

Southern, R. W. *The Making of the Middle Ages.* New Haven: Yale University Press, 1953.

Spectorsky, Susan, tr. *Chapters on Marriage and Divorce: Responses of Ibn Hanbal and Ibn Rahwayh.* Austin: University of Texas Press, 1993.

Spellberg, D. A. "Marriages Made in Heaven and Illustrated on Earth: A Note on the Disjunction Between Verbal and Visual Images in An Ottoman Manuscript." *Bulletin of the Harvard Center for the Study of World Religions* 26 (1989–90): 47–54.

—— "Nizam al-Mulk's Manipulation of Tradition: Women in the Islamic Government." *The Muslim World* 77, no. 2 (April 1988): 111–17.

—— "Political Action and Public Example: `A'isha and the Battle of the Camel." In N. Keddie and B. Baron, eds., *Women in Middle Eastern History: Shifting Boundaries in Sex and Gender,* pp. 58–74. New Haven: Yale University Press, 1991.

—— "The Politics of Praise: Depictions of Khadija, Fatima, and `A'isha in Ninth-Century Muslim Sources." *Literature East and West* 26 (1990): 130–49.

Spiegel, Gabrielle M. "History, Historicism, and the Social Logic of the Text in the Middle Ages." *Speculum* 65, no. 1 (1990): 59–86.

Stern, Gertrude. *Marriage in Early Islam.* London: Royal Asiatic Society, 1939.

Stowasser, Barbara F. "The Status of Women in Early Islam." In F. Hussein, ed., *Muslim Women,* pp. 11–43. London: Croom Helm, 1984.

Stuard, Susan M. "The Chase After Theory: Considering Medieval Women." *Gender and History* 4, no. 2 (1992): 135–45.

Al-Tabari, Abu Ja`far Muhammad ibn Jarir. *The History of al-Tabari: The Foundation of the Community.* W. Montgomery Watt and Michael V. McDonald, trs. Albany: SUNY Press, 1987.

—— *Jami` al-bayan `an ta'wil ay al-Qur'an.* 30 vols. Matba`at Mustafa al Babi al-Halabi, 1903–1910.

—— *Tafsir al-Tabari Jami` al-bayan `an ta'wil ay al-Qur'an.* 16 vols. M. Shakir and A. Shakir, eds. Cairo: Dar al-Ma`arif, 1955–69.

—— *Ta'rikh al-rusul wa al-muluk.* 15 vols. M. De Goeje et al., eds. Leiden: E. J. Brill, 1879–1901.

al-Tabari, Muhibb al-Din Ahmad Ibn `Abd Allah. *Al-Simt al-thamin fi manaqib ummahat al-mu'minin.* Cairo: Kulliyat al-Zahiriyya, 1983.

al-Tabarsi, Al-Fadl ibn al-Hasan. *Majma` al-bayan fi tafsir al-Qur'an.* 5 vols. Qumm: Mataba`at al-`Irfan, 1937.

Tahmaz, `Abd al-Hamid. *Al-Sayyida `A'isha.* Damascus: Dar al-Qalam, 1975.

Tanindi, Zeren. *Siyer-i Nebi: Islam Tasvir Sanatinda Hazreti Muhammed'in Hayati.* Istanbul: Hurriyet Vakfi Yayinlari, 1984.

al-Tirmidhi, Muhammad ibn `Isa. *Sahih al-Tirmidhi.* 5 vols. `Abd al-Rahman `Uthman, ed. Cairo: Matba`at al-I`timad, 1967.

Van Ess, Dorothy. *Fatima and Her Sisters.* New York: John Day, 1961.

Vansina, Jan. *Oral Tradition as History.* Madison: University of Wisconsin Press, 1985.

Veccia Vaglieri, L. "`Ali." *Encyclopaedia of Islam.* 2d ed., 1:381–86.

—— "al-Djamal." *Encyclopaedia of Islam.* 2d ed., 2:414–16.

—— "Fatima." *Encyclopaedia of Islam.* 2d ed., 2:841–50.

Waldman, Marilyn. "The Otherwise Unnoteworthy Year 711: A Reply to Hayden White." In W. J. T. Mitchell, ed., *On Narrative,* pp. 240–48. Chicago: University of Chicago Press, 1981.

—— *Toward a Theory of Historical Narrative: A Case Study in Perso- Islamicate Historiography.* Columbus: Ohio State University Press, 1980.

Wansbrough, John. *Qur'anic Studies: Sources and Methods of Scriptural Interpretation.* Oxford: Oxford University Press, 1977.

—— *The Sectarian Milieu: Content and Composition of Islamic Salvation History.* Oxford: Oxford University Press, 1978.

al-Waqidi, Muhammad b. `Umar. *Kitab al-maghazi.* 2 vols. Marsden Jones, ed. London: Oxford University Press, 1965.

Watt, W. Montgomery. "`A'isha." *Encyclopaedia of Islam.* 2d ed., 1:307–8.

—— *The Formative Period of Islamic Thought.* Edinburgh: University of Edinburgh Press, 1973.

—— *Muhammad at Mecca.* Oxford: Oxford University Press, 1953.

Wensinck, A. J. et al. *Concordance et Indices de la Tradition Musulmane.* 8 vols. Leiden: E. J. Brill, 1962.

Wilson, Adrian and T. G. Ashplant. "Whig History and Present-Centred History." *The Historical Journal* 31, no. 1 (1988): 1–16.

al-Ya`qubi, Ahmad ibn Abi Ya`qub. *Ta'rikh*, 2 vols. T. Houtsma, ed. Leiden: E. J. Brill, 1883.

al-Zarkashi, Muhammad ibn Bahadur. *Al-Ijaba li-irad ma istadrakathu `A'isha `ala al-sahaba*. Cairo: Matba`at al-`Asima, 1965.

index

St. Louis Community College
at Meramec
Library